The Simbas who had been on the truck came up behind the Americans and beat them with rifle butts, forcing them through the violent mob. They halted in front of Olenga's office. A trial was in progress when they arrived. Two Simba officers were judging the fate of four Congolese civilian prisoners. The prisoners' hands and feet had been tied together behind their backs in an agonizing fashion.

One of the "judges" was the big, heavily bearded captain who had been ordered by Olenga, the day before, to protect the consular corps.

"Aren't you the man who is supposed to be protecting us?" Hoyt cried out.

"Why do Americans come to the Congo and interfere in our affairs?" the captain shouted.

The Simbas told the Americans to remove their shoes and socks.

"Dance," they shouted and began beating at their bare feet with clubs. The Simbas laughed hilariously while the Americans hopped around trying to avoid the blows.

Major Nasor bulled his way through the mob. He came close to Hoyt and shouted: "I am immune to bullets because of my *dawa*! Watch—I'll show you."

While a hundred Simbas watched in rapt fascination, Nasor opened the breech of his Fal automatic rifle. He saw that there was a bullet in it. Then he snapped the breech closed and laid the weapon on the ground at Hoyt's feet.

"Pick it up and shoot me!" Nasor cried. "Shoot me! You'll see—nothing will happen because of my *dawa*!"

The Simbas murmured.

"Shoot me!" Nasor screeched.

SAVE THE HOSTAGES!

DAVID REED

BANTAM BOOKS
TORONTO • NEW YORK • LONDON • SYDNEY • AUCKLAND

SAVE THE HOSTAGES!

*A Bantam Book / published by arrangement with
the author*

PRINTING HISTORY
First published in Great Britain 1966
Previously published as 111 Days in Stanleyville
Bantam edition / December 1988

*Illustrations by Greg Beecham and Tom Beecham.
Maps by Alan McKnight.*

*The lines on page 64 are from "The Congo," by Vachel Lindsay.
Copyright 1914 by The Macmillan Company; renewed 1942 by
Elizabeth C. Lindsay.*

ISBN 0-553-27605-0

Published simultaneously in the United States and Canada

*Bantam Books are published by Bantam Books, a division of
Bantam Doubleday Dell Publishing Group, Inc. Its trademark,
consisting of the words "Bantam Books" and the portrayal of
a rooster, is Registered in U.S. Patent and Trademark Office
and in other countries. Marca Registrada. Bantam Books,
666 Fifth Avenue, New York, New York 10103.*

PRINTED IN THE UNITED STATES OF AMERICA

O   0 9 8 7 6 5 4 3 2 1

Contents

AUTHOR'S NOTE

This book was made possible by the unique, world-wide facilities of *The Reader's Digest*. *Digest* offices in several European cities and especially the European Editorial Office in Paris assisted me in locating and interviewing more than three hundred people involved in the events reported in this book. Interviews were held in the Congo, Belgium, Germany, Switzerland, France and Kenya. Then, with the help of the Pleasantville, Washington and New York City offices of the *Digest*, I was able to track down and interview nearly fifty other people in the United States. With half a dozen editors and researchers at work on three continents, we were able, in just ten weeks, to record the complete details of a moment in history while the events were still fresh in the minds of the participants and while it was still possible to trace them.

D.R.

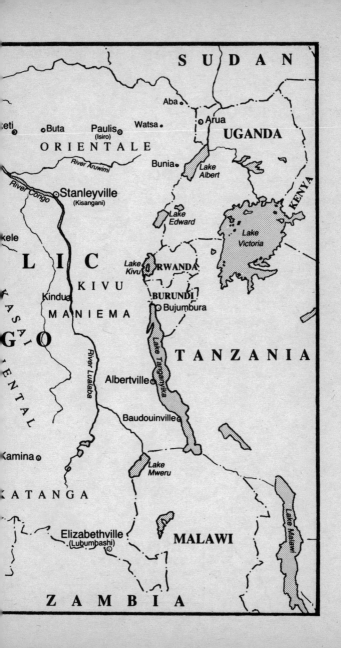

1

SEVEN FIRES IN STANLEYVILLE

Stanleyville is in dead center of the African continent, halfway between Cairo and Cape Town, halfway between the Atlantic and Indian oceans. The city is surrounded by the great rain forest of the Congo basin, a wilderness that is wild, luxuriant and mysterious. And it is no ordinary jungle; it is one of the two great tropical forests which remain on earth, the other being that which covers the Amazon basin.

On a plane bound for Stanleyville, one flies for hours without seeing a sign of human existence. Then a road appears, a forlorn ribbon of dirt that seems to wind from nowhere to nowhere. But the road is gone as quickly as it came into view. Once in a while, a plantation flashes beneath. Or one glimpses a native village, a pathetic huddle of crude huts, surrounded by a tiny patch of cultivation. But then absolute greenness closes in again.

The jungle is a haunting place. The immensity and wildness of it evoke a sense of awe, mixed with dread. It is as if you were accidentally whisked back through thousands of years of time to find yourself staring at the forest primeval. You experience an absurd panic; it is as if you had lost your bearings, or you had lost touch with reality. Or perhaps it is that the jungle suggests an even more disturbing thought: that of eternity itself. For the jungle has been there, unchanged, from the beginning. And it will be there for a long, long time.

If you venture into the jungle on foot or in a canoe, you find yourself in a place of great beauty. But the beauty is overlaid with foreboding. Trees soar higher than fifteen-story buildings, each wrapped in the murderous clutch of lianas and parasites. The canopy of foliage is so dense that a twilight gloom, much like that of a great cathedral at sunset, prevails on the jungle floor. The crush of trees is so great that when one dies it rarely falls; it remains propped up for years by its neighbors.

The jungle is vivid, and intense. Gorgeous orchids and other flowers bloom in rank profusion. Brilliant-hued birds flit through murky thickets. Monkeys screech as they leap high overhead. Occasionally one sees an elephant barging through the undergrowth like a bulldozer. Each river and stream is filled with crocodiles which wait patiently, only their eyes showing, for the moment to murder. Brown and yellow pythons, some twenty feet long, glide through stagnant pools. There are dozens of other species of snakes as well, some of them most deadly. Day and night, one hears the insistent whine of the mosquito, the carrier of fatal fevers.

After the jungle, Stanleyville comes as a jolt. As the plane circles to land, a lovely little city appears, as if by magic. At least in former times, Stanleyville was a delight to the eye. Clusters of pastel-colored office and apartment buildings gave it the suggestion of a modern skyline. Some of the resident Europeans had built palatial villas. Several pretty little boulevards had been laid out, each lined with palm and mango trees. In Stanleyville's shops, one could purchase an expensive camera, a Parisian frock, an American automobile or just about anything else. There were comfortable hotels and there were restaurants where one could dine on oysters or châteaubriant that had been flown in that day from Brussels. A university had even been founded.

Stanleyville was an anomaly, but there was a reason for it—the great brown flood that is called the Congo River. Like the jungle, the river is an enormous thing. It rises in the southern Congo, close by the border of Zambia, and crosses the equator twice as it knifes through the jungle in a great arc on its 2,700-mile journey to the sea. Stanleyville is at the head of navigation for the middle portion of the river; just beyond the city there is a 60-mile stretch of wild water,

2

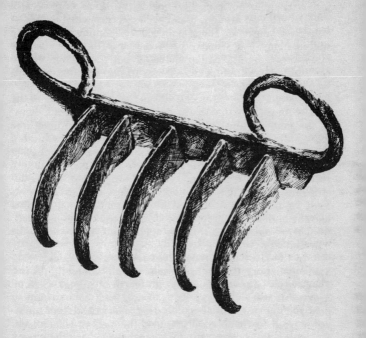

Leopard Man's Claws

known as the Stanley Falls. Stanleyville grew up as the great transshipment point for all goods moving into and out of the interior. Here upbound cargoes were transferred to a little railway, to be taken around the rapids to Ponthierville, where navigation resumes. And here, too, downbound cargoes were transferred from the railway to boats and barges, to be carried a thousand miles downstream to Léopoldville, the capital of the Congo.

No one ever bothered to count the population of Stanleyville in recent years, but one guess was that it had risen to 150,000. For European and Congolese alike, life there was, for the most part, dreamy and idyllic. The city was

3

just forty miles north of the equator and there were no real seasons. All year around, Stanleyville was drenched in golden equatorial sunshine. The sweet scents of jasmine and mimosa wafted along the streets. Each day was the same as the last—warm, humid and punctuated now and then with a refreshing shower. Indeed, life was so pleasant that one was scarcely aware of the passage of time.

And yet there was uneasiness in Stanleyville, even in the best of times. The jungle was never far away; it began almost at the edge of town, a great, glowering, incomprehensible wilderness. In Stanleyville itself, there were many educated Congolese, but out in jungle villages, witchcraft, cannibalism and ritualistic murder still flourished. From time to time a secret society of tribesmen, known as the *Anyoto*, the Leopard Men, carried out savage and senseless murders at night. They would fasten steel claws to their hands; then, howling like the animals they represented, they would fall on a child, woman or old man—never an able-bodied male—and rake him to death.

In the last half of 1964, a bizarre drama was enacted in Stanleyville, one that had repercussions all around the world. That drama began on Tuesday the fourth of August. Several Americans were gathered that morning next to a swimming pool on the grounds of a villa that overlooked the white-water rapids of Stanley Falls. One of the men struck a match. He stepped up, gingerly, to a steel drum that had been placed next to the pool, touched the match to a fuse and jumped back. With a whoosh, the barrel exploded into a ten-foot pillar of flame. The man went down a row of similar barrels, igniting one after another. The flames leaped up so high that they scorched leaves in nearby mimosa trees and threw several tame monkeys into an uproar. Soon seven fires were burning fiercely.

The men were members of the staff of the U.S. consulate in Stanleyville. They were burning their code materials and classified papers. The drums—called "destruction barrels"—are kept in U.S. consulates and embassies for just such emergencies; they are lined with chemicals that explode into intense flame. The consul, a tall, husky, mild-mannered man named Michael Hoyt, had ordered the files destroyed as a precaution. An army of Congolese rebels who called themselves

4

Simbas—the Swahili word for lions—was advancing on Stanleyville.

Hoyt and the other Americans spent nearly an hour trudging back and forth from the consulate to the fires. They scooped up papers from vaults, filing cabinets and desks, carried them out and consigned them to the flames. Eventually only smoldering ashes remained of what had been the consulate's most precious bureaucratic treasures.

The destruction of the consular documents was made particularly urgent by the fact that the Simbas were violently anti-American. Only a few weeks before, a rebel leader declared that the Simbas would not "guarantee the safety" of any Americans who were found in rebel territory. But the Simbas did not seem to be particularly antiwhite at that time. The same leader urged the Belgians and other white foreigners to remain in the city and keep the economy going.

One reason for the anti-Americanism of the Simbas was that the United States was supplying military aid to the central government in Léopoldville—the government against which the Simbas had rebelled. Another reason was that the Simbas had been influenced by Chinese and Soviet propaganda that had sought to blame the Congo's woes on "American imperialism."

The Simba threat to Stanleyville had materialized with the sudden fury of a tropical storm. In early July, a motley column of tribal dissidents, which probably numbered no more than a few hundred men at the start, moved out of Albertville, a town on the shores of Lake Tanganyika, and headed north and west, gathering recruits along the way. They seized town after town without opposition. In each case the troops of the central government—the Armée Nationale Congolaise (ANC), or Congolese National Army—fled without a fight.

On July 22, the provincial capital of Kindu, 250 miles south of Stanleyville, fell to the rebels, who now began to call themselves the Simbas. Thousands of local tribesmen flocked to the cause. Setting out from Kindu in trucks, the Simbas moved toward Stanleyville, encountering little resistance from the demoralized ANC. On Sunday, August 2, Michael Hoyt heard reports that the Simbas had reached Wanie Rukula, a village only twenty-four miles from Stanleyville. At first, the

5

ANC headquarters in Stanleyville scoffed at the report. A Belgian officer who had been serving on loan to the ANC went to Wanie Rukula to investigate, but he was never seen again. Much later a group of Simbas boasted to Hoyt that they had killed and devoured the officer.

Now the Simbas were nearing the gates of Stanleyville. The city was defended by four to five hundred heavily armed ANC troops. They were considered elite troops, at least by Congolese standards. With the assistance of Belgian military advisers, they had drawn up elaborate plans for the defense of the city. But no one was sure that these plans would work.

Having destroyed the consulate files, Hoyt turned to his next task. With the concurrence of the U.S. embassy in Léopoldville, he decided to evacuate all dependents and all nonessential personnel. He radioed to Léopoldville for evacuation planes; he was told they would arrive in a few hours. The only dependents in Stanleyville at the time were Hoyt's wife, Jo, and one of their four children, the other youngsters having been sent back to the United States for a summer holiday.

"I want to stay," Mrs. Hoyt said, over and over, as she followed Hoyt around the consulate.

"No, you can't," Hoyt kept replying.

Mrs. Hoyt finally gave up and began packing her clothing.

Hoyt told the American secretary, two radio operators and two officials of the U.S. Information Service to be ready to leave. Then he had his Congolese chauffeur drive him to the airport to meet the first evacuation plane.

Ordinarily, Hoyt was a member of the economics staff of the embassy in Léopoldville. He handled commercial matters and worked on problems relating to American aid for the Congo. He had been sent to Stanleyville just three weeks previously to fill in as temporary consul for two and a half months. Then, having completed a two-year tour of duty in the Congo, he would have been sent home for two years' service in the State Department in Washington.

Hoyt liked what little he had seen of Stanleyville. Instead of being an obscure junior officer in a large embassy, he now found himself in charge of a consulate. It was a small consulate, but Hoyt was an ambitious man and he knew that if he handled the job well he would be in line for bigger and better posts.

The consulate was as picturesque as Stanleyville—a one-story villa with white walls and a red roof. It had a large lawn, planted with a cloverlike herb, and a long, curving driveway. Stanleyville could be hot and humid at times, but the consulate was air-conditioned and, in any event, Hoyt and the others could always cool off in the swimming pool. The previous Saturday night, Hoyt had held a diplomatic reception on the grounds—the first he had hosted in Stanleyville—and he had shown his Congolese and European guests a U.S. Information Service film which depicted the Vietcong takeover of a Vietnamese village.

Hoyt, thirty-four years old, was one of the most promising young diplomats in the U.S. Foreign Service. Six feet tall, he normally weighed two hundred pounds. He had close-cropped brown hair, beginning to gray. An affable, easygoing man, he was soft spoken and had a quiet sense of humor. In conversation, he paused frequently to think out answers. People who were with him in Stanleyville say that he never lost his composure or his mild mannerisms.

Hoyt grew up in the heady intellectual atmosphere of the University of Chicago. His father, Frank C. Hoyt, was a noted theoretical nuclear physicist, and his mother, Elizabeth, was an artist. The elder Hoyt was an associate professor of physics at the university for nineteen years and, as a Manhattan Project scientist, helped develop the first atomic bomb. During Michael's boyhood, the late Enrico Fermi and Harold C. Urey, both Nobel-prize-winning scientists, were frequent visitors at the Hoyt home. So, too, was Edward Teller, who played a major role in the development of the hydrogen bomb.

Michael entered the university at the age of fifteen under an accelerated program and, after receiving a bachelor's degree, took a master's degree in modern European history from the University of Illinois. Then came four years of service in the Air Force, as a staff sergeant and ground control approach operator. Hoyt joined the Foreign Service in 1956 and served in Pakistan and Morocco before arriving in the Congo in 1962.

* * *

7

When Hoyt arrived at the airport, he ran into a Congolese friend, Captain Henri Tshimala, a small, intense man who was head of intelligence for the Third Army group, which had its headquarters in Stanleyville.

"Where's your wife?" Tshimala asked excitedly in French. He was even more nervous than usual.

"She's at the consulate—she's going to be evacuated later this afternoon," Hoyt replied, surprised at Tshimala's agitation.

"No, you'd better put her on a plane at once," Tshimala said. "The Simbas are almost here. The situation is very, very bad."

Hoyt sent his chauffeur hurrying back to the consulate. Mrs. Hoyt had already finished packing and she was at the airport in ten minutes, together with their son, Evans, three years old, and Joan Allen, the American secretary. Hoyt put the two women and the child on a small two-engine plane that the U.S. Army attaché had sent up from Léopoldville.

"Don't be a hero—come back to me—I need you," Mrs. Hoyt shouted amidst the roar of the engines.

Hoyt went to the airport control tower. As the plane zoomed down the runway and took off over the jungle, Hoyt spoke to his wife on the radio.

"Bye bye, baby doll," he said.

In less than a minute, the plane was out of sight.

Captain Tshimala put his own family on another plane. He stayed on to defend Stanleyville. A few days later, he was captured by the Simbas and executed.

Hoyt was relieved that he had gotten his wife and children out of Stanleyville, but he had no desire to follow them. The show was about to start, and Hoyt did not want to miss it.

Among the whites who were leaving were five Belgian military advisers. Even more than the Congolese, they could never run the risk of capture; to do so would mean death by the most fiendish tortures.

Several United Nations personnel were also leaving. Gaston Soumialot, the rebel leader who had given the warning about any Americans found in rebel territory, had also said he would not "guarantee the safety" of any UN officials. Soumialot's hostility to the UN stemmed from the fact that the world organization had maintained a military force in the Congo for four years—until June 30, 1964—in an effort to keep down just such revolts. No one, of course, loves his policeman. But Soumialot and the Simbas were also influenced by Communist radio broadcasts, as well as by a flood of written propaganda which was widely circulated in the Congo—propaganda which had all along portrayed the UN mission as an "imperialist plot to enslave the Congolese people."

While Hoyt was still at the airport, several planes arrived, bringing reinforcements for the ANC. The new troops were paracommandos from Léopoldville, eager to have a crack at the Simbas. Many were veterans of a campaign against other rebels in the Kwilu province. They had fought well in the Kwilu and it was hoped they would do the same in Stanleyville.

Strangely enough, there was no panic among Stanleyville's white residents, who included 29 Americans—almost all of them missionaries and their families. The whites were uneasy. But, although Hoyt had contacted all Americans in Stanleyville and had offered to evacuate them, all chose to remain. The Belgian consulate also advised its people that planes were available to take them out. But only 165 Belgians—the 5 military advisers and 160 women and children—decided to go. The Belgian consulate offered to take anyone else who wanted to leave. But only the same number of people—165 of them, French, Italians, Greeks, Indians, Pakistanis and some Congolese—accepted the offer.

About 1,600 foreigners remained in the Stanleyville area—500 Belgians, 700 people of other European nationalities and 400 Indians and Pakistanis. Many had been in the city during the chaotic days of a secessionist movement in 1960 and 1961. Although some had been roughed up then, none had been killed. They figured that difficulties would probably arise if the Simbas took Stanleyville, but they felt that they would manage somehow. Many had all of their money tied up in businesses and plantations. To leave would mean abandoning everything they owned.

Only a week before, Soumialot had sent a radio message to Stanleyville urging Belgians and other foreigners to remain. "You have nothing to fear from us," Soumialot said. "Stay here and continue to work. We need you. You will be

9

happier under our government than under the Léopoldville regime. Nothing will happen to you if you remain in Stanleyville."

And so, for one reason or another, there were sixty empty seats when the last plane took off from Stanleyville that evening.

At that time, the Simbas were pretty much an unknown quantity. They could be savage with their own people, or, more precisely, with Congolese who were identified with the central government or with those Congolese who, by virtue of having had some education, were regarded as "intellectuals." There had been reports that the Simbas had killed four Europeans in Kindu, but they were unconfirmed. Otherwise, as far as anyone knew, the Simbas had not harmed any whites.

The Simba army was something which could happen only in the Congo. It was composed of primitive tribesmen who were led into battle by witch doctors, or sorcerers. Each recruit was put through an elaborate ceremony which conferred *dawa*, or medicine, on him—*dawa* that was supposed to make him immune to bullets. If the warrior took the precaution of waving palm branches and chanting, *"Mai, mai"* (water, water), as he went into battle, looking neither to the right nor left, enemy bullets would simply turn to water. Inevitably some got bumped off, but the sorcerers had a quick explanation: the deceased had violated some taboo—perhaps he had looked to one side or the other—and thus he had lost his *dawa*. In order to bolster their courage still further, the Simbas smoked marijuana before going into action.

Anywhere else, the Simbas would have been mowed down by opposing troops, but in the Congo they proved to be more or less effective as a fighting force. For one thing, the ANC was, for the most part, little more than a mutinous rabble, with no taste for a real fight. ANC troops seldom took aim. Why bother? Most of them knew, as a fact, that it is the noise, not the bullets, which kills. Many also believed that the Simbas really were immune to bullets. Time and again the soldiers dropped their weapons and ran as the Simbas approached chanting, *"Mai, mai."* At first the Simbas were armed mostly with spears, arrows and clubs, but eventually they captured a considerable quantity of modern firearms from the army.

As Michael Hoyt rode back to the consulate, he heard the rattle of machine guns in the distance; the Simbas were now at the outskirts of the city. The firing grew louder, more insistent. Occasionally Hoyt saw an army vehicle in the streets, but otherwise Stanleyville was deserted. The whites had closed up their offices and shops and had drawn the shutters of their homes. The Congolese had disappeared into the native communes.

It was 2 P.M. when Hoyt reached the consulate. He ordered the nonessential personnel to go to the airport. He had already decided that the radio operator who would remain would be James Stauffer, thirty years old, of Findlay, Ohio. Stauffer was due to leave Stanleyville in a few days after completing a two-year tour of duty, but since he was the most experienced of the three Hoyt decided that he should remain for the time being. The two men who were to be evacuated were Ernest Houle, fifty-two years old, of Providence, Rhode Island, and Donald Parkes, thirty-four, or Bloomfield, Indiana. Houle had been in Stanleyville for only a few months. Parkes had arrived a few days previously, as Stauffer's replacement. All three of the radio operators were bachelors.

Hoyt instructed Phil Mayhew, one of the U.S. Information Service men, to take two American women tourists who happened to be in Stanleyville to the airport and put them and himself on the next plane. Mayhew and the women got into a jeep and made a dash through the streets, which now were reverberating with heavy firing. They reached the airport safely and were soon aboard a plane. Then Hoyt told the other USIS man, Max Kraus, to pick up Houle and Parkes at their apartments in the Immoquateur, an eight-story building in downtown Stanleyville, and take them to the airport. Kraus found that Houle was still packing. Houle told him to go on ahead; he would come out to the airport with Parkes. In the meantime, Parkes had driven back to the consulate to pick up a diplomatic pouch. But while he was at the consulate the firing increased to the point where it was dangerous to try to make a dash for the airport.

And so Houle was stranded at the Immoquateur and

11

Parkes at the consulate. They were still there when the last plane left that night.

At 4 P.M., the vice-consul, David Grinwis, thirty-four, of Maplewood, New Jersey, arrived at the consulate after a tour of the city. Grinwis, a bachelor, was tall (a shade under six feet), thin (132 pounds normally) and had blond hair. He wore expensive, well-tailored suits. He was tense and reserved, with an analytical mind, and he habitually viewed even the most hectic events with quiet, scientific detachment. His hobbies included playing classical piano music.

The son of a prosperous physician, Grinwis graduated from Hamilton College in 1952 and did postgraduate work at Georgetown University in Washington. He joined the Foreign Service in 1960 and, after some months in Washington, was sent first to Léopoldville and then to Stanleyville. At the time he welcomed the assignment to Stanleyville because he felt it would be a quiet post, thus giving him plenty of spare time to complete a Ph.D thesis on African history which he had planned to submit to Georgetown.

As Hoyt and Grinwis were exchanging news of what they had seen, they were interrupted by a tremendous racket. Peering out the windows, they saw ANC troops advancing along the road in front of the consulate—it was called Avenue Eisenhower—firing wildly at Camp Ketele, a military base not far from the consulate. This was ominous; it indicated that Camp Ketele, which was at the edge of the city, on the road in from Wanie Rukula, had already fallen to the Simbas. The troops fired at Camp Ketele for several minutes, then they retreated. Now the street was empty. Silence.

A moment later, the four men—Hoyt, Grinwis, Stauffer and Parkes—received a shock. If men from Mars had suddenly appeared, the impact could hardly have been greater. A bare-chested Simba sorcerer came walking slowly up Avenue Eisenhower, waving a palm branch back and forth. He looked neither to the right nor to the left as he strode resolutely along. In single file, a considerable distance apart, seven or eight other Simbas followed. Each was in similar battle undress, naked to the waist. None carried a weapon—only a palm branch. But the palm branches were enough; the Simbas had succeeded in scaring the daylights out of the government troops.

The column of sorcerers paused for a minute in front of the consulate. They pointed at it and talked among themselves. Then they marched on in the direction of the wharves and disappeared from sight.

Five minutes later, another tremendous racket was heard close by. It sounded, Hoyt said, as if the world were coming to an end. The government troops had screwed up their courage and were shooting at the sorcerers with everything they had.

And then—Hoyt and the others could scarcely believe what they saw—the column of sorcerers reappeared, walking slowly and deliberately in single file, heading back along Avenue Eisenhower toward Camp Ketele. They looked neither to the right nor the left. They paid no attention to the bullets that were flying around them. In a moment they disappeared from sight.

Once more the street was silent and deserted. Soon, however, the ANC reappeared, firing machine guns and a recoilless rifle. The troops moved onto the lawn of the consulate and took up positions behind a low wall. For half an hour, they kept up a furious fusillade. Then, inexplicably, they withdrew.

Hoyt and the others were stunned. No one said anything. The telephone jangled. It was an American colonel, the pilot of the last American evacuation plane, calling from the airport. He begged Hoyt and the rest of the men to leave.

"No," Hoyt said. "We're going to stay." As far as Houle and Parkes were concerned, it was too dangerous for them to try to make a dash for the airport through the lines of the trigger-happy ANC.

"Go ahead," Hoyt told the pilot. "No one else will be leaving."

Now it was 6:30 P.M. Night came with the suddenness it always does near the equator. There is virtually no twilight in that part of the world. Darkness arrives with the abruptness of a curtain banging down in a theater at the end of a performance. A torrential downpour followed. The storm halted the battle for the night—the Simbas considered it taboo to fight in the rain.

Vice-consul Grinwis telephoned ANC headquarters. They

told him that the situation was not as bad as it seemed and that the Americans should remain in the consulate. If they were threatened, headquarters would send a column to the consulate and move them to safety. Most of the city, the army said, was still in government hands. In the morning they were going to mount a large-scale counterattack which they were certain would be successful.

The four men felt somewhat better, but they remained in the consulate, sleeping fitfully, that night. From time to time they heard gunfire, but the rain kept up all night long, and the Simbas were quiet.

The next day—Wednesday—was a bad day for Michael Hoyt and the other Americans. It was a bad day, too, for the honor and prestige of the United States.

As the morning wore on, Hoyt's fears for the safety of the consular personnel rose. He telephoned repeatedly to army headquarters and asked that they send troops to escort the Americans to a less-exposed part of the city. Headquarters agreed and told them to wait. They waited. At 10 A.M., the ANC appeared in front of the consulate, not to rescue the Americans, but rather to resume the battle. The troops took up positions on the lawn of the consulate and on the road and fired hundreds of rounds from heavy machine guns and from a recoilless rifle in an attempt to take back Camp Ketele. A bullet cut the rope on the flagpole in front of the consulate, making it impossible to lower the flag.

During the battle, an American military plane appeared over the city. It was bringing Colonel Léonard Mulamba, the military commander of the Stanleyville region, back from Bukavu, a city three hundred miles to the southeast which is the capital of Kivu province. Mulamba, a man of extraordinary military abilities, was highly respected by blacks and whites alike. He had been directing operations against other rebels in the Kivu. Later on, he turned back the Simbas after fierce fighting in the streets of Bukavu itself. Many people thought that if Mulamba had been able to land in Stanleyville that morning he might well have saved the city by the sheer force of his personality. But the pilot of his plane was hit in the leg by a sniper's bullet and the plane flew on to Léopoldville without landing.

14

Gradually the firing died down. From telephone calls to friends, Hoyt and Grinwis learned that the Simbas had been spreading out across the city. Walking slowly, single file, waving palm branches and changing, *"Mai, mai,"* they had taken the post office, the radio station, the wharves and the airfield. Many government troops were killed. Some surrendered, only to be executed, after torture. Some retreated down the river, commandeered a steamer and made it to safety.

The Congolese civilians remained hidden in the native communes for several days. They ventured out only after the shooting was over. Some welcomed the Simbas—and joined the Simba army. Others regarded the newcomers with indifference. Few of the Congolese civilians moaned the passing of the old regime. Like most provincial governments in the Congo, it had been hopelessly corrupt and incompetent. Frequently the authorities had been brutal with the civilian population. If nothing else, some of the civilians thought, the Simbas could hardly be worse.

At 1 P.M., Hoyt and Stauffer went to the consul's residence next door to have lunch while Grinwis and Parkes remained in the consulate. The lunch was prepared by Hoyt's cook, an elderly half-deaf Congolese named Tata Paul. Tata Paul belonged to an earlier Congolese generation. For many years he had been the cook for a Belgian colonial governor. To him, those were the good old days; nothing had been right since the governor left. Such were his views that he was reluctant to cook good food when Hoyt was having Congolese guests. "They wouldn't appreciate it," he would say.

That day Tata Paul served Hoyt a favorite dish—*capitaine*, a Congo river fish that resembles perch. Battle or no battle, Hoyt was a man who appreciates food and he dug in heartily. Stauffer, by contrast, picked at his food, still shaken by the events of the morning. It was a good lunch and it was the last one Tata Paul ever cooked. While riding home on his bicycle that day Tata Paul was struck and killed by a stray bullet.

At 1:30 P.M., as Hoyt was finishing his lunch, the phone rang. It was Grinwis.

"Come over quickly," Grinwis said. "The Simbas are coming up the road toward us."

"Okay," said Hoyt. He hung up and went back to the table for one last bite.

The phone rang again.

"Hurry," Grinwis shouted. "They're attacking."

Hoyt dashed over to the consulate, followed by Stauffer, entering by the back door. As they came into the foyer they saw ten or eleven Simbas coming across the lawn, firing automatic weapons point blank at the consulate. The glass doors and the front windows shattered under the impact of the bullets. Broken glass flew through the air. Bullets tore holes in the walls and ripped into furniture.

The day before, Hoyt and Grinwis had decided that if there was an attack on the consulate they would lock themselves in a vault. And so, when Hoyt and Stauffer dashed into the consulate, Grinwis and Parkes were already in a large vault, one that was used to house the communications equipment. Three Congolese employees of the consulate were crouched in a second, smaller vault, one that was used to store documents. Stauffer dived into the vault with Grinwis and Parkes. Hoyt was about to follow when he noticed that a fourth Congolese employee was huddled by a window.

Crouching to avoid the bullets, Hoyt ran over, grabbed the man and pushed him into the smaller vault. He shouted orders for the Congolese to lock the door from the inside. Then he dived into the larger vault with Grinwis and the other Americans. As bullets whizzed past his head, he pulled shut an outer wooden door and slammed an inner steel door, locking it from the inside. Then he and the other men shoved a safe against the steel door.

As the four men listened, the Simbas shot open the locked front door of the consulate. Other Simbas went around the sides of the building, firing into the windows. Then that group too came into the consulate. They searched the rooms and finally came to the door of the smaller vault, the one in which the four Congolese employees were hiding.

"*Fungua*," a Simba shouted in Swahili—"open it."

The four Congolese sat motionless, frozen in terror.

"If you open it, we won't hurt you. Otherwise we'll kill you."

The Congolese opened the door and stepped out.

"Where are the Americans?" a Simba, who appeared to be the leader, asked.

"What do you want with them?"

"We have come to kill them."

The Simbas realized that the Americans were in the other vault. They beat on the outer wooden door with rifle butts. They chopped at it with a shovel. After ten minutes, they succeeded in breaking through the wooden door. Then they saw the steel door. Enraged, they sprayed it with bullets, which bounced off harmlessly.

Hoyt, huddled in the vault, thought that his time had come. Several years before he had given up smoking. Now he borrowed a cigarette and took a long drag.

When the four Americans entered the vault, it was lighted by an electric bulb and an air conditioner was running. But suddenly the chamber was plunged into utter darkness and the air conditioner stopped. What happened was that Grinwis's Congolese chauffeur, hoping to protect the Americans, told the Simbas that they should not touch the steel door. "It's electrified—it'll kill you," the chauffeur said. But the Simbas were not to be taken in so easily. They forced the chauffeur to cut the consulate's master switch.

The Simbas got a sledgehammer and began bludgeoning the door. There was an ear-splitting report each time the hammer struck the steel. The Simbas knocked off the dial of the combination lock; the Americans heard it clatter to the floor. To the horror of the men inside, they started to see a band of light along the edges of the door every time the Simbas banged on it. The door was beginning to give.

After bludgeoning the door for more than an hour, the Simbas gave up. The door frame was weakened, but it still held. The Americans could hear the Simbas moving around in the consulate. And they heard rain. This was something of a consolation; rain always calmed the Simbas down.

The Simbas found wine and some emergency rations and had a meal. They discovered a typewriter and amused themselves by banging on it. They also found—and made off with—a pair of binoculars belonging to Grinwis, and Hoyt's spectacles.

On two occasions, the Congolese employees came close to a small slot that led between the two vaults—the slot was

17

used to pass messages to the radio operators in the large vault—and whispered in French, "*Ne bougez pas!*—don't budge!"

The hours ticked away. With the air conditioning shut off, the vault grew very hot and stuffy. But the Americans were able to breath; a little air came through the cracks around the air-conditioning installation. At 6:30 P.M. they heard a loud argument between one of the Congolese employees and a Simba. Then silence.

Was this a ruse to lure them out so that they could be gunned down? Rather than run the risk, they decided to remain. Another hour passed, then two. Still no sounds outside the vault. Was a grinning Simba waiting there with a cocked weapon?

Finally the men could stand it no longer; there comes a time, after living through too much tension and suspense, when one wants to end it, come what may. Slowly and cautiously, so as to avoid making the least sound, they rolled the safe away from the door. The Americans took a deep breath. Then, an inch at a time, they swung the steel door back. Hoyt looked out.

There was no one there.

2

CALL STANLEYVILLE 2904

Michael Hoyt was not the only diplomat in Stanleyville who had come as a temporary consul for what he thought would be just a matter of weeks. Four days before the city fell to the Simbas, a jaunty and unkempt young man came trotting down the steps from an Air Congo DC-4 which had just landed in Stanleyville after a four-hour flight from Léopoldville. A crowd of Congolese surged forward and burst into a welcoming applause. "Thank you, thank you," the young man shouted, waving back at them. "*Merci, merci.*" He beamed affection for the Congolese and for the human race in general. What a nice gesture! But then—*horrors!* He realized that the Congolese had not come to welcome him, but rather to cheer a Congolese politician who was coming in on the same plane. Crestfallen, the young man trudged into the terminal.

Thus did Patrick Nothomb, the twenty-eight-year-old Belgian consul, make a somewhat less than triumphal entry into Stanleyville. Nothomb was not only an eager-beaver junior diplomat, but a hereditary baron as well. For nearly two years, he had worked as the private secretary of the Belgian ambassador in Léopoldville and as the number two man in the political section of the embassy. The regular Belgian consul in Stanleyville was due to leave on August 1 and his replacement was not scheduled to arrive until August 15. So, why not? The ambassador sent the young baron to fill in for the two weeks.

19

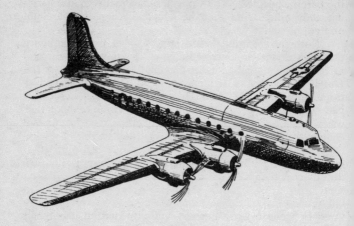

DC-4 Skymaster

In the months that followed, Patrick Nothomb would become a hero. But he was a rather improbable hero as well as a rather improbable baron. Nothomb was short and pudgy, with a barrel chest, tiny legs and tiny feet. His manner of dress was anything but elegant: the baron's necktie was always askew. His shoes were scuffed and the laces were usually untied. His trousers did not appear to be pressed too often. One or more buttons frequently were missing from his shirt and his hair flew about in great disarray.

Nothomb was anything but the icy aristocrat. A man of great energies, he radiated happiness and good will. He seemed to like everybody and everybody seemed to like him; to do otherwise would have been impossible. Almost everything in life seemed to amuse and delight Nothomb. He joked about even the worst misfortunes. A voluble talker, he was equally at home orating in the most sophisticated salons in Europe and in the mud huts of the Congolese. Nothomb had a great liking for the Congolese and the Congolese (who also are effervescent and a trifle unkempt) seemed to recognize a kindred spirit: they were fascinated by him. On one occasion, the baron explained: "The Congolese are really good, charming and polite." And then he added: "When they are not excited, of course."

Nothomb's family owned large estates in Luxembourg province, in the far south of Belgium. There was rebel blood in the baron's veins; a great-grandfather fought against the Dutch for Belgium's independence in 1830 and served as prime minister for a time. He was awarded the hereditary baronetcy for his services to the nation. Patrick's grandfather was a senator and his father a cavalry officer. The Jesuits had charge of the young baron's early education. Then he took a doctorate of law at Louvain, the five-hundred-year-old Catholic university in Belgium. While there he wrote and produced several satirical comedies. Since then he has written some other works but, alas, the powers-that-be in the Belgian entertainment world have, for their own selfish reasons, refused to produce them. Never mind. Undaunted, the baron still writes them. Nothomb's fellow students at Louvain remember how he often kept them up all night in wild arguments. What, Nothomb was asked, were these arguments about?

"All the madnesses that the people of our age found interesting! Building back the world!" Nothomb exclaimed in English with a beatific smile.

"What? You mean building a *better* world?" he was asked.

"Hah, hah, yes, that's it. A *better* world."

On Wednesday, August 5, when Hoyt and the other Americans were in the vault because of the Simba attack, Nothomb was in an apartment on the third floor of the Immoquateur. The day before he had evacuated those Belgians, and people of other nationalities, who chose to leave. He did not have to worry about his own wife and two small children; they had remained in Léopoldville. But he was concerned about the fact that most of the Belgians had refused the evacuation offer. Then, he caught his first glimpse of the invaders. A column of Simbas, naked to the waist and chanting *"Mai, mai"* passed by the Immoquateur. "Dreadful people," Nothomb muttered.

The Simbas were not exactly elegant in appearance.

Some had bits and pieces of military uniforms or khaki slacks; many were clad only in tattered shorts. A few, having liberated some panties from a lady's boudoir, wore them over their trousers. They sported a bewildering array of headgear— ANC caps, cowboy hats, steel helmets left behind by the UN troops. Some even wore lampshades or women's hats which they had pilfered from European homes.

Many of the Simbas were armed with automatic weapons and rifles, but quite a few had only spears, sticks and palm branches.

A short while later, they returned and entered the Immoquateur. They banged on the door of the apartment in which Nothomb was staying—the apartment belonged to a Swiss named Raymond Meier. After a moment's hesitation, Nothomb and Meier opened the door. Several Simbas were in the corridor. They seemed drunk, or drugged.

"Give us the keys to your car," they said in French.

Nothomb had no car, but Meier did. The two men hesitated, then decided it was not worth risking their lives for a car. Meier handed the keys over and the Simbas left.

The telephone rang. It was a Belgian who lived with his family at the outskirts of the city. The Simbas were shooting around his house. The man was frantic. "Please come and get us," he wailed to Nothomb.

Nothomb had enough problems of his own. But, underneath the aura of confusion that surrounds the little man, there is courage. And so, accompanied by a Belgian who spoke Swahili, he went down to the street, which was crackling with gunfire. They saw a Simba and went up to him.

"This is the Belgian consul," the man told the Simba. "He has to go and rescue some of his people who are in danger. Will you come with us and protect us?"

"All right," the Simba said. "But I want your car."

The Belgian said he could keep the car after they had rescued the family. They drove through deserted streets at high speeds with gunfire coming from all directions, picked up the family and brought them safely back to the Immoquateur, where they gave the car to the Simba.

Later that afternoon, Nothomb went out again and brought

back another Belgian family. Again he took a Simba escort—at the price of another car, which had belonged to another Belgian.

No one objected to giving his car up. The Simbas were taking them anyway.

Back in the Immoquateur, Nothomb began ringing up other Belgians to see if they were safe. He made about two hundred calls that day. Miraculously the telephone system stayed in good working order all through the Simba occupation. Nothomb's number—Stanleyville 2904—was to become one of the busiest in the city. Each day he was on the phone for hours, checking to see if anyone was in trouble. If, as often happened, they were in trouble, Nothomb went dashing to the rescue.

All afternoon, more and more Belgians crowded into Nothomb's apartment. By nightfall, there were fifteen frightened people in the flat.

When Hoyt and the three other Americans came out of the vault at nine o'clock that night and found to their relief that the Simbas had departed, Jim Stauffer turned on the master switch. The consulate was flooded with light again. The men felt almost elated; it was as if they had awakened from a bad dream. Hoyt composed a radio message to the embassy in Léopoldville saying that they had just emerged from the vault after an attack on the consulate.

"The United States," Hoyt said, flippantly, "should not hide while things are going on."

Hoyt felt that the attack on the consulate might well have been carried out by individual Simbas, without permission from the Simba authorities. He thought that in a day or two, when he had made contact with the Simba leaders, an apology might well be made and measures would be taken to protect the consulate against any more attacks by individual Simbas. Surely, Hoyt felt, even the Simbas would respect the immunity of diplomats from foreign countries and the sanctity of diplomatic establishments.

The men prepared a light supper. Stauffer and Parkes spread blankets on the floor of the vault. They slept there in case they should have to send a message quickly. Hoyt and Grinwis slept on office couches.

But the next morning—Thursday—it become all too clear that the bad dream had not ended. Scattered firing was heard as the last government troops tried to beat a retreat to the river. Two truckloads of Simbas passed the consulate, and yelled, "Americans!" The American consulate was evidently very much on their minds.

A call came in on the radio from the American embassy in Léopoldville. The embassy told the men that a daring rescue operation was being considered. First, T-28 propeller planes would buzz the area around the consulate. Then an armed helicopter would land on the consulate lawn, pick up the men and, while the T-28's provided cover, carry them away to safety.

A great feeling of relief surged over Hoyt. Then he froze. He remembered that Ernie Houle was still stranded in his apartment in the Immoquateur.

"I can't leave him," Hoyt said.

"We understand, but we would like to go ahead with it," an embassy official said.

"I'll try to get Ernie here," Hoyt said.

Hoyt told the embassy that he would give a signal from the ground; he would park a green car in the consulate driveway if it was all right for the helicopter to come in.

Stauffer and Parkes spent the day locked in the vault. The idea was to maintain constant communication with Léopoldville. Inasmuch as the Simbas had knocked the outer lock from the door, it could only be opened from the inside.

Early in the afternoon, a group of Simbas appeared in front of the consulate. They fired a few shots in the air and honked the horns of cars parked there. Then the Simbas stole Grinwis's car—an air-conditioned Rambler Classic—and a Chevy II that was owned by the U.S. government and used by Hoyt.

Soon after, four Simbas approached the consulate. One of them, who appeared to be their leader, seemed to be under the influence of marijuana. He had glazed eyes and moved with a sort of dance step. The Simbas came up to Hoyt and Grinwis, who happened to be standing in front of the consulate, and pointed rifles at them.

"Give us the keys of your cars," the leader said in crude French.

Hoyt protested that this was an official consular establishment. But he might just as well have tried to explain the theory of relativity to the wild man.

"The keys," he shrieked.

Hoyt saw it was useless to resist. He handed over the keys to two cars.

"The keys to that one, too," the Simba said, pointing to Stauffer's Ford.

Hoyt said he didn't have those keys. Stauffer had them and he was in the vault.

The Simba thrust the rifle against Hoyt's body. "I'm quite capable of killing you, you know," he said.

"I know—what do I have to gain by not giving you the keys?" said Hoyt.

The wild man pondered that for a moment, then seemed to accept it.

A Simba pushed Grinwis into the consulate. They came to the locked vault door.

"*Fungua*—open it," the Simba said.

Stauffer and Parkes kept still.

"I can't open it—the lock's broken off," Grinwis said. "Anyway there's no one in it. It's empty."

The Simba shoved Grinwis against the door and put the tip of the rifle barrel against his chest.

"Open it or I'll kill you."

Death was only a few millimeters away; all the Simba would have to do would be to squeeze the trigger ever so lightly. Grinwis felt that it could not really be happening to him. It was as if he were entangled in a nightmare. But he managed to reply, very calmly: "Go ahead. You might as well kill me. I can't open the door."

The Simba paused. His mind seemed to be wandering. Perhaps his attention span was impaired by hemp. In a moment, he forgot about the vault. The Simbas left with the cars.

Hoyt's spirits sank. He realized that he was not dealing with a revolutionary government, but rather with a gang of wild men to whom diplomatic immunities and civilized behavior meant nothing. He was thankful at least that he had made his wife and child leave Stanleyville before the Simbas arrived.

During the evening the American consulate was shaken by concussions. It was mortar and artillery fire, as well as constant machine-gun fire, coming from the general direction of the Immoquateur apartments, where Nothomb and the Belgians, as well as Ernie Houle, were hiding.

The Immoquateur was typical of the absurdities of Stanleyville—an elegant apartment building in the middle of nowhere. It looked as though it had been transplanted from a city in Florida or California, or from the French Riviera. It consisted of two blocks of flats which were completed, or rather nearly completed, just before the Congo became independent in 1960. There was a row of shops on the ground floor, with air-conditioned apartments above. Each apartment was a triplex, with a living room, dining room, kitchen and three bedrooms, all on various levels. There were two balconies in each apartment—one looking out across the Congo River and the other giving onto a square. The only thing that was lacking in the Immoquateur was that some of the lighting fixtures and other little details had never been installed. Independence came before the building was completely finished and the owners did not care to risk any more money on the venture. And so the apartments often had gaping holes in the plaster where a fixture should have been. But the delight of finding a luxurious apartment building in the heart of Africa was such that no one minded a few holes.

Ernie Houle, the radio operator who was to have been evacuated but who had been stranded in the city, lived on the fourth floor. He stayed there all day Wednesday, when the other Americans were hiding in the vault during the Simba attack, and all day Thursday, when the Simbas stole the cars. Although he was cut off from the other Americans, he was able to keep in contact with Michael Hoyt by telephone. Hoyt told him to stay put for the time being. Most of the time he dozed, read or drank beer. One afternoon he peeped out from his balcony and saw about fifteen canoes filled with Congolese fishermen and their wives and children slip away from the bank and head downstream. They were, quite obviously, trying to escape from the Simbas. Houle was not the only person who saw them: Simba machine gunners opened fire from the shore. With many of the occupants dead or wounded, the canoes drifted on downstream until they were out of sight.

After Houle had been in the apartment a couple of days, there was a knock on the door. It was Peter Rombaut, the honorary British consul and manager of the local branch of the Britch-American Tobacco Co. Rombaut lived outside of town and had decided to come to the Immoquateur for greater protection. Houle brought out a welcoming bottle of beer for his guest and the two men waited it out together.

Now it was Thursday afternoon. On the floor below, Stanleyville 2904 was busy as usual. Baron Nothomb, his clothing in great disarray because he had even less time than usual to attend to sartorial details, was telephoning everyone he knew, trying to find out what was going on.

The baron learned that one unit of the ANC was still holding out—on the left bank of the river. The main part of Stanleyville is on the right bank, but there is a smaller settlement on the other shore. There is no bridge across the Congo at Stanleyville and so the ANC unit was reasonably safe for the moment.

The other apartments in the two Immoquateur blocks were filled not only with the usual tenants, but with Europeans who, like Rombaut, had come in from outlying areas in the hope of finding some protection. In all there were about 160 people in the two blocks when darkness came that evening.

At about 8 P.M., the ANC troops opened up with a tremendous barrage from the left bank, directly across from the Immoquateur. They let loose with everything they had, including mortars and at least one artillery piece. Fortunately for the people in the Immoquateur, the ANC is not noted for the excellence of its marksmanship. Not only are they convinced that it is the noise that kills, but many of the ANC troops shut their eyes when they fire their weapons. The mortar and artillery shells fell in the river. But the troops fared somewhat better with their machine guns and rifles. Soon bullets were raking the Immoquateur.

Nothomb and the people who had taken shelter with him hit the floor. So, too, did Houle and Rombaut and everyone else. Picture windows on the riverfront balconies shattered and broken glass flew across the rooms. Plaster cracked and crumbled. Pictures fell off the walls and lamps tumbled over.

For four agonizing hours, the 160 people in the Immoquateur clawed at the floor, prayed to God, cursed the ANC, and regretted that they had not accepted Nothomb's offer of evacuation to safety in Léopoldville.

All the while, there was a large contingent of Simbas in the streets near the Immoquateur. They, too, had taken cover during the barrage. Looking up at the Immoquateur, they saw bullets coming out of the street-side windows. Actually these were bullets fired by the ANC on the left bank; they had passed through the apartments to emerge from the street-side windows. But to the Simbas it was all too plain: the ANC, they concluded, had hidden in the Immoquateur and now was firing at them.

Midnight came. The ANC stopped shooting. They had either exhausted their ammunition or themselves, or both. The people in the Immoquateur got to their feet. They turned on the lights. Some of them wept, some laughed. The ordeal was over. Or so they thought.

While the whites in the two blocks were rejoicing that the ANC attack was over, the Simbas were fanning out around the street side of the Immoquateur, getting ready for their revenge against what they construed as an ANC attack on them. Then, screaming battle cries, they opened fire at the two blocks point blank.

Windows on the street side shattered under the impact. The people in the two blocks hit the floor once more.

A Belgian, worried over what the Simbas might do to his wife, took her to the roof of an adjacent apartment building. But the Simbas caught them there, beat the man and broke his glasses, then dragged his wife downstairs and raped her.

Screaming and cursing, the Simbas smashed shop windows on the ground floor. They tried to enter the block where Nothomb, Houle and Rombaut were hiding, but were stopped by an iron gate. They shot at the lock and battered it

28

with rifle butts, but the lock held. They turned to the iron gate at the other block. This time the lock gave way. Whooping victoriously, they poured through the gateway.

Some of the Europeans in that block jumped into elevators, then stopped them between floors. Others hid beneath beds and in cupboards. One group ran to the roof, moments ahead of the Simbas, and, one at a time, climbed down a ladder into an airshaft. The building manager, who was the last to enter the airshaft, bolted a door from the inside. The door had a skull and crossbones painted on it—there was high-voltage electrical equipment in the airshaft—and the Simbas did not go near it.

The Simbas ran up and down the stairs for hours, shooting into the ceiling and walls. They smashed down doors and burst into apartments, looking for nonexistent ANC troops. They pummeled the whites whom them found in the apartments. They smashed furniture and other belongings and set several small fires.

The Simbas rounded up fourteen Europeans, put them on a truck and drove them away. No one knew where they would be taken, but they feared the worst.

It was Patrick Nothomb who averted what would otherwise have been a massacre. Crawling across the floor of his apartment with bullets whizzing past overhead, he reached for the telephone and soon Stanleyville 2904 was in action. Nothomb rang up all the ministries, all of the military camps and everyone else he could think of. But he could get through to no one in authority. Then he made one more effort to reach an officer in Camp Ketele.

To Nothomb's astonishment, General Nicolas Olenga, the commander in chief of the Simba legions, came on the phone.

"You have hidden ANC troops in your apartment buildings!" Olenga thundered.

"No, no," Nothomb protested.

"I have just given the order," said Olenga. "We're bringing mortars up. We're going to blow your buildings to pieces." Nothomb was aghast. He argued and pleaded with the general for half an hour while bullets whizzed overhead.

Finally Olenga said: "All right, you have convinced me.

I'll give the order to stop the mortar attack and I'll pull all of my men back. Wait five minutes—you'll see."

It was 6 A.M.—Friday. Dawn was breaking over Stanleyville. The Simbas still were ransacking apartments and racing up and down stairs firing guns wildly. A jeep pulled up in front of the Immoquateur. A Simba officer got out and blew a whistle. Instantly there was silence.

Peeping from his balcony, Nothomb saw an incredible sight. Dozens of Simbas came pouring down out of the other block. They assembled in the street. The officer who had blown the whistle gave the order. The Simbas trudged back to Camp Ketele, looking neither to the right nor the left. In two minutes, the street was empty except for the officer and two other Simbas who had come in the jeep.

"Where is the Belgian consul?" the officer called out. There was nothing threatening in his manner; rather he seemed pleasant and relaxed.

The diminutive Nothomb trotted out to meet the savior.

"I am Commandant Sengha," the officer said. The rank of commandant was borrowed by the Simbas from the Belgian army and indicates an officer ranking between a captain and a major. "General Olenga wants to see you and the English consul at Camp Ketele at once."

Nothomb, accompanied by a Simba, went up to Houle's apartment to get Peter Rombaut. The Simba pointed at Houle. "You come, too," he said. Houle, who was wearing slacks and a T-shirt, started out the door with Rombaut and Nothomb. The Simba noticed that Houle, who was an ex-Navy man, had a tattoo on his arm.

"You go put a shirt on," the Simba said. "If the men at Camp Ketele see that tattoo, they'll shoot."

Houle gulped. He went back and put on a shirt. When he returned to the front door of the apartment he found that Nothomb, Rombaut and the Simba guard had gone on downstairs in the elevator. With the wisdom of the long-suffering enlisted man—never volunteer for anything and particularly for trouble—he went back into the apartment and shut the door.

The Simba forgot about Houle. Nothomb and Rombaut got into the jeep with Commandant Sengha. They rode along in silence through the empty city. The sun had come up out of the jungles to the east and Stanleyville was bathed in the golden glow of morning. The baron's usual jauntiness was gone. He was full of foreboding. He had just survived one nightmare, but now Camp Ketele presented a new danger. The Simbas might well tear him and Rombaut to pieces.

On the way to Camp Ketele, Baron Nothomb saw many corpses of ANC soldiers along the road.

3

THE LORD OF THE SIMBAS

When Baron Patrick Nothomb neared Camp Ketele, the place looked, from a distance, the same as ever—a collection of buildings in an open field, surrounded by a wire fence. But when the jeep rolled through the gates, Nothomb wondered for a moment if he had lost his sanity. It was as if he had been whisked back fifteen centuries to find himself in the camp of Attila, king of the Huns, lord of the barbarians. Camp Ketele was one vast sea of Simbas. There were well over a thousand of them. Most were in the frenzy of a drunken victory celebration. Bare-chested, they were decorated with feathers and bits of leopard and monkey skins. They fired guns into the air. They shouted. They danced and pounded on drums. Women whooped. Children and dogs ran around wildly.

In the midst of the uproar, one group of Simbas was going through a drill exercise, marching smartly back and forth while an officer barked commands. Nearby, a group of forlorn ANC prisoners was sitting under guard. No one paid much attention to them. Later on, the lucky ones would be impressed into the Simba legions. The rest would be executed, after appropriate torture.

The jeep stopped in front of the guardhouse. The mob swirled around the vehicle. The noise was deafening. Nothomb wondered if he would ever get out of the place alive. Then a man dressed in the uniform of a Belgian general stepped from the headquarters building. A hush fell over the riotous camp.

T-28 "Trojan"

It was Nicolas Olenga, the self-styled lieutenant general and lord of the Simba legions.

Olenga was a striking figure. He was in his early thirties, and nearly six feet tall, with a lean, hard body. He walked erectly but not stiffly; he carried himself with the grace and ease of a man who knew that he was born to command. Olenga had a handsome, intent face, with dark, piercing eyes. He had a mustache and goatee. The khaki-colored uniform—no one knew how he had acquired it—was a bit too big for him but nevertheless he wore it well. There were three gold stars, the insignia of a lieutenant general, on his jacket lapels. Gold braid was draped over one shoulder. The cap was a regular officer's cap with one exception; on it he wore a piece of leopard skin, the symbol of authority. And then, to heighten the effect, he carried a ceremonial officer's sword on a Sam Browne belt.

Olenga strode toward the jeep. The throng of Simbas parted in reverence. Nothomb had a moment of panic, but then he saw that the general was smiling. Olenga, as it turned out, could be the most charming of men—when he

33

was victorious. When he was losing, the lord of the Simbas took on another personality.

"I'm glad to see you, Mr. Consul," Olenga said in excellent French, nodding to Nothomb. He did not offer to shake hands; it was taboo for a Simba to touch a European. "And you, too," he added, beaming at Peter Rombaut.

"I'm very sorry about what happened last night," Olenga went on. "It was a stupid mistake. It will never happen again; I can assure you of that. I will do everything that is necessary to protect you. I promise you."

Nothomb and Rombaut felt relieved. Perhaps the nightmare was over.

"I am glad to inform you," Olenga said, "that since we began our campaign we have never met a Belgian or an English mercenary fighting against us. I appreciate this act of friendship on the part of your governments."

Suddenly Olenga's face knotted. "But it is not the case with the Americans," he said. A murmur went through the mob of Simbas. "The Americans!" they shouted. "Down with the Americans!"

"Every day we fight two hundred American soldiers," Olenga cried. "These are regular American soldiers, not mercenaries, because the American army is here in the Congo! They are attacking us!"

The Simbas screamed: "Yes! yes!"

"We have killed two hundred American soldiers," Olenga shrieked. "You see, we are not afraid of the American army. All the American army is here in the Congo, but, since we are victorious, we are the best army in the world. We are stronger than the American army. What a pity we have no ships because if we had them we would go and invade America!"

The Simbas roared approval.

"I want to see the American consul, and I am going to tell him this," Olenga was shouting.

Nothomb screwed up his courage and interrupted the general. "The American consulate has been attacked by your troops," he said. "You can think what you want about the United States, but you can't attack a country's consulate. It is a dreadful thing. We are obliged to protest in the name of our American colleagues."

34

Olenga stared at Nothomb. Perhaps he was measuring him. Then he smiled. "Of course," he said. "I will call the American consul and tell him that I did not order the attack on the consulate." Then his tone changed. "My soldiers are so furious against the Americans that I could not prevent the attack," Olenga cried.

The Simbas whooped in approval.

Camp Ketele was hardly the place for diplomatic negotiations, yet Patrick Nothomb was a tenacious young man. There was another matter he wanted to discuss with the general. Nothomb would like to have a Red Cross plane come to Stanleyville to evacuate some of the whites—women, children, the elderly and those who were sick. Nothomb hoped that this, if successful, might lead to a general evacuation later on of everyone else who wanted to go.

The general eyed Nothomb coldly. "We shall see," he said. "But not immediately. No, I can't authorize this immediately."

Then the general brightened. "I can't spend any more time with you now," he said. "I have to organize the occupation of the city. But I will try to meet with the consuls and the directors of the business firms tomorrow. In the meantime, we will put Simba sentries in front of all the houses where the white people live. You will be protected."

With that, the general turned and strode back into the headquarters building. Nothomb and Rombaut were driven back to the Immoquateur. There they found the fourteen Europeans who had been taken away in the truck during the nighttime attack—the Simbas had taken them to Camp Ketele, but then had brought them back unharmed.

Olenga was as good as his word about the guards. Nothomb, Rombaut and the other consuls were provided with Simbas who accompanied them whenever they had to travel about the city on business. So, too, were managers of local companies given protection. Everyone got a guard—except the Americans.

General Olenga was, of course, mad. From time to time he would rant that he had captured one hundred American soldiers and that he had killed "thousands." There were no American combat troops in the Congo, but that made little difference to Olenga. Indeed, his grasp on sanity was so tenuous that he later accused the Belgian government of dropping an atomic bomb on a Congolese town, killing "100,000 people."

But Olenga's anti-Americanism was real enough. One reason for it was the U.S. support for Prime Minister Moise Tshombe, the new head of the central government. This was a new and somewhat embarrassing role for the United States. The State Department had backed the UN "peace-keeping" force to the hilt when it waged three wars that finally succeeded in crushing a secessionist movement, led by Tshombe, in Katanga province. Indeed, it was the American government which largely financed these operations. The State Department's position then was that it opposed all secessionist movements and that it strove, instead, for a strong and unified central government in the Congo.

During the Katanga wars, the State Department gave its all-out support to Cyrille Adoula, as prime minister of the central government. But Adoula lost control. After a bout of furious politicking that makes sense only in the Congo, if it makes sense even there, the renegade Tshombe was invited back from exile in Spain and became prime minister of a government against which he once had rebelled. The U.S. embassy in Léopoldville seems to have been caught unawares by the move. Tshombe took office. And the United States, like the United Nations, had no choice but to support a man whom it once had so righteously denounced.

What made the American position all the more painful was that Tshombe was greatly disliked by many other African leaders. They regarded him as a "puppet" of European interests and particularly of Belgian mining companies in Katanga. The American "image" in Africa suffered accordingly. After having basked for years in the rosy glow of friendship with new African states, the U.S. now found itself the target of mounting vilification, not only from radicals, but from moderate elements as well.

So much for Tshombe's international reputation. As far as the Congo itself was concerned, Tshombe seemed to be as effective as the other Congolese politicians, perhaps even more so.

Another and even more important reason for the Simbas'

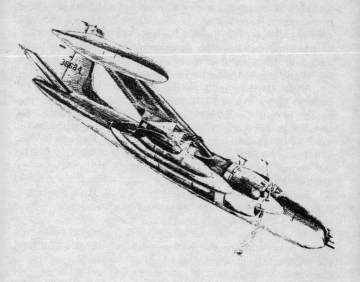

B-26K

anti-Americanism was that the United States supplied the Tshombe government with some propeller-driven airplanes for use in suppressing the Simba revolt and other disturbances. These airplanes included single-engine T-28 trainers, equipped with rockets and machine guns, and twin-engine B-26 fighter-bombers. They were piloted by anti-Castro Cubans who were recruited by the Central Intelligence Agency. There were never very many of these planes—at one time there were four B-26's and six T-28's, plus some cargo planes and helicopters. But they proved most effective in the jungle fighting of the Congo.

The Simbas developed a great fear of the planes; they invoked their most powerful magic in an attempt to ward them off. Bridges and other likely targets were festooned with palm branches and other talismans. When a plane appeared, the Simbas would chant, "*Mai, mai.*" They would assume ferocious expressions that, in other circumstances, would drive an enemy to despair. But nevertheless the planes would come down out of the sky, screaming like a thousand devils, and reduce festooned bridges, vehicles and other targets to rubble in a matter of seconds. Then they would soar back into the sky and disappear, leaving the Simbas raging in impotent fury against "the Americans."

Quite apart from the planes, Americans have become the number one devils in a cult that is widespread in the eastern Congo—a cult which seeks to deify the late Patrice Lumumba, the first prime minister of the Congo, who was murdered in 1961 while in the custody of Tshombe in Katanga. When Lumumba was an up-and-coming young politician, he sought the support of gullible tribesmen by promising that, when independence came, they would all "turn white." They would be rich—they would live in big houses, just like the Europeans, and they would drive European cars. No one would have to work. Or so Lumumba said.

All over the eastern Congo, masses of ignorant tribesmen are convinced that it was only Lumumba's death which kept the promise from coming true. They blame the death on American and Belgian "imperialists." They believe that Lumumba will return to earth in a second coming to make good his word. Naturally, the Belgian and American imperialists —but particularly the rich and powerful Americans—will do their best to try to foil Lumumba. But Lumumba inevitably will win.

In other circumstances, the Lumumba myth might have died out eventually, but Communist China and the Soviet bloc have done their best to keep it alive. Even in outlying villages, at least one person owns a transistor radio, around which everyone gathers to hear, among other things, propaganda from high-powered Communist radio stations. Day in and day out the Congolese are told that all of their troubles are due to the American imperialists. Day in and day out, Moscow and Peking strive to portray themselves as great friends of Lumumba, and of the Congolese people in general.

General Nicolas Olenga, smarting under the air attacks and probably himself a prisoner, at least to a degree, of the Lumumba myth, was, of course, unable to produce any American soldiers that he said he had captured in combat. But the general did have five officials of the American government in his grasp—Michael Hoyt and the other consular personnel.

When Patrick Nothomb returned to the Immoquateur that Friday morning, Michael Hoyt was wrestling with the toughest decision he ever had to make. A helicopter rescue of the American consular personnel still was possible. But, inasmuch as the Immoquateur had been under attack all night long, it had been impossible to bring Ernie Houle to the consulate. In any case, Houle was not the only other American in Stanleyville; there were, in addition, twenty-four—most of whom were missionaries and their families. The Simbas would be furious if aircraft came to snatch the American consular personnel from their hands. Even if Houle could be saved, it was possible that the Simbas would retaliate by murdering the missionaries.

And there was another problem. The Simbas were fairly well armed. Perhaps they might succeed in shooting down the helicopter, killing everyone aboard. Should they take the risk? After all, it was still faintly possible that Hoyt could secure their release through negotiation.

Hoyt lighted a cigarette and inhaled. After that one cigarette in the vault, he was back on the habit again.

The temptation to go through with a helicopter rescue was, of course, almost overwhelming. If all went well, Hoyt and the others would be back that evening in Léopoldville. Hoyt thought about the joyous reunion with his wife and son, about how pleasant it would be to spend a day without having to fear for his life.

But it was impossible. Hoyt crushed out the cigarette. He got on the radio with the embassy in Léopoldville. The plan was dropped.

During the day, several Simbas came to the consulate. There was no rough stuff this time; they simply took another car, leaving only a Volkswagen. The Volkswagen was of little use to them at the moment. It had a flat tire.

The Americans spent the day feeling gloomy. But then, at 7 P.M., a car came up the driveway and a welcome face appeared—that of Baron Nothomb. He seemed to have forgotten the terrifying events in the Immoquateur the night before and was back in form, bubbling over with enthusiasm and good humor. A meeting of the consular corps was set for that evening in the Belgian consulate general on the second floor of the Immoquateur. General Olenga had promised to come and discuss the situation with the consuls. Nothomb had come to the American consulate to escort Hoyt and Vice-Consul Grinwis safely to the meeting.

There were a dozen or so men at the meeting; along with the consuls, several business leaders were present. Hoyt, Grinwis, Nothomb and Paul Duqué, the Belgian vice-consul, were the only professional diplomats present. The rest were honorary consuls—local businessmen who represented their governments in routine matters. In addition to Peter Rombaut, the Briton, there were honorary consuls for France, Italy, Holland, Greece and Cyprus.

While the consuls and businessmen waited for Olenga, they talked about their plight. Many were extremely nervous; all were worried about the future. They had just learned that a white man who had worked as a local contract employee for the United Nations had been badly beaten by the Simbas. Although no one knew the details of the attack, they recalled that the rebel leader Soumialot had said that he would not "guarantee the safety" of any Americans or UN personnel.

The consuls talked about the plight of the Americans. They suggested that Hoyt and the others remain in their consulate for the time being. They should not circulate around the city; that would only exacerbate the anti-American feelings of the Simbas and might bring on violence. The consuls cautioned the Americans that they should especially avoid going near Camp Ketele. "Olenga is so crazy that he might well shoot you if he sees you," Nothomb said.

Anyone who has lived in Africa knows that Africans are seldom punctual and frequently do not bother to keep an appointment at all. And so it came as no surprise when General Olenga failed to appear. The meeting broke up. Nothomb took Hoyt and Grinwis back to the American consulate. The two men agreed that they should remain discreetly in the background for the moment. But their hearts were heavy. They realized that they were being isolated from the rest of the white community.

It was an isolation that was to grow progressively worse.

* * *

The next few days were peaceful—or peaceful at least by Stanleyville standards—as far as the Americans were concerned.

In the morning, two Simba officers visited the consulate. They greeted Grinwis warmly. Grinwis blinked and looked again. Sure enough, it was Frédéric and Evariste. Grinwis had hired them two years before as night watchmen for the consulate. Then, some months previously, another consular official had fired them for fighting between themselves. Frédéric and Evariste seemed to have settled their differences —they were the best of friends now—and they had, since their dismissal as night watchmen, risen far in the world. The two men had been ANC soldiers before becoming watchmen, and because of their military experience the Simbas had made them officers. They bore no grudge against the consulate and, after exchanging pleasantries, they went away, saying:

"Don't worry—we'll look after you."

Later on, Grinwis's customary composure was shaken when a servant came to the consulate to tell him that a group of Simbas was waiting for him in his house, at the edge of own. They had found a chauffeur's khaki uniform in the nouse. To the Simbas, this was conclusive evidence that Grinwis had been hiding ANC troops. There was only one penalty for hiding ANC troops; everyone knew that. And so he Simbas were waiting patiently for Grinwis to come back o his house so they could kill him.

Next evening—it was Sunday evening—Hoyt concluded hat they would be trapped in Stanleyville for some time to come. His wife and son had been waiting in Léopoldville; since there was no knowing when he could join them, it would be best if they returned to the United States.

Hoyt got on the voice radio. Inasmuch as anyone could listen in on voice transmission, Hoyt talked in a roundabout vay.

"Tell my Number One to go to Jerome," he said. By this ne meant that his wife should to return to Jerome, Arizona, vhere the couple had a vacation home.

"Jerome?"

"Yes, Jerome."

There was a pause. An embassy official puzzled a mo-ment. He concluded that Hoyt was talking about Jerome

Anany, a former minister of defense of the central government. The embassy telephoned Anany. He was even more mystified.

Mrs. Hoyt, who had been maintaining a vigil at the communications center in the embassy ever since the evacuation, cleared up the confusion, then came on the radio.

"You'd better go back to Jerome," Hoyt said.

"I don't want to go home," she said.

"You've got to," he said. "I don't anticipate being relieved right away."

After some argument, Mrs. Hoyt agreed. An embassy official came back on the radio. He wanted to know if all five consular personnel were safe, so he asked: "What do you do in your spare time?"

There were only four Americans at the consulate then, Houle being still at the Immoquateur.

"We can play bridge," said Hoyt, "but we have to contact our kibitzer by telephone." Then he signed off and went to bed.

SIXTEEN HUNDRED TRUMP CARDS

Nicolas Olenga was nervous. The long-awaited meeting between him and the leaders of the European community had finally convened—in the Immoquateur offices of the local Chamber of Commerce. Now, as the great chieftain sat at a table, looking out at a roomful of white faces, he seemed to have lost some of his regal mannerisms. He fidgeted. He cleared his throat. He whispered nervously to his aides. It was probably the first time in Olenga's life that he had ever addressed such a large gathering of Europeans. He had, of course, the power of life or death over them. But that was not enough to erase a lifetime of psychological attitudes. Like many other Africans, he was uncomfortable in the presence of people with more education, wealth, skills and worldly experience.

Olenga was dressed in his Belgian general's uniform. In addition to a sword, he wore a pistol on his belt. He was flanked by what might be called his general staff, a group of bearded men in their twenties and thirties who were dressed in bits and pieces of military uniforms. Along with the officers, two ancient harpies stood next to Olenga, glaring ferociously at the Europeans. They were members of a paramilitary organization called the "Nationalist Women." The organization had flourished during the 1960–61 secession in Stanleyville; its members had served as a sort of bodyguard to Antoine Gizenga, the secessionist leader. After the Gizenga regime was toppled, nothing more was heard of the Nationalist Women until the Simba conquest, when they reappeared, as if by magic. The two who attended the meeting in the Immoquateur were dressed in trousers and they had feathers in their hair. To give themselves the proper military appearance, they wore the blue-colored steel helmets of the UN troops. And, to top it off, each lady carried a pistol—not a real pistol, but a toy one—on her belt. "Dreadful women—remedy against love," Nothomb muttered. They upset even General Olenga. He confided to Nothomb on another occasion that he had not recreated the movement and that he wished the ladies would leave military matters to him.

Some one hundred Europeans—consuls, businessmen, physicians and others—had gathered for the meeting. The atmosphere was akin to that of an Irish wake. The reason for the gathering was anything but joyous, but a certain festive mood nevertheless prevailed. Many of the men had not seen each other since the Simba conquest. They had been worried about the safety of friends and colleagues. Now, if nothing else, they found that their friends and colleagues were safe and sound, at least for the moment.

The business community had selected as its spokesman a small, wiry man named José Romnée, who was the manager of a petroleum company. Romnée, then fifty-one years old, was a long-time settler in the Congo and his face was bronzed by nearly twenty years in the equatorial sun. He fought with Belgian forces during World War II, first in Africa and then in Europe and wound up as a paratroop officer. Romnée knew just about everyone of consequence in the eastern Congo, including many of the rebel leaders.

When Olenga opened the meeting, he seemed to have recovered his composure. He made a short speech. "I want the Europeans to go about their work in a normal fashion," he said. "The conflict that is going on in the Congo now is an internal one, between the Congolese. It does not concern you. You will be protected."

Romnée complained that several Europeans had been beaten by Simbas. The general appeared to be upset when he heard this. He assured the meeting that if any Simba abused a European he would be severely punished.

Next Romnée brought up the question that was foremost in everyone's mind: were they free to go to Léopoldville?

Olenga thought. "No, not for the moment," he said. "Not until my troops conquer the entire Congo."

The Europeans were stunned. They knew now that there would be no quick escape from Stanleyville. There was always the hope that they would get out later—that the lord of the Simbas would relent. But, although he was most reasonable at this point, he nevertheless was closing the exit door in their faces. The Congolese "internal conflict" would, after all, concern them very much.

After Romnée had recovered his composure, he asked the general if they could send messages to relatives and friends in Léopoldville.

"Oh, yes," Olenga said. "But, of course, there will be censorship. You can send cables saying that you are in good health." He paused, then added: "But that's all."

The screw was tightening. The Europeans realized that they were not only going to be held captive, perhaps as hostages, but that they were prevented from alerting the outside world to their plight. It was as if they were being enveloped in the soft, lush greenery of the jungle, helpless, unable to cry out.

Having dispensed with those matters, Olenga turned to some economic problems that had been bothering him. The economy was plainly in trouble, he said. There had been a great deal of inflation since the Congo became independent in 1960. But the solution was easy. From that moment on, all prices in Stanleyville would be rolled back to the 1960 level. Wages, however, would remain the same.

Romnée and the other businessmen squawked loudly.

"Why not?" said Olenga. "A franc is, after all, worth a franc."

Protests from the businessmen were so voluble that for a moment no one could be heard. Olenga silenced them: the decision was final; prices would be rolled back to the 1960 level.

Next the general abolished taxes. When Romnée pointed out that governments could not exist without an income from taxes, Olenga hushed him with the observation that inasmuch

45

as this was a "people's revolution," taxes were no longer necessary.

Olenga at that time was quite rich. When his men overran the Air Congo office in Stanleyville, they discovered a shipment of around 200 million Congolese francs in worn banknotes that had been withdrawn from circulation and were to be flown back to Léopoldville. At the black market rate this would amount to more than half a million dollars. And, if that ran out, Olenga knew that he could always help himself to whatever was on hand in Stanleyville's banks—and in the pockets of the Europeans.

Later Olenga amended his tax decree: only the Congolese were excused from taxes. Foreigners were told they must continue to pay.

When General Olenga announced his economic decrees, the European-owned trading firms in Stanleyville were still well stocked. A few months previously, a large amount of consumer goods had been imported. But, once word of the new decrees got out, Congolese entrepreneurs descended on the stores and bought up manufactured goods at the new bargain prices, then made windfall profits by selling the same goods in the native markets at inflated prices. The foreign merchants were ruined. In a matter of days, Stanleyville ceased to have a functioning modern economy. "Maybe Olenga is a very great soldier," Baron Nothomb lamented, "but about the economics, he is dreadful."

After dealing with Romnée and the business community, Olenga summoned the consular corps to a meeting in the next room. Nothomb opened the session by informing the general that the consuls were very worried about the safety of the foreign community and the foreign consulates.

"Unfortunately I have too few Simbas to provide an adequate guard," Olenga said. Then his voice hardened. "The reason is that my soldiers are being killed by the Americans!" Olenga's voice grew shrill. "Where is the American consul?" he said.

Hoyt indicated that he was the American consul.

"We have killed 250 American soldiers who were trying to defend Wanie Rukula," Olenga cried.

Several Simba officers who were standing behind the general started to chant in unison: *"États-Unis d'Amérique* . . .

États-Unis d'Amérique . . .—United States of America . . . United States of America . . ."

"I myself have seen thousands of American troops fighting us," Olenga continued. "I have captured them and I am going to bring them to Stanleyville. You will see."

The Simbas chanted: *"États-Unis d'Amérique* . . . *États-Unis d'Amérique* . . ."

Hoyt interrupted. He denied that there were any American troops fighting in the Congo.

"I have evidence!" Olenga thundered. He did not look directly at Hoyt; rather he addressed the speech to the other consuls. "I have papers taken from American soldiers whom I have captured."

"May I see the papers?" Hoyt asked.

Olenga ignored him. The Simbas chanted: *"États-Unis d'Amérique* . . . *États-Unis d'Amérique* . . ."

"We have shot down many American planes. We have captured their crews," Olenga said. "As soon as I capture Léopoldville, I will declare war on the United States. I will invade the United States as soon as I get the necessary transport."

"États-Unis d'Amérique . . . *États-Unis d'Amérique* . . ."

Olenga told Hoyt that he was expelling him and the other American consular personnel. They would have to leave on the first available transportation.

"États-Unis d'Amérique . . . *États-Unis d'Amerique* . . ."

"If you want us to leave, we have no choice," said Hoyt. "But what about the American missionaries?"

"I am only against the military and civil representatives of the American government," Olenga replied. "I want the American missionaries to remain."

Nothomb broke in to ask Olenga if he would allow a Red Cross plane to bring in medicines and take out women, children, the elderly and those who were ill.

"It's possible; we'll talk about it later," Olenga said.

It was the second time that the general had evaded the request that a Red Cross plane be permitted to land. Nothomb was very worried now. As a diplomat he would, of course, continue to plead the case with Olenga. But even then he was convinced that Olenga had no intentions of allowing Stanleyville's sixteen hundred white and Asian foreigners to leave. They had fallen into his hands quite unexpectedly. Now he had sixteen hundred trump cards to be played at the appropriate time.

Olenga did make one concession to the consuls. He assigned a big, heavily-bearded captain to look after their protection. The meeting was about to break up when Olenga said he had one more announcement. He declared that he was going to set up a "People's Republic," composed of civilians, which would govern the rebel-held territories. The president of this new government, he announced, would be Alphonse Kinghis.

It was as if the consuls had been struck in the face. Kinghis was known to all of them as a madman and as the fanatic leader of an antiwhite, anarchistic religious cult. The cult, known as the Kitawala movement, was a weird mixture of teachings of the Watchtower group and African paganism. Kinghis, who was a giant of a man physically—well over six feet tall and weighing two hundred pounds—was the "bishop" of the Kitawalists. He had been in prison in Stanleyville for two years and had been released only recently by the Simbas. He had on one occasion distinguished himself by declaring that the Americans had bewitched the Congolese twenty-franc note, that the Americans had made it radioactive, and that if anyone slept in a room with a twenty-franc note he would be contaminated. When the Congo became independent in 1960, Kinghis and his wild-eyed followers tore down several monuments to explorers and colonial governors that the Belgians had erected in Stanleyville. The mob went to the cathedral and attempted to topple a statue of Christ. "That isn't Christ," Kinghis shrieked, pointing at the statue, "that's King Albert." A Congolese priest rushed out of the cathedral and succeeded in driving the mob away, but only after they had broken a hand from the statue.

For a brief time after independence, Kinghis had been one of the provincial authorities. He was deposed by Léopoldville. When soldiers came to arrest him, they found him and his followers in the act of crucifying a man.

The consular meeting broke up. The consuls congratulated Hoyt on the fact that he was to be expelled from Stanleyville. "You're really lucky to be getting out," Peter Rombaut remarked.

But, as Hoyt returned to the consulate, he was anything but elated. Common sense told him that he and the other Americans were far from being out. He radioed the embassy in Léopoldville and told them that he and the four other consular personnel had been ordered to leave Stanleyville. But he cautioned the embassy not to send an American plane to pick them up. It would be too risky in view of the Simbas' anti-Americanism and also in view of their fear of airplanes. They might shoot the plane down. Or, even if they did allow it to land, they might "requisition" it. Hoyt felt that if the Americans were to get out at all it could only be done in a Red Cross plane.

That was the last time that Hoyt was in direct communication with the embassy.

Later that day, Hoyt rang up the consul general of the Sudan and asked him if he would take responsibility for the administrative affairs of the consulate. The thought was that perhaps he also would intercede with the Simbas. As an African, he would in all likelihood have more influence with the Simbas than his European colleagues would have. The Sudanese evaded the plea. He never gave Hoyt a flat no, but it added up to the same thing.

Hoyt telephoned Peter Rombaut. Rombaut was not a diplomat—he was only the honorary British consul—but he said he would be delighted to help.

The Sudanese consul general disappeared from Stanleyville soon after. General Olenga gave him a pass allowing him to return home by road. The Sudan, as it turned out, supported the Simbas. Later it assisted in the airlift of Communist-made weapons to them.

Early in the afternoon of August 11, a Belgian contractor arrived at the consulate with several of his Congolese workmen. Hoyt had asked them to repair the glass front door, which had been shattered by the gunfire of the Simbas six days previously. The men fixed the door. Hoyt asked if they could take the flag down. It had been flying day and night ever since the rope was cut by a bullet during the battle on the consulate lawn.

Just then a car pulled up and Ernie Houle got out. Hoyt and the others greeted him warmly; they had not seen him since the Simbas overran the city a week previously, leaving

Houle stranded in the Immoquateur. A carload of Simbas happened to be passing by the consulate at that moment and their attention was attracted by the man on the flagpole.

"What are you doing?" they asked as they pulled into the driveway.

Hoyt explained that this was the American consulate and that General Olenga had guaranteed that it and the other foreign consulates would be protected. The Simbas looked around the consulate, then ordered the five Americans to sit on the front steps. Two Simbas with automatic weapons were told to guard the Americans. The others said they were going to Camp Ketele to see what General Olenga had to say about it.

The five Americans waited for what seemed an eternity. As they learned later, the Simbas did not find General Olenga at Camp Ketele. And so they went to the airport, another Simba command post, where they met Major Lambert Nasor. The major was a short, stocky and fierce-looking man. He wore a cap that had been fashioned from the mane of a lion. And it was no ordinary brown mane; it came from a magnificent black-maned *simba*.

Nasor and the Simbas arrived at the consulate in an auto and a truck. They tumbled out of the vehicles. "We've come to search this place," they said. And then, without further explanation, they began beating the five Americans with rifle butts and the flat side of bayonets.

The Simbas were careful in administering the beating. They wanted to cause as much pain as possible, but they did not want to kill or permanently maim their victims—at least not yet. They smashed their rifle butts against the shoulders, backs, buttocks and legs of the Americans. They also hit them in the kidneys, which is particularly painful. But the Simbas took care not to hit them on the head or the back of the neck—blows in either place could cause permanent disability or death.

Some of the Simbas flailed at the Americans with the flats of bayonets. But sometimes their weapons were turned slightly. Soon small cuts were opened on the Americans' arms and legs. Blood oozed out.

One Simba came up behind Houle and smashed a rifle butt between his shoulder blades. It knocked Houle to his knees.

"You open that vault or we'll kill you," Major Nasor shrieked in bad French.

The Simbas drove Hoyt into the consulate with a flurry of blows, leaving the other four men outside.

"*Fungua, fungua,*" they shouted, pointing at the vault door.

Hoyt protested that diplomats and diplomatic offices are entitled to immunity. A Simba replied by raising a rifle and smashing the butt into Hoyt's side.

"*Fungua!*"

"I can't open it—the knob's broken off," Hoyt wailed as the Simbas worked over him with rifle butts.

In desperation, Hoyt got a hammer and chisel. "Okay— I'll try to break into the vault," he said. Hoyt began chipping at the lock, trying to jimmy it open. Every few minutes, the Simbas urged him on with more blows.

The other Simbas, meanwhile, had ordered Grinwis, Houle, Stauffer and Parkes to line up at attention in the driveway. The Simbas found two large flags in the consulate— one the Stars and Stripes and the other the American consular flag, which is a sea of stars on a blue background. Whooping with glee, they made the men hold the two flags while they were beaten. A Simba found some small American flags which are flown on consular automobiles. They made the four men chew on these flags while they continued to rain blows on them.

Then the Simbas invented a new game. They brought two typist's chairs out into the driveway. While a Simba sat in a chair, another would roll it into one of the Americans, knocking him out of line. Each time the man then would be knocked back into line with a rifle butt wielded by a Simba standing behind him.

Although the Simbas were well armed and outnumbered the Americans by more than two to one, they displayed a curious cowardice. They always hit the Americans from behind.

None of the Americans said a word while he was beaten. They figured that if they protested the Simbas would interpret it as a challenge. And they knew they could not fight back—they would be gunned down if they tried. They could only stand there and take it.

The Simbas pointed to the little flags that each man had in his mouth and cried, *"Mangez, mangez—eat, eat."*

The men chewed on the cloth. They found that it would not come apart, even if they chewed hard. Grinwis had a moment of panic. He feared that the Simbas might try to stuff the flags down their throats—they would surely have choked to death. But the Simbas did not appear to be particularly interested in whether anyone was actually eating the flags; they just wanted them to chew on them.

Inside the consulate, Michael Hoyt finally succeeded, after twenty-five minutes of frenzied work, in breaking into the vault. He stepped back so that the Simbas could enter. "No, you go first," Major Nasor said. The major was very nervous;

perhaps there were armed men in the vault. He chanted, *"Mai, mai"* several times before he followed Hoyt into the chamber.

Nasor stared dumbly at the radio equipment for several moments. Then he shouted: "The attic—open the attic!" Nasor was convinced that ANC troops were hidden somewhere in the premises—perhaps, he now thought, in the attic.

Hoyt, followed by the Simbas, climbed a ladder into the attic. The Simbas looked around and found nothing.

"Take off your tie," one of them shouted.

Neckties were another Simba taboo. Hoyt took it off and dropped it on the floor.

On the way down, Hoyt fell from the ladder, cutting a large gash in his hand. Blood poured out.

The Simbas pounded on the floor.

FAL Auto Rifle

52

"Fungua!" they shouted, indicating that they wanted Hoyt to show them the cellar. Hoyt protested that there was no cellar in the building. When Nasor was out of sight, a Simba told Hoyt to take his watch off and lay it on the floor. The man snatched it up. It was taboo for the Simbas to steal, but if someone "voluntarily" laid a watch on the floor, that was different.

One Simba spotted the Volkswagen in the driveway. The flat tire had been repaired and the Simba demanded the keys. Hoyt told him that his chauffeur had the keys and that the chauffeur was not there at the moment. Another Simba came up behind Hoyt and hit him in the back with a rifle butt. They chased Hoyt around the consulate, raining blows on his back and shouting, "The keys!" One Simba cracked him on the top of his head with the barrel of a rifle. Hoyt staggered.

Major Nasor rammed the barrel of a Fal—a Belgian automatic rifle—into Hoyt's chest. Calmly and deliberately, Nasor snapped a cartridge into the breech. He took off the safety catch. Then he pointed down at the nonexistent cellar.

"Fungua!"

"What do I have to gain by lying about a cellar?" Hoyt cried. "There's no cellar, no cellar."

Hoyt was not certain how much French Nasor understood. But in a moment the major lowered the Fal. He shoved Hoyt outside. The Simbas ordered the Americans into the truck, beating them with rifle butts. The truck was one that had been given to the Congolese government by the American government. On it was painted the standard symbol of trucks that are given as foreign-aid gifts: a pair of hands, clasped in everlasting friendship.

The Americans were forced to hold the two big flags as they stood in the back of the truck and to keep the smaller flags in their mouths. Then the Simbas got another idea. The floor of the truck was littered with dried fish. *"Mangez,"* the Simbas exclaimed in glee. The Americans chewed on the fish. Some of the men retched and spat the fish out.

Major Nasor, grinning from ear to ear, declared: "We are taking you to the Lumumba Monument. We're going to kill you there."

The American-donated friendship truck started up, the

flags flying in the wind. Michael Hoyt happened to glance at his shirt front. Although he had removed his tie in the attic and had left it there, he saw that he still had on his tie clasp—an expensive one that his wife had given him as a present. He took it off and threw it on the floor of the truck. "No more use for it," he said to himself. As the truck rattled along, they passed a group of white people standing by the side of the road. The Americans stared at the whites; the whites stared back. No one said a word.

After going a few blocks, the truck reached the junction of Avenue Eisenhower and a main thoroughfare called Route de Bafwaboli. The Lumumba Monument was to the left. But, instead of turning in that direction, the driver turned to the right. For a moment the Americans felt relieved, but then a new horror came over them. They realized that they were being taken to Camp Ketele. They remembered that the other consuls had warned them that they might be killed if they went to the camp.

When the truck rolled through the gates of Camp Ketele, the Americans were confronted with the same wild, incredible scene that Patrick Nothomb had witnessed four days previously. There were more than a thousand people in the camp—Simba warriors, women and children. A deafening cry went up when the mob saw the American prisoners. The five men were pushed off the truck into the mob. They were still carrying the American flags. The Simbas who had been on the truck came up behind the Americans and beat them with rifle butts, forcing them into the mob. The mob tore at their clothing and tried to pull out their hair. The Americans were devils, but they were very powerful and clever devils. In accordance with the wisdom handed down from their ancestors, they wanted to get a little bit of the devil's clothing, or, better still, a lock of his hair, or some other part of his person. This little souvenir would then become a wonderful fetish. It would confer on its possessor all of the powers of the American devil from whom it was wrenched.

After being forced through the mob, still carrying their flags, the Americans halted in front of Olenga's office. A trial was in progress when they arrived. Two Simba officers were judging the fate of four or five Congolese civilian prisoners. The prisoners were rolling in the dust. Their hands and feet had been tied tightly together behind their backs in an agonizing fashion. They groaned. Their faces were contorted.

One of the "judges" was the big, heavily bearded captain who had been ordered by Olenga, the day before, to protect the consular corps.

"Aren't you the man who is supposed to be protecting us?" Hoyt cried out.

"Why do you Americans come to the Congo and interfere in our affairs?" the captain shouted.

The Simbas told the Americans to remove their shoes and socks.

"Dance," they shouted and began beating at the bare feet with clubs.

The Simbas laughed hilariously. The Americans hopped around trying to avoid the blows. All the while, the captain was shouting: "American troops are fighting us in the Congo!"

Major Nasor bulled his way through the mob. He came close to Hoyt and shouted: "I am immune to bullets because of my *dawa!* Watch—I'll show you."

While a hundred Simbas watched in rapt fascination, Nasor opened the breech of his Fal automatic rifle. He saw that there was a bullet in it. Then he snapped the breech closed and laid the weapon on the ground at Hoyt's feet.

"Pick it up and shoot me!" Nasor cried. "Shoot me! You'll see—nothing will happen because of my *dawa!*"

The Simbas murmured.

"Shoot me," Nasor screeched.

"I can't—no, I can't do that," Hoyt said.

"Ah, hah," Nasor shouted. "You see—the white man acknowledges that my magic is more powerful than bullets!"

The Simbas burst into applause. They shrieked and danced around.

The hulking figure of Kinghis, the fanatic whom General Olenga had named as president of the Simba regime, loomed up. He accused Hoyt of having behaved in a condescending fashion toward him by addressing him as *"tu,"* the familiar form of "you" in French, instead of the more polite *"vous."*

Hoyt protested that he had never used the *"tu"* form in addressing Kinghis or any other Congolese. But Kinghis waved aside the protest.

"I'll get you," he told Hoyt. There was an icy tone to his

voice. Hoyt swallowed back a burst of fear. Kinghis was one of the most malevolent of all the new rulers of Stanleyville.

The Americans were pushed into Olenga's headquarters. The big, heavily bearded captain took the flags and flung them into a corner. Then, all of a sudden, the captain underwent a change of personality. He returned the men's shoes and socks. "Don't worry about a thing," he said in a pleasant tone. "I'll talk to the general; I'll take care of everything."

The Americans lighted cigarettes. They looked around the room. It was crammed with "requisitioned" goods—radios, typewriters, tape recorders and other such things. Hoyt felt almost elated; it was such a relief to be alive that the beatings had become unimportant.

After the men had waited half an hour, Commandant Oscar Sengha, the Simba officer who had stopped the attack on the Immoquateur by blowing his whistle, came into the room. He said he had been appointed chief of Olenga's secretariat. He chatted in a friendly way with the Americans, then left. Of all the Simbas whom the Americans met, Sengha seemed to be the most reasonable.

Looking out the window, the Americans saw General Olenga talking with Major Nasor, the man who had ordered their beating and who had brought them to the camp. As the Americans watched, Olenga handed a little sack to the major. The Americans concluded that this was Nasor's reward for what he had done.

General Olenga came into the room. He appeared groggy. "I have a terrible headache," he said.

Olenga noticed that the five men were cut and bruised. "Oh—you've been beaten?" he said. "I'm very sorry. It's Major Nasor's fault—he's drunk."

The Americans did not believe that Olenga was as blameless as he claimed, particularly inasmuch as they had seen him slip the little sack to his underling.

"I have decided that I do not want to break diplomatic relations with the United States," Olenga declared. "You won't be expelled. We want you to remain in Stanleyville and operate normally. We'll give you whatever protection you need."

In a way, the Americans were disappointed that they were not going to be expelled. But it was only a faint disappointment; they had never really expected that they would be allowed to leave.

Olenga called Nasor into the room. If the general had been angry at Nasor for beating the Americans, he had forgotten it now. He told Nasor to provide a Simba guard for the American consulate, to be billeted on the premises twenty-four hours a day. At six o'clock, the Americans were told to get into automobiles. They were driven back to the consulate accompanied by a truckload of Simbas who were supposed to guard them from the others.

The Americans had supper. They ached from the beatings. Even worse, they realized that they were utterly helpless. There was nothing they could do to influence their fate.

At eleven o'clock that evening a car rolled up the driveway and an important visitor stepped out. It was Olenga's new puppet president, Alphonse Kinghis. Had he come to apologize for the assault on the five Americans that afternoon? No, Kinghis had something else on his mind. He wanted Grinwis's car. But the president went away empty-handed. Someone else had already stolen it.

5

"THE CONGO HAS RETURNED"

When two Simbas met on the streets of Stanleyville, they greeted each other with cries of "Simba!" And if a white man approached, they shouted, *"Mateka!"* Not many Europeans in Africa ever bother to learn the native language, but soon all the whites in Stanleyville knew what *mateka* meant. In a dialect of Swahili, it was the word for "butter." And it was also the word for "dead flesh."

Despite the macabre gibes of the Simba soldiers, General Olenga and his top officers made a determined effort during the first weeks of the occupation to restore law and order and to get the economy cranked up again. They gave repeated assurances to managers of the European-owned firms that they wanted them to resume operations and that they would be protected. In view of some of the things that happened, the managers were skeptical. But they had little choice: they were captives; they could not leave the city. And so work resumed, but only after a fashion.

Peter Rombaut's tobacco factory went back into production. So, too, did a soft-drink bottling plant and a number of other little industries. Bakeries resumed operations. All plane and river-boat service to the outside world had been suspended, as had mail service, and telecommunications were censored. But the local telephones still functioned and the city was still supplied with electricity and water. Even more important, the city's breweries were back in action. To the whites, wilting in the tropical heat and humidity, beer was something of a necessity. To the Congolese, it was the arch symbol of the good life, if not of civilization itself.

One of the strangest things about the Simba occupation was that the sale of Bibles in church bookshops suddenly soared. It was not the worried Europeans who were buying them, but the Simba soldiers themselves. The movement was based on pagan witchcraft, but many of the Simbas had been baptized by Catholic and Protestant missionaries and still regarded themselves as Christians. They had money in their pockets for the first time in their lives and now they wanted Bibles. One missionary bookstore did a land-office business. It took in 40,000 francs a day—or $260 at the official rate of exchange—in selling Bibles and religious literature. The missionaries suspected that at least some of the Simbas regarded the Bibles as powerful fetishes, but they nevertheless were overjoyed. For years they had been trying with only limited success to get Bibles into the hands of ordinary Congolese.

The Simbas were perplexing in other ways as well. Although they often used Marxist jargon and although "nationalization" is a favorite game these days in the underdeveloped world, the Simbas never talked of taking over foreign-owned enterprises. Many leading officials in the Simba-installed government looked with favor on foreign firms and congratulated the managers on what they had done in developing the economy. On one occasion, a high-ranking official lamented: "The majority of our brothers, not having the slightest notion of the revolution we are undertaking, are behaving in an inadmissible way toward their employers, displaying insolence, absenteeism and even threatening outright takeover."

But, despite the assurances from the Simbas, the economy never got back on its feet. Retail trade had been pretty much destroyed by Olenga's decree rolling prices back to the 1960 level. And, whatever their intentions, the new officials had only the vaguest ideas of how a modern economy operates.

In a typical case, the Simbas "requisitioned" so many trucks that factories found it impossible to operate. Foreign businessmen protested and asked that they be allowed to keep at least a few vehicles. "All right," a government official said, "come to my office at two o'clock tomorrow afternoon and we'll discuss your problem.

Next morning, Simba troops confiscated what few trucks still remained in private hands. When the businessmen showed up for the afternoon meeting, the official was not there.

"The meeting is canceled," an assistant told them. "General Olenga has decided to seize all the trucks. Therefore, it is our opinion that you no longer have a problem."

As elsewhere in Africa, the Europeans supplied the skills to keep the economy going. But they had no heart for it. They reported for work at eight o'clock each morning, but then they closed for the day at noon. Each afternoon, Stanleyville was all but deserted.

During the first few weeks, the Simbas showed much more discipline than the ANC had ever displayed. General Olenga in particular strove to stamp out thievery and lawlessness among both the civilians and the rank-and-file Simbas. Almost every day, accused criminals were taken to Camp Ketele for drumhead trials. If they were found guilty, they usually were shot.

On one occasion, a Simba invaded a Congolese home and demanded that a Congolese woman submit to him sexually. When she refused, he shot her dead. The woman's family complained to the Simba officers. They arrested the murderer and brought him to the scene of the crime.

"Where did he shoot the woman?" an officer asked.

"Right there," a civilian said, pointing to the spot.

The Simbas told the killer to stand there. Then they shot him dead.

General Olenga was not the only man who had the power of life or death over the Simbas. For, in the weird world of Simba justice, that power soon was shared by none other than Baron Patrick Nothomb. Whenever Nothomb went to Camp Ketele to protest that a Belgian had been robbed or beaten by a Simba, he discovered to his horror that those Simbas whom he had denounced often were shot. If Nothomb had been a Congolese, this would have been only just—after all, had not General Olenga decreed that there would be no thievery and that Europeans were to be protected? But Nothomb was a man from another world. He struggled with the problem—should he have a man killed if the man had only punched a Belgian nose or perhaps had taken a few francs? Nothomb finally decided to remain quiet about any but the most flagrant attacks.

In the first weeks after occupation, the Simbas created a

government that was a marvel to behold. Ministries were formed and intricate hierarchies of officialdom were appointed to staff them. Perhaps not even Tammany could have created so many jobs so quickly. Each minister was surrounded by deputies, by chiefs of cabinet, by private secretaries. And each deputy, each chief of cabinet and each secretary had his own followers, who lived off him and, therefore, were highly devoted to him.

The new rulers had a great passion for bureaucratic red tape. Each day, in halting French, they typed out mounds of communiqués and other documents—always in quadruplicate. Officials sent a steady stream of letters to each other and, it is said, sometimes they wrote letters to themselves. They also set up—on paper—an air force of their own. They had no planes, no pilots, but that made no difference in the make-believe world of the new government.

In former years, during colonial times, many of the Simbas had, undoubtedly, peered through the windows of the offices of Belgian colonial administrators. They had seen mounds of papers, covered with markings. It was all strange and all very wonderful. It was, no doubt, the secret of the white man's power.

Soon after he conquered Stanleyville, General Olenga took over its radio station. Now, with his voice ringing from transistor sets throughout the jungle, he vowed that he would never rest until he had conquered Léopoldville and all the rest of the Congo. Olenga also took over a local newspaper and renamed it *Le Martyr*, in honor of Patrice Lumumba. It, too, proclaimed that total victory was near.

Stanleyville's foreigners were stunned by the advent of the Simbas. Their attitude might be compared with what the Romans undoubtedly felt when the Vandals seized that city in the fifth century. All of a sudden, their tidy little world had fallen apart. They found themselves at the mercy of a horde of wild tribesmen.

As time went on, the foreigners in Stanleyville got a better idea of what the Simba movement was. They learned that the hard-core members of the movement were Batetela*

---

*As with other Bantu tribes, *tetela* is the stem of the tribal name. An individual is a Mutetela, or Otetela. The plural is Batetela, or Atetela. But for the sake of convenience, only the plural form is used in referring to this and other tribes.

and Bakusu—tribes which are closely related to each other and which are found in the Maniema and Sankuru provinces to the south of Stanleyville.

The Batetela and kindred groups are a remarkable people. They are not very numerous—there probably are fewer than a million of them—yet the history of the Congo had been shaped in large measure by them. The Batetela are, for example, great warriors. Before the coming of the Belgians, their armies ranged far and wide over the eastern Congo, destroying or subduing any lesser mortals who got in their way. During colonial times, the Batetela formed the backbone of the Force Publique, the brutal army that the Belgians used to police the Congo. The Batetela and their tribal relatives also are known and feared as sorcerers. So great is their fame that when someone in Stanleyville or some other city wants to devastate an enemy he often will send to the Maniema for the appropriate charm.

Few people in the outside world have ever heard of the Batetela. Yet one of their tribal sons managed, in a period of just ten weeks and three days to jolt the entire world. And that man was Patrice Emery Lumumba, the Congo's first premier.

The Maniema and other regions of the eastern Congo have long been lands of horror and suffering. During the nineteenth century, much of that region was ravaged by Arab slavers and their African allies—allies that included the Batetela. Indeed, few other places in Africa were so heavily raided for what was known as "black ivory." The Arabs and their African allies surrounded villages of weak, peaceful tribesmen at night. Huts were burned. The elderly and infirm were massacred. Able-bodied adults were chained and they and their children were yoked together by the neck with heavy wooden poles. Then they were driven under the lash for a thousand miles or more to the coast of the Indian Ocean, where they were taken by ship to the Middle and Far East.

The slave trails led out across what is now Tanzania, and there are old men there who say that the trails were blazed with bones. But the Arabs were not worried about the loss. When Henry Morton Stanley, the journalist-explorer, reached the Maniema in 1876, the leading Arab slaver in the region declared: "Slaves cost nothing. They only require to be gathered." Stanley found that a sheep or an elephant tusk was worth far more than a Congolese. In one area that Stanley visited, he was told that one could purchase a tusk for a sheep. But if he had only slaves to offer, he would have to give twelve Congolese for each tusk.

As a result of the slave raids, much of the Maniema was greatly depopulated by the end of the nineteenth century. Ritualistic cannibalism—the eating of certain parts of the human body, such as the heart or liver, so as to acquire the powers or virtues of the deceased—had long been a respectable custom in the Maniema. But now cannibalism took on a new meaning. With cultivation at a standstill, people ate each other from sheer hunger.

Even today, a large part of the Maniema is still a wasteland.

When Stanley visited the Maniema, he was on his epic, three-year journey across Africa. He had come to the Lualaba River, the upper Congo, thinking that it might be the parent stream of the Nile. And he set out to follow it to the sea. Almost every day he fought pitched battles with local tribesmen who feared that Stanley had come to enslave them. After many difficulties, the explorer managed to descend a series of rapids and arrive, in January, 1877, at the site of the future city that would be named in his honor. Stanley thus was the first white man to visit the region. He was greeted by a band of tribesmen who stood on the banks of the river, howling curses and brandishing spears. War drums throbbed. Going ashore at one island not far from the future city, Stanley found this scene: "Human skulls ornamented the village streets of the island, while a great many thigh bones and ribs and vertebrae lay piled at a garbage corner, bleached witnesses of their hideous carnivorous tastes."

Stanley's visit led to the formation of what was airily known as the "Congo Free State." The territory was governed as the personal domain of Belgium's King Léopold II. The natives were obliged to collect wild rubber for Léopold's agents. Those who failed to meet their quota had their hands cut off. After a storm of international protest over these and other atrocities, Léopold surrendered his fiefdom to the Belgian parliament in 1908. A few years later, Vachel Lindsay, in his poem "The Congo," wrote:

Listen to the yell of Leopold's ghost
Burning in Hell for his hand-maimed host.
Hear how the demons chuckle and yell
Cutting his hands off, down in Hell.

The Congo as a Belgian colony was an economic miracle
The industrious Belgians created several modern cities such
as Stanleyville. They carved plantations from the jungle, opene
industries and organized vast transportation networks. Whe
independence came, the Congo had one of the best "infra
structures," or foundations for further development, of an
territory in Africa.

But the Congo was a political disaster. It was held to
gether only by the heavy hand of the Force Publique. Tha
army, the forerunner of the ANC, was formed in Free Stat
days, with a large share of its recruits drawn from the Batetel
tribe. The Batetela staged a series of mutinies just before th
turn of the century after the Belgians hanged their chief. I
the process, the Maniema was once more drenched in blood
But then the Batetela settled down and helped the Belgian
pacify the other tribes.

The Force Publique and ANC have been the curse of th
Congo to this day. In colonial times, it was a color-bar army
Officers were Belgians; the troops Congolese. Most of th
soldiers were illiterate roughnecks; some were cannibals. Man
were conscripts. Chiefs were told to supply certain quotas c
men and usually they took the opportunity to get rid o
criminals and troublemakers in their villages. The troop
were kept in line by brutal punishments. Privates were pai
only a pittance; they were not only allowed but expected t
live off the land. If they indulged in a little pillage, well, th
officers just shrugged.

The Congo was totally unprepared for independence
The Belgians did give large numbers of Congolese a primar
education, but it was designed only to make them good clerk
and dutiful helpers. There was virtually no opportunity for
Congolese to acquire a higher education. When indepen
dence came, there were fewer than thirty university gradu
ates in a population that then numbered 13.5 million. Wors
still, the Belgians never gave the Congolese any training i
the arts of self-government. In every other African colony

en or fifteen years of intensive preparation preceded self-government. But in the Congo the Belgians handed over the reins less than two weeks before independence.

Patrice Lumumba's life was a reflection of the topsyturvy world of the colonial Congo. Born in 1925 in a mudhut village in Sankuru Province, which adjoins the Maniema, Lumumba got about six years of education in a mission school. At the age of nineteen, he went to Stanleyville to seek his fortune. For a time he prospered. He got a job as a postal clerk, acquired a car and many expensive suits. But then in 1956 his postal career came to an abrupt halt; investigating Lumumba's mysterious affluence, the Belgians discovered that he had embezzled more than $2,000 in postal funds.

After serving a year in prison, Lumumba went into politics. He was a success almost from the start. A handsome and lean six-footer with a small goatee, Lumumba radiated charm and self-assurance. Unlike most of his countrymen, he bubbled over with nervous energy. After building up a large following in Stanleyville, principally among the Batetela, Lumumba moved to Léopoldville. There he peddled beer—the brewery remembers him as the best salesman it ever had—and he founded a political party known as the Mouvement National Congolais.

Time was running fast in the Congo. In 1954, a Belgian professor was hooted down when he suggested that the colony should be granted independence in thirty years. But in 1957 the Congo and all the rest of Africa was electrified by Britain's grant of independence to Ghana. The French territories, too, were moving toward internal self-government. Political riots broke out in Léopoldville in 1959 and again in early 1960. And then, to the dismay of knowledgeable onlookers, the Belgians simply abdicated their responsibilities in the Congo. They announced that independence would come on June 30, 1960. After much confusion, Lumumba was installed as premier. A president was also named—Joseph Kasavubu, a long-time political enemy of Lumumba's. The president would be partly a figurehead, as chief of state, but he also would have some reserve powers.

Independence day was marked with bitterness. King Baudouin, a great-grandnephew of Léopold II, was on hand for the ceremonies. While riding in an open car, Baudouin

65

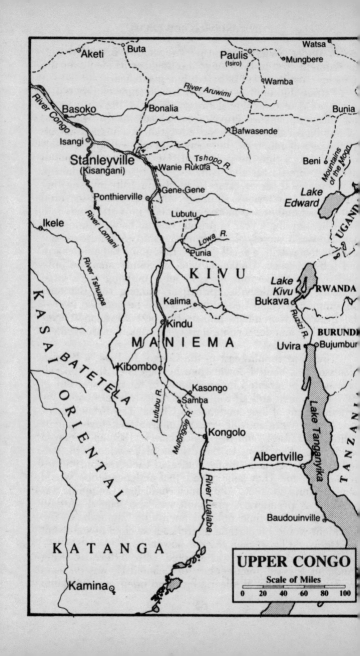

UPPER CONGO

Scale of Miles

0   20   40   60   80   100

suffered the humiliation of having his sword snatched from him by a Congolese bystander. (The Force Publique beat the man senseless and returned the sword.) At the formal ceremonies, Lumumba rose to make an acceptance speech. Instead of the usual pleasantries that one expects on such an occasion, Lumumba glowered at the Belgians and denounced everything they had done in the Congo. "Slavery was imposed on us by force," the thirty-four-year-old Batetela politician shouted. "We have known ironies and insults. We remember the blows that we had to submit to morning, noon and night because we were Negroes." Baudouin went home in a huff.

A short while later, the Force Publique mutinied and the Congo exploded into anarchy. Tens of thousands of Belgians fled the country. United Nations troops were brought in to restore order. But chaos nevertheless continued. Lumumba made virtually no effort to try and govern the country, but instead spent much of his time holding windy press conferences during which he rained abuse on the UN and the Belgians and other Western powers. After ten weeks, President Kasavubu deposed Lumumba from the premiership. Lumumba later tried to flee to Stanleyville to form a separatist government with Gizenga. But he was caught by the ANC, and beaten savagely and imprisoned. In early 1961, Kasavubu had Lumumba flown to Katanga, where he was turned over to Moise Tshombe. Soon after, Tshombe's government announced that Lumumba had escaped and had been killed by villagers. Most people suspected that Lumumba had, instead, been executed by Tshombe's men.

The UN peace-keeping force remained in the Congo four years. At peak strength, the UN army numbered 20,000 men. Because of rotations, some 93,000 soldiers from thirty-three different countries saw service in the Congo under the UN flag. But the results were not very impressive. The Congo was in just as great a turmoil on June 30, 1964, when the UN withdrew, as it had been four years earlier. In that time, the Congo had all but bankrupted the UN. It spent more than $500 million—half of it supplied by the American taxpayer—and the UN ran up enormous debts. Because of the refusal of the Soviet Union and France to pay their share of the costs, the UN was weakened politically and it lost considerable prestige. The UN mission had, all along, been defended as a means of keeping the cold war from the Congo. But, after four years, the cold war continued unabated. By then, not only the Soviets, but the Chinese Communists as well were meddling in the Congo.

The Simba uprising had its origins in June of 1964, a few weeks before the final withdrawal of the UN from the Congo, when Albertville, a port on Lake Tanganyika, was seized by a group of tribal rebels. Several unemployed politicians and malcontents from the Maniema flocked to Albertville, eager for jobs and favors from the new regime. Among them was Nicolas Olenga, who assumed the rank of "lieutenant colonel" in what was sometimes spoken of as the "People's Army."

With a following that probably numbered no more than a few hundred at the start, Lieutenant Colonel Olenga moved out of Albertville in early July. His tattered troops soon overran the town of Kasongo; the ANC fled in panic. After taking Kasongo, Olenga's men established what was to be a pattern in each town they took: some two hundred Congolese who had been identified with the old regime, or who had some education, were assembled and clubbed to death.

Riding in vehicles that they had commandeered in Kasongo, Olenga's column set out for Kindu. They took that town, too, without a fight—and then staged another mass execution. And Olenga promoted himself to lieutenant general.

Olenga had appeared on the scene like a meteor. Until Kindu fell, few people had ever heard of him. Piecing the story together later, it was learned that he was a Batetela tribesman. Like Lumumba, he had had only a few years of education and, again like his hero, he was a convicted thief—Olenga served two months for theft in 1959 or 1960. It seems that for a time Olenga worked as a railway clerk in Kindu. Later on he became an organizer for Lumumba's Mouvement National Congolais. For a brief time he enjoyed power, or at least a glimpse of it, as a minor functionary in Gizenga's regime in Stanleyville. After the collapse of the Gizenga regime, Olenga returned to the Maniema. For a time, he attempted to resurrect a Batetela kingdom. Congolese who knew Olenga in Kindu said that he spent much of his time in riverfront bars and that he organized bands of young men who terrorized the countryside.

Olenga was a heavy drinker. The Congolese who knew him recalled that when he was drunk he was very cruel.

The Simba movement as such apparently was formed at Kindu. It was a beggars' army. Olenga and his sorcerers sought out the poorest and most primitive elements from among the Betetela, Bakusu and other local tribes—people with many resentments and little or nothing to lose.

Like much of the Congo, the Maniema was a fertile place for revolution. The local administration, as elsewhere, was corrupt and incompetent. Teachers, soldiers and other government functionaries went unpaid for months; the provincial authorities simply pocketed the payrolls. Trade and commerce had withered and unemployment was rife.

Then Olenga came along. He promised the poor and suffering that when the cause was victorious they would have all the things that the provincial authorities and, before them, the Belgians had had—jobs, cars, big houses, money and, of course, beer. Recruits were given advances of a thousand francs—$6 at the official rate of exchange—and promised salaries that for ordinary soldiers could amount to as much as $200 a month. Many of the recruits were children—ten to fifteen years old. Often they proved to be the most sadistic of all the Simbas.

The ANC helped Olenga considerably. Wherever there was an ANC garrison, there had been looting and violence. Much of the population was bitterly anti-government, and so they flocked to the Simba cause. But Olenga was not choosy about recruits; he signed up large numbers of ANC renegades as well.

The Simba movement and particularly some Congolese politicians who later flocked to Stanleyville to help run the rebel government were backed by the Chinese Communists. Chinese propaganda turned up all over the eastern Congo and it is possible that the Chinese shelled out cash to get things started. Later on, Communist-made arms were supplied to the Simbas by leftist African states. Olenga and his associates were violently anti-American and they often spoke of the Communist countries as their friends. And they frequently used Marxist jargon.

Yet, despite all this, there is no evidence that Olenga and the others were real Communists, or even political radicals. The Simba movement was basically an uprising of the Maniema tribes—a struggle between the ins and outs, between those who got the spoils and those who did not. If they used Marxist jargon, it was only because they had no ideology or political labels of their own. Neither Olenga nor any of his top aides had ever visited the Communist countries, and their knowledge of Marxism, like their knowledge of most other things, was faint. The Communist countries, of course, knew this. But to them the Simbas represented an opportunity to stir up trouble for the West and so the Communists supported them.

Witchcraft, not ideology, was the glue which held the Simba army together. There had never been any dearth of sorcerers in the Maniema and now they flocked to the Simba cause, grateful, perhaps, that somebody really appreciated them. With the sorcerers officiating, recruits were put through a mumbo-jumbo initiation ceremony. The recruits were scarred on the forehead and chest. Then the learned men rubbed charcoal dust or other powerful potions into the cuts. A recruit was draped in an animal skin and told to walk away. After he had taken a few steps, a Simba fired a shot in the air. The recruit was brought back. "You are a Simba!" the sorcerer proclaimed. "You have *dawa*. You are immune to bullets."

The Simba recruits were warned that there were several taboos that they had to observe or they would lose their *dawa*. Along with the prohibitions against stealing and looking sideways when going into battle, the Simbas were told that they could not sleep with women in the daytime. Nor could they eat food prepared by a pregnant woman.

Some of the Simbas sported little pieces of fur on their heads, which they called "Air Congo." This protected them against attack by planes. Other wore fetishes on their necks which were designed to beef up the anti-bullet power of the *dawa*. And, at least in some cases, the sorcerers polished off the ceremony by sprinkling everyone with holy water.

A crafty organization man, General Olenga reserved the most powerful *dawa* for himself. His *dawa* was administered regularly by a wrinkled hag named Mama Onema, who served as the general's personal sorceress. Mama Onema was not exactly an engaging person. She was about four and a half feet tall and she had a face like a shriveled prune. When she spoke, she whistled and hissed through holes where teeth presumably had once been. Her breath made a strong man wince. No one knew how old Mama Onema was—perhaps Mama Onema did not know either, or care. But she had been feared and revered throughout the Maniema for a long, long time as one of its greatest witches.

To use a Cold War expression, Mama Onema "defected" much later to the ANC. It was not a matter of ideology or conscience, but rather one of cash. Mama Onema complained that Olenga had promised her the equivalent of $20,000 for keeping him in *dawa*. But the great man, she said, had coughed up only $13. "That," the lady bitched, "isn't enough for *my* magic."

Although much of the Simba initiation ritual was nonsense of a sort that is dear to the hearts of lodge joiners everywhere, there was method in it. By promising the recruits an immunity to bullets, Olenga and his sorcerers gave them a courage they would not otherwise have had against well-armed ANC troops. And by setting up a long list of taboos, such as the one against looting, Olenga was able to impose some discipline on what would otherwise have been an ungovernable rabble.

Although General Olenga struggled against lawlessness during the first weeks of his rule in Stanleyville, he found it was no easy task. One problem was that in order to give the Simba movement a broader base and made it acceptable to the people in Stanleyville, he was forced to recruit local elements to his army. Many of these had been members of the *jeunesse,* the youth group, of Lumumba's old party, the MNC. Most independent African countries have a youth wing of its ruling party. In Africa they are known as "young nationalists"; anywhere else they would be regarded as young hoodlums. They furnish the strong-arm squads which break up opposition political meetings and on occasion break opposition heads.

Olenga was able to keep tight control on the original Simbas from the Maniema. But with the *jeunesse* it was another matter. They began stopping Congolese on the streets, demanding that they produce MNC membership cards. If the person did not have a card, he either bought one or was beaten senseless. Some of the newly-recruited Simbas, particularly in the outlying towns, carried out executions so as to satisfy personal grudges. And some, even in Stanleyville, helped themselves to homes and cars without securing permission from Olenga or anyone else.

Soon things got to a point where Olenga broadcast a warning over the radio against a "certain group of local youths who want to sow an atmosphere of terror among the masses." He promised he would punish them with the "utmost energy." But he never got full control of them.

Although Olenga had his problems, his first weeks in Stanleyville were ones of great exhilaration. For Stanleyville undoubtedly represented more than just a military victory to him. What he and Simbas had done was to reaffirm themselves as Africans, and as men. Stanleyville had always been, to them, an alien city, part of their homeland, but a place in which they had walked as strangers. White foreigners had built Stanleyville's hotels and its office and apartment buildings. White foreigners had constructed its factories and wharves and had laid out its pretty, tree-lined avenues. White foreigners had governed the Congolese for more than half a century and, even after independence, had continued to lord it over them.

But now black men had Stanleyville, black men who, accompanied by their sorcerers, had come pouring out of the jungles of the Maniema, much as their ancestors had done in the great and glorious days of the past. General Olenga was not made enough to drive the whites away. They were valuable as hostages and, in any case, he knew that Stanleyville needed them to keep the place running. But now the boot was on the other foot.

Sitting in Stanleyville's cafés—cafés from which they would have been unceremoniously hustled during the color-bar days of colonialism—the Simbas composed a little song in Swahili which they sang as they guzzled life-giving beer:

Congo ilipotea;
Sasa inarudi.

In English the words are:

The Congo, it was lost:
Now it has returned.

6

AT THE ALTAR OF THE
GOD LUMUMBA

The Simba army was like a column of *siafu*—the Swahili
name for driver ants. They devoured everything that got in
their path. Under the leadership of their brilliant if somewhat
demented general, they brought off one dazzling victory after
another. Striking out from Stanleyville, the Simbas quickly
overran all of the northeastern Congo—to the borders of
Uganda and the Sudan. Other columns, speeding westward
in trucks, took the towns of Bumba, Lisala and Boende. With
the Maniema, which had previously been conquered, Nicolas
Olenga, the one-time railway clerk, was now master of one-
fifth of the Congo—an area the size of New England, New
York and Pennsylvania.

Olenga's goal was Léopoldville. When it fell, he would
be master of all, or at least most, of the Congo. His Simba
legions would be in control of one of the richest countries in
Africa. They would be a sovereign government, entitled to
send diplomats abroad and to be represented in the United
Nations. By mid-August, General Olenga had every reason to
believe that Léopoldville would soon be his.

But a detail remained. The town of Bukavu, on the
Congo's eastern borders, was still in government hands. With
the assistance of American planes, the government had been
supplying it by air, but no one was sure whether the ANC
could hold it. Tiny though it was, Bukavu was a humiliation
that could not be ignored.

And so General Olenga spent little time rejoicing over the capture of Stanleyville. Instead he busied himself with plans for the attack on Bukavu. He sent messages by radio to his troops in Kindu and other towns, telling them to get ready. In a few days, the assault would begin.

Baron Patrick Nothomb, all the while, was similarly busy. Stanleyville 2904 rang day and night with complaints from Belgians who had been robbed or beaten by the Simbas. Each day Nothomb, accompanied by Paul Duqué, his vice-consul, traveled around the city, picking up isolated families and bringing them to the Immoquateur and other apartment buildings in the downtown area.

The authorities provided Nothomb with a young Simba who served as his bodyguard. The Simba, whose name was Christophe, took a great liking to Nothomb. And he took his duties seriously. Whenever another Simba annoyed Nothomb, Christophe kicked the man smartly in the shins.

As time went by, food stocks in Stanleyville's stores began to dwindle. To make it easier to cope with the problem, Nothomb organized a common mess for thirteen Belgians —nine men and four women—who lived in the Immoquateur. Although they continued to sleep in their own flats, they had all of their meals in Nothomb's apartment. The women prepared the food and everyone shared the expense.

Life in Stanleyville was full of absurdities. One was that Nothomb became highly popular with the Simbas at Camp Ketele. The reason was that each time Nothomb wanted to make a trip outside of the city he always requested, and was given, extra guards. The Simba officers let Nothomb choose the men. This was a very pleasant assignment for the Simbas. If they accompanied Nothomb, they would eat European food and sleep in European houses; more important, they would not be sent to the front. And so whenever Nothomb appeared at the camp he was quickly surrounded by a mob of clamoring applicants, each of whom tried his best to win the baron's favor. Nothomb, for his part, enjoyed his new role hugely.

On one occasion, Nothomb set out in a car for the town of Paulis, 357 miles to the northeast, to check on the safety of the Belgian community there. As they bounced along over unpaved jungle roads, one of Nothomb's Simba guards exclaimed: "Monsieur Tshombe is my god."

Nothomb wondered if he had heard the man correctly. Tshombe, the prime minister of the central government in Léopoldville, was, of course, the number one devil of the Simbas—or rather the number two devil, first place being reserved for the American imperialists. It was Tshombe, after all, who was blamed for the murder of Lumumba and who, as every Simba knew, had "sold" the Congo to the Americans.

"You, ah, *admire* Monsieur Tshombe?" Nothomb asked.

The Simba poured out a tale of woe. He had been an officer in Tshombe's Katanga gendarmerie when Tshombe was staging his own rebellion against the central government. When Tshombe's secessionist movement collapsed, the then prime minister of the central government, Cyrille Adoula, invited the Katangese gendarmes to join the ANC. They would keep the ranks they held in the gendarmerie. But then—*treachery*. The officer was busted to sergeant. So, to get revenge against Adoula, he defected to the Simbas.

"But now," the Simba wailed, "Monsieur Adoula is gone from Léopoldville. He has been replaced by Monsieur Tshombe. So now I am a rebel against Monsieur Tshombe, who is my god. How is this possible?"

When they reached Paulis, Nothomb and his Simba guards, together with a local Belgian businessman, were walking down a street when suddenly a drunken Simba officer approached and told the Belgian businessman to take off his glasses. The man did. The Simba officer punched him in the face.

"You hate the People's Army!" the officer shouted.

Nothomb and the businessman—and the two Simba guards—were hustled before a Simba major.

"They are mercenaries!" the drunken officer told the major. "They are Englishmen coming from Uganda." Then, spitting contemptuously at the Simba guards, he added: "And these two blacks are traitors!"

Well, that was enough. A group of Simbas fell on the Belgians and the two Simbas from Stanleyville, beating them with clubs. The Stanleyville Simbas howled in protest, and finally succeeded in producing identity papers.

The major was really annoyed by now. It was plain to

him that everyone was wasting his time. So he set about to make things right. First he ordered the drunken officer tossed into jail. Then, turning to Nothomb and the Stanleyville Simbas, he barked: "It's finished—you can go."

The men did not argue or demand apologies; they left, nursing their bruises.

On another occasion, when Nothomb visited the town of Punia, about two hundred miles southeast of Stanleyville, he was confronted by an angry twenty-two-year-old Simba who was the local police chief.

"Prove that you are the Belgian consul!" the Simba cried.

Nothomb presented a special pass that had been issued by the Simba authorities in Stanleyville.

"I don't want to see that—I want to see Belgian papers," the young man declared.

Nothomb produced his passport. The police chief studied it for a moment, then cried triumphantly: "There's no stamp in it giving the date of your arrival in Stanleyville."

"They didn't stamp it when I arrived," Nothomb said.

"You lie!" the cop said. "You're not the Belgian consul. You're under arrest."

A less tenacious man might well have given up in face of such monumental stupidity. But the baron is not only a tenacious young man but a great talker to boot. He sat down and talked. The Congolese, like all Africans, also are great talkers. And so Nothomb and the police chief yakked and yakked and yakked—for six hours!

The police chief knew that he had met his match. He gave up. "All right, I'll let you go," he said, gazing in admiration at the loquacious white man.

Nothomb beamed triumphantly.

But first there was a little detail. The cop wanted to copy some information from Nothomb's passport. For two hours he sat at the desk, laboriously copying every last word, in both French and Flemish, in Nothomb's passport, filling page after page of paper.

"Now I believe that you are the Belgian consul," the police chief declared, smiling brightly at Nothomb. "Where are you going now?"

Nothomb said he intended to visit a nearby village.

"Come—I'll take you in my car," the young man said.

The two men got into the car. As they rode along, the police chief took Nothomb's thumb and squeezed it.

"You are my friend," he said. "I love the Belgians. Can you get me a scholarship to study in Belgium?"

When Nothomb reached his destination, he got out of the car. "Please write to me every week—I want to have letters from you," the police chief called out as Nothomb walked away.

But the ignorance of the Simbas was not always so amusing. One European in Paulis wore a hearing aid; the Simbas concluded that he was using it to send messages for American planes to come and bomb the town. And for that they executed him.

A Belgian in Boende had a gold tooth; often he tapped on it nervously with his finger. To the Simbas it was clear: he was sending radio messages. So they shot him.

About two miles from downtown Stanleyville, in a modest residential neighborhood, there was an outpatient clinic. The doctor who ran it was a very busy man during the Simba occupation; he had to look after the health not only of his regular Congolese and European patients, but also of the Simba invaders.

One day the Simbas "requisitioned" the doctor's car. He did a slow burn. Soon a sign appeared on the front door of the clinic:

SINCE YOUR SOLDIERS HAVE STOLEN MY CAR,
ALL FEES WILL NOW BE DOUBLED.

That really hurt. In a few days the Simbas returned the car.

The doctor was Alexander Barlovatz, a man who was constantly at the side of just about all of the foreigners in Stanleyville as a physician, counselor and friend. He reminded one of a country doctor in an earlier America. He was nearly seventy years old, but he had more energy than many a man half his age. Barlovatz had white hair, a white mustache and wore glasses; he was slight of build and dignified in his bearing. He was a kindly man, but his temper had a low boiling point. On one occasion several rebels approached and demanded that he give them five thousand francs. Barlovatz threw a wet paint brush at them and shouted, "Get out." They left, in a hurry.

A Serbian by ancestry, Barlovatz was born in Hungary in 1896. His father was the Serbian consul general in Budapest. Barlovatz grew up in the glittering world of eastern Europe's aristocracy. His godfather was King Alexander of Serbia, who was assassinated in Marseilles in 1934. Eventually Barlovatz's father lost his diplomatic post in a Balkan political shuffle and the family was forced into exile in France.

During the First World War, Barlovatz served as a medical assistant in the Serbian army during the bloody campaigns at Salonika. After the armistice, he completed his medical studies in Brussels and acquired Belgian citizenship. But the prospect of life as a doctor in Belgium proved too tame for him and in 1923 he set sail for the Congo. These days the Congo is anything but a haven of peace and civilization, but when Barlovatz arrived there more than forty years ago it had scarcely changed from the savage land of Conrad's *Heart of Darkness*.

Barlovatz plunged into his work with a passion. Often he was the only doctor in hundreds of miles. He opened hospitals and dispensaries and trained many young Congolese as medical assistants. A man of great scientific curiosity, he conducted research into improved techniques for treating the Congo's two great scourges—sleeping sickness and malaria. And he imported fruit tree seeds from East Asia and Central America and set about developing new strains that the Congolese could grow.

Barlovatz opened his outpatient clinic in Stanleyville fifteen years ago. The demand for his services was so great that he hardly ever had time for a vacation. Each year he treated ten thousand patients, most of them Congolese, but including Europeans as well. The clinic, in fact, became something of a social center. Everyone was welcome, sick or not.

One visitor in former times was a young postal clerk by the name of Patrice Lumumba. Barlovatz remembers him as a rather likable and somewhat impatient young man who was full of ambitions. Barlovatz became the godfather of Lumumba's young son and Mrs. Barlovatz the godmother of one of Lumumba's daughters.

One day Lumumba burst into the clinic full of enthusiasm and asked Barlovatz if he would help him form a Belgian-Congolese "friendship" society. There was still a rigid color bar in the Congo and Lumumba said it would be nice if educated Africans could get to know the Belgians personally. Barlovatz agreed and meetings were held in the clinic. But the other Belgians showed little interest and the friendship society withered away.

Barlovatz's home became something of an international salon. Whenever an important visitor arrived in Stanleyville—a colonial governor, the head of a trading firm or a foreign diplomat—he usually went straight to the Barlovatz home, where the doctor and his wife, Lucy, entertained with vintage wines, good food and, even rarer in Africa, brilliant conversation. The Barlovatzes were fluent in French, German, Italian, Spanish, Hungarian, Serbian and Swahili. Neither of them spent more than just a few weeks in English-speaking countries, yet they spoke excellent English as well. They learned it from reading. They had a library of several thousand well-worn volumes in English and several other languages.

Soon after Stanleyville fell, a group of Simbas came to the Barlovatz home. "What's that?" one of them said, pointing to a grand piano. Mrs. Barlovatz is an accomplished pianist and she used to entertain her guests with Mozart sonatas. She tried to explain what a piano was. The Simbas glared at it with fierce suspicion. "It's a radio for calling the American planes!" one of them exclaimed. Mrs. Barlovatz succeeded in convincing them that the strange contraption was not a radio and they left. But then she closed the keyboard and never played the piano again. Her heart was not in it.

Dr. Barlovatz took the Simba occupation pretty much in stride, with the stoicism that comes from a long and eventful life. Fortunately the couple's teen-aged daughters were in school in Belgium at the time, so he did not have to worry about them.

A few days after the Simbas arrived, Barlovatz was summoned to Camp Ketele by General Olenga. The two men had never met before, but the doctor's fame in the Congo was such that Olenga knew about him. Olenga was almost deferential to Barlovatz. With great politeness, he asked if the doctor would care for the Simba wounded.

Barlovatz agreed. But caring for the Simbas proved to be a bit trying at times. Once a fourteen-year-old major demanded that Barlovatz operate on him for a minor complaint. When the doctor told him he did not need an operation, the child whipped out a pistol and threatened to kill him. It took an hour to persuade the young major that he did not need surgery.

One evening a Simba captain died while being treated for a venereal disease. The Simba grabbed the Congolese male nurse who had given the captain an injection of penicillin, tied him to the body and said they would shoot him in the morning. Again it took much patient talk before Barlovatz got the Simbas to release the nurse.

Barlovatz encountered what might be called "professional jealousy" from the Simba sorcerers. Sometimes they invaded the clinic after he had performed an operation, tore the bandage from the patient and poured dust and other witchcraft charms into the wound.

Although the other Belgian nationals were glad to get special passes from General Olenga to allow them to circulate in the city, Barlovatz refused to carry one. Often he was stopped by Simbas and told to produce a pass. "You know me," the doctor would say in an angry and exasperated voice. Each time they stepped back and let him pass.

Both Patrick Nothomb and Dr. Barlovatz managed fairly well during the first days of the Simba occupation. The Simbas were not particularly anti-Belgian then. They reserved their fury, instead, for the Americans—and particularly for Michael Hoyt and the other consular personnel.

After the incident in which the Americans were beaten and forced to chew on the flag, General Olenga assigned ten Simbas to live in the consulate and protect the Americans. But the Simbas were more than bodyguards; they were jailers as well. Hoyt and the other Americans could not leave the premises. They were prisoners in their own consulate.

Hoyt knew that he and the others were helpless and that their lives depended upon the caprice of the Simbas. But he was determined to remove any possible points of friction. One thing that worried him was that he still had the two-way voice radio transmitter in the consulate. In view of the Simbas' fear of radios, he decided to get rid of it. So he rang up Olenga's office at Camp Ketele.

Kinghis, the demented provincial president, answered the phone. This was the one man Hoyt particularly wanted to avoid. But now there was no way out: he told Kinghis about the radio and asked that he send someone to pick it up.

"Wait there—I'll come," Kinghis said.

While Hoyt waited he decided that it might be safer for the three radio operators if they were to leave the consulate and stay in their apartments in the Immoquateur. The Simba guards agreed that the three men could leave, as long as Hoyt and Grinwis remained in the consulate. So, at Hoyt's request, Patrick Nothomb took the three men back to the Immoquateur in his car.

At 1:30 P.M. Kinghis drove up to the consulate with some Simbas.

"Get in the car," he told Hoyt and Grinwis.

"Where are you taking us?" Hoyt said.

"You'll see," Kinghis muttered.

The car pulled up in front of a red brick building with a high wall around it. It looked very much like a fort. It was Stanleyville's Central Prison.

Kinghis marched the two diplomats into the prison and pushed them into a cell.

"We're foreign diplomats," Hoyt protested.

"I'll take care of your case later," Kinghis said, as he turned and left.

The cell door was not locked. Looking around, they could see that there were only a few other prisoners in the place—bloody and ragged Congolese who appeared to be former ANC troops. There were three or four pallets in the cell, covered with straw, and a small table. Everything was filthy.

Two young Simbas sat at the table, guarding the Americans. They were obviously dead tired from some exertion or other and they were slumped against their spears. The Simbas seemed friendly, but they were too tired to talk. The Americans were too shocked to think of anything to say.

A prison official came into the cell. "As you can see, the prison is empty," he said. "Most of the prisoners have been taken out. There have been some terrible massacres."

A man whom they knew as an announcer from Radio Stanleyville stuck his head in the door. "What are you doing here?" he said.

"That's what we'd like to know," said Hoyt. "It's an international crime to put foreign consuls in prison."

The announcer shrugged and left.

The afternoon ticked by. Then it was 8:30 P.M. Night, a magical Congolese night, had descended on Stanleyville. A soft breeze caressed the little city. The sky blazed with a hundred thousand stars, pinpoints of brilliance in a cold and indifferent universe. The scent of night-blooming jasmine wafted along the darkened streets.

A guard came to the cell. "Come with me," he said to Hoyt. He was taken out to a car parked in front of the prison. The car was filled with guns and ammunition and there were two Simbas in it. Hoyt fought down a burst of panic. Were they going to execute him?

"*Bon soir,* Monsieur Hoyt," one of the Simbas said. It was Commandant Oscar Sengha, the man who had stopped the attack at the Immoquateur and who had befriended the Americans at Camp Ketele.

"Come on along—let's go have some supper," Sengha said.

When Hoyt recovered his composure, he remembered Grinwis. "Can the vice-consul come too?" Hoyt asked.

"Fine," Sengha said.

Hoyt went back into the prison and got Grinwis.

Sengha radiated good cheer as they drove through the sweet-scented night. "Let's see—where'll we go for dinner?" he said. "What about the Sabena Guest House—is that all right with you?"

The two Americans grunted a faint assent.

"It's a shame you were put in prison," Sengha said. "I just can't understand it."

When the car neared the Congo Palace Hotel, the fanciest one in town, Sengha told the driver to stop. "I think General Olenga is having dinner here now—I'll ask him about you," Sengha said.

In a minute, Sengha was back, grinning happily. "The general says it was a mistake—you're free," he said. "I'll take you back to the consulate right now."

When they reached the battered consulate, Hoyt brought out several bottles of beer. The four men drank, talked, exchanged jokes. Good fellowship welled up, like bubbles in the glasses. Grinwis brought out a Polaroid camera—the type that turns out a finished print in a few moments—and took snapshots of Hoyt and their new friend. Sengha and his driver were amazed; the Americans were truly great magicians.

"I visited your house this morning," said Sengha. "I'd like to buy some of your liquor and food and the air conditioners, the refrigerator and maybe some of the furniture."

Grinwis's residence was some distance from the consulate. He had not been able to live in it since the Simbas arrived in the city and he had worried that the place might be looted. Now he had an idea.

"The appliances and the furniture are the property of the American government and I can't sell them," he said. "But why don't you move into the place? You can pay me rent."

The advantage to Grinwis, of course, was that Sengha would keep looters out.

"Marvelous," Sengha said. "But how much will the rent be?"

"Oh, we can settle that later," Grinwis said.

The two men drew up an agreement and each solemnly affixed his signature to the document.

After another round of beer, Hoyt checked and found that Parkes, Stauffer and Houle were missing from the Immoquateur. The Simbas had taken them away, but no one knew where. Hoyt rang up Patrick Nothomb. True to form, he promptly came to the rescue. He learned that Kinghis had put the three men in prison that evening, just after Sengha had freed Hoyt and Grinwis. Nothomb drove to Camp Ketele, and persuaded the Simba authorities to release them.

When the baron brought the three men back to the consulate, Hoyt ran out and hugged them. The three were in good spirits. They had been in jail only an hour and a half. It had been a lark as far as they were concerned.

On the evening of August 13, a Simba convoy of autos and trucks that had been "requisitioned" from the Europeans moved out of Stanleyville on the road to Kindu. At the head of the convoy was General Olenga. With him rode his best officers and his most powerful sorcerers. Olenga was going to Kindu first to pick up more men. Then they would move on Bukavu.

Just behind Stanleyville's post office there was a lovely little park. It was ringed with coconut palms that swayed ever so gracefully in the warm tropical breezes. There were gorgeous flowers in the little park—flowers that were blood red in color. The flowers and lawns were tended with reverence by the Simba authorities for the park was a very special one. In the center, on a raised concrete platform, there was a full-length color photograph, nearly life-sized, of a rather dour-looking young man: Lumumba. The platform and photograph comprised what was known as the Lumumba Monument. To the Simbas, Lumumba was a deity; everyone knew that he would return to earth soon to right all wrongs. And so the monument was no ordinary memorial. It was a shrine, an altar to the god.

When General Olenga left Stanleyville for Bukavu, Kinghis saw his chance. On the morning of August 16, he ordered about a dozen Congolese prisoners to the monument. Most of them were moderate politicians, of minor functionaries of the Léopoldville regime. Kinghis also summoned a mob of several thousand civilians. The stage was set; now the show would begin.

Kinghis's giant body towered over the mob. His voice crackling with rage, he harangued them into a frenzy. Then the Simba soldiers dragged the first victim to the altar.

"Is he guilty or innocent?" Kinghis shrieked.

"Guilty!" the mob roared.

The Simbas riddled the man's body with bullets. They kept on firing in a frenzy until the body had been cut into pieces. Blood spurted onto the monument, onto the clothes of the Simbas and the civilians, onto the beautiful red flowers.

"Guilty or innocent?" Kinghis cried as the next man was taken to the monument.

"Guilty!"

It went on for perhaps an hour. Sometimes the Simbas

riddled their victims with bullets; sometimes they fell on them with spears and machetes.

Then a very important man, a very powerful man, was brought out. It was Sylvere Bondekwe, who had been the head of a moderate political party in the Stanleyville region. Bondekwe had to die, of course, but Bondekwe had *power*.

The mob became even more restless. Something as ancient as Africa itself was stirring in their minds. And then what was left of decades of work by missionaries and teachers suddenly fell away. Bondekwe's liver was cut from his body while he was still alive. Pieces were snatched up by the mob and devoured eagerly. They screamed triumphantly. Now they too had *power*.

With Kinghis presiding, the executions continued for five days. In all, about 120 men were killed, or, rather, offered up as human sacrifices to the god Lumumba, during that time. The executions at the monument were halted by Kinghis after a delegation of Congolese women marched into his office and demanded that they be stopped. Kinghis may well have wanted to continue the killings at the monument. But he knew it was dangerous to oppose the women, since they undoubtedly reflected a growing revulsion among the civilian population.

Although those executions were stopped, others went on almost every day during the Simba occupation. They were carried out from a bridge that spans the Tshopo River just above a roaring cataract. The Simbas tied their victims' hands and feet or sewed them into bags. Then they flung them into the cataract. Or sometimes they simply shot or speared them, then threw them into the torrent. Almost every day the crocodiles feasted.

Most of those who were executed at the Tshopo bridge were killed because they were regarded as "intellectuals." Their intellectual accomplishments were rather pathetic; they were clerks, teachers, nurses, postmen, small merchants, small farmers, foremen and artisans. No one kept track of the toll, but people living near the bridge said that one to two thousand were done away with.

Executions of "intellectuals" and former politicians went on in the other cities that were occupied by the Simbas. At Kindu, as estimated eight hundred were slain at the local

Lumumba Monument, many of them burned alive. At Paulis an estimated two to four thousand were killed.

What made the executions all the more tragic was that the Simbas were systematically killing off the very class of people who, given time, might have lifted the Congo to the level of a modern and civilized country. Some Europeans in Stanleyville felt that the Chinese Communists had prompted the slaughter of the "intellectuals"; the Chinese were, after all, masters at the art of killing off entire classes of people. But a more likely explanation is that the Simbas singled out the "intellectuals" simply because they were a part of the old establishment. The Simba movement was a beggars' uprising; anyone who was not a beggar was clearly an enemy.

Whenever a Congolese gets a smattering of an education, he finds a job as a minor clerk and immediately starts wearing a necktie: the outward and visible sign that a man has arrived in the world. But a tie could either make or break you in the Congo. After the Simbas took Stanleyville, no one dared wear a tie. It would identify him as an "intellectual" and guarantee him a one-way trip to the Tshopo bridge.

One afternoon while Kinghis was still conducting his executions at the Lumumba Monument, a happy-go-lucky man named Théo Papazoglakis decided to take a stroll through the city. Papazoglakis, a Belgian subject of Greek origin, had been born in Stanleyville and had spent most of his life there. His family owned a soft-drink bottling plant. Papazoglakis knew what had been going on at the monument, but even that did not dampen his spirits. Anyway, it was his thirty-third birthday. He whistled as he strolled along.

Papazoglakis met a friend on the street—an old Congolese man.

"*Jambo, mzee*—Greetings, old man," Papazoglakis said in Swahili. The Bantu tribes of eastern Africa look with great reverence on their elders and *mzee* is a highly honorific mode of address.

The ancient looked glum.

"What's wrong, *mzee*?" Papazoglakis asked.

"Life is hard, life is hard," the *mzee* grunted.

"Old friend—tell me, what is wrong?"

"Hear the words. They killed Matabo at the monument this afternoon," the *mzee* said. (Matabo had been a former burgomaster, or mayor, of Stanleyville.) "I cut a very nice piece from his back because I wanted to get meat. Then I took it home. But when I left the piece near the fire to get some salt, some accursed dog passed by and grabbed it and so I have no meat to eat now. I am hungry."

"Yes, that is too bad," Papazoglakis said.

The ancient trudged woefully on. Another white man might have been horrified by the *mzee*'s problem. But Papazoglakis had been born in Africa. He burst into laughter. And, whistling merrily, he resumed his stroll.

7

JUDGMENT WITHOUT PITY

Bukavu is situated on five hilly peninsulas that reach out into the deep blue waters of Lake Kivu, one of the great lakes of Central Africa. Lake Kivu is one of the sources of the Congo River (the headwaters of the Nile also are nearby), but the climate and terrain have nothing in common with the rain forests. Bukavu is nearly a mile high. The days are cool and the nights are chilly. The lake is ringed with steep mountains, the slopes of which are covered with forests not too different from those in Maine or Michigan. At the north end of the lake there is a range of volcanos. At night, low-lying clouds glow red from the fires that smolder within the great cones.

In colonial times, Bukavu flourished as a holiday city. Belgians from Stanleyville and other sweltering jungle settlements flocked to Bukavu in great numbers to revel in the highland chill and to bathe and boat in the lake. Several resort hotels and good restaurants were opened. Shops were stocked with expensive goods that had been flown in from Europe. The future of Bukavu and the Kivu seemed so promising that a guidebook published by the colonial government declared: "When it is better known, the Kivu will one day become the playground of Africa in the same way as Switzerland has become the playground of Europe."

But things did not work out quite that way.

Bukavu was defended by about 650 ANC troops. Like

most ANC units, they were demoralized and undisciplined. They had received one pasting after another from the Simbas. Many of their comrades had defected to the Simbas. The remainder had retreated to Bukavu. They would have liked to retreat further, but their backs were at the wall. Bukavu is right on the eastern border of the Congo; only a river, the torrential Ruzizi, separates Bukavu from newly independent Rwanda. And there were Simbas all around the city.

In other circumstances, the ANC garrison might well have given up; Bukavu might have fallen to General Olenga with hardly a struggle, as so many other cities had fallen. But Bukavu was different in one respect: the best officer—indeed, some said, the only good officer—in the ANC was defending it—Colonel Léonard Mulamba. Mulamba had been the garrison commander in Stanleyville and had been in Bukavu on temporary duty when the Simbas conquered Stanleyville. It was he who tried to return to the city in an American military plane, the time that the pilot was hit by a sniper's bullet and had to continue on to Léopoldville without landing. Many people thought that if Mulamba had succeeded in landing in Stanleyville he might have saved it. Now, as the Simbas closed in on Bukavu, Mulamba would have a chance to even the score with Olenga.

Mulamba was a remarkable man. He came from Luluabourg, capital of the Kasai province, many hundreds of miles from either Stanlèyville or Bukavu. A man in his mid-thirties, he was short and stocky. He wore a steel helmet most of the time. He was stern, silent and in complete control of himself and others. Much later he found himself in command of several hundred white mercenaries, many of them white supremacists from South Africa. He demanded, and got, instant obedience from them. Curiously enough, they held him in great respect, albeit of a rather grudging nature.

Mulamba was one of the few men who could exact a degree of discipline from the ANC. He had no officers he could rely upon, so he had to be everywhere at once, urging his reluctant soldiers into a battle for which they had no heart.

The Simbas, led by General Olenga, came on the afternoon of August 19. There had been skirmishes around Bukavu for weeks, but now the big push was on.

C-130 E

As the Simbas neared the city, three Americans went out in a jeep with Captain Shimanga of the ANC to inspect an ANC position on the road that led in from Kindu. The Americans were Colonel William A. Dodds, fifty, of Alexandria, Virginia, a counter-insurgency expert who had been serving as a military adviser to Mulamba; Lieutenant Colonel Donald V. Rattan, thirty-nine, also of Alexandria, another counter-insurgency expert and a member of the American military aid mission to the Congo; and Lewis R. Macfarlane, twenty-five, of Seattle, vice-consul in the Bukavu consulate. Macfarlane spoke Swahili and had gone along as an interpreter.

At 3 P.M. that afternoon the Simba column clashed with ANC troops on the outskirts of Bukavu. There was a brief but furious fire fight. Alerted by the sound of gunfire, Bukavu's white community fled over the border into Rwanda. The State Department, mindful of what had happened in Stanleyville, ordered Richard C. Matheron, the American consul, and four members of his staff to go to Rwanda. But the two American colonels and Vice-Consul Macfarlane failed to return. Fears rose that they had been killed by the Simbas.

The Simbas quickly routed the ANC troops at the edge of the city. Then, giddy with success, they poured into the main part of the city. They reached the main street, which goes down one of the peninsulas. The main body of ANC troops now were trapped in the peninsula, their backs against the lake. With Mulamba urging his men on, they laid down a murderous fire. But block by block they were forced back to the tip of the peninsula, where Mulamba had his headquarters.

It looked as if Mulamba was finished. But he did not give up. He snatched up a rifle—he is an excellent marksman—and fired point blank at the oncoming hordes. He himself killed about a dozen Simbas within fifty yards of his headquarters. And his men cut down others by the scores.

Two of the Cuban-piloted T-28 planes strafed the Simbas with machine-gun and rocket fire, inflicting heavy casualties.

The Simbas began to weaken. They drew back.

When night came, there was a lull in the fighting. Mulamba radioed to Léopoldville. "I think I can hold Bukavu, but I will have to have more men and more ammunition," he said.

Early the next morning, three huge C-130E turboprop transport planes took off from Léopoldville's N'Djili Airport, loaded with 150 former Katanga gendarmes and with ammunition. The C-130E's were American Air Force planes, flown by American crews with American soldiers aboard as guards. They had arrived in the Congo only eight days before, having been put at the disposal of the central government in its campaign against the rebels. The C-130E's landed at Kamembe airport in Rwanda, only a few miles from downtown Bukavu. Then the gendarmes poured across the border and eventually linked up with Mulamba.

There was heavy fighting all day, but by now the tide of battle had turned. With support from the T-28's, Mulamba drove the Simbas from the downtown area and pursued them into the outlying native communes. Mopping-up operations continued for a few more days, but the main battle was over by the afternoon of August 20. Some three hundred Simbas lay dead in the streets of Bukavu. Mulamba had won.

When the members of the American consular staff returned from Rwanda, they could find no trace of the two American officers and the vice-consul who had gone out to inspect the ANC position on the 19th. A helicopter was sent from Léopoldville; it fluttered along all of the valleys and mountain slopes in the region, but found nothing. And the ANC made a dismaying discovery: blood-soaked identity papers, that had belonged to Macfarlane, on the body of a dead major. Hopes of ever finding the men alive dwindled still further.

But the Americans were very much alive, although in grave danger. Late in the morning of the 19th, they were rounding a bend in the road, about thirty-five miles from Bukavu, when they saw a truck filled with armed men approaching rapidly. Colonel Dodds suspected that they were Simbas. He turned the jeep around. The Simba vehicle opened fire with several automatic weapons. A bullet disabled the engine of Dodds's jeep. The three Americans and Captain Shimanga jumped out and dived into the bush.

They ran through the bush, trying to work their way back to the ANC. But, as they approached an ANC position, the ANC opened fire on them, having mistaken them for Simbas. This was no time to argue about their identity; they fled deeper into the bush. Then they stopped and took stock of the situation. If they set out in a northeast direction they could reach the Ruzizi River and cross into safety in Rwanda. But it was too dangerous to travel by day. They waited for darkness, then, navigating by the stars, spent the night trudging through the bush.

It was a wild, mountainous and scarcely populated region. Sometimes they had to cross over rugged peaks that reached to seven thousand feet. They had no food, but they found some wild pineapples and bananas and they drank water from mountain streams.

During the second day, while they were hiding and trying to sleep, Macfarlane awoke to find a three-foot viper coiling around his leg. He killed it with a rock. The men heard dozens of drums being beaten close by. "I could just imagine the message: 'Three whites and a black. Big reward,' " Dodds recalled later.

Late that afternoon, while the men were still hiding, five Bashi tribesmen stumbled upon them. The Bashis were anti-Simba, but they were highly suspicious about the three white men and the Congolese. The Bashis took the four men to their village. Some of the villagers urged that they be killed. But a Bashi interceded. "No, no—I know these men," he said, pointing to Dodds and Rattan. The colonels stared incredulously, but then they recognized the man. He was the nephew of Queen Astrida, a local potentate. They had met her and the nephew at her court in a nearby village a week before.

The Bashis were terrified of going near Bukavu, because of the fighting that had been going on. But, after the Americans agreed to pay the equivalent of $260, they finally furnished a guide. The men set out with their guide immediately and spent the night trudging over the mountains. In the morning, they reached a Catholic mission station a few miles from Bukavu. An ANC truck drove them the rest of the way. When the men arrived in Bukavu, their clothing was in tatters. But they were safe at last.

Just after the battle of Bukavu, the government radio announced that Olenga had been killed during the fighting. The report was picked up by transistor receivers all over the eastern Congo, to be relayed by word of mouth from one jungle village to another: the general is dead!

But Olenga was not dead. He retreated in disorder with his surviving Simbas to Kindu. When he arrived there, the populace took this as one more proof that the great man was, indeed, immune to bullets. His magic clearly surpassed that of anyone in the world.

Olenga, however, was in no mood to exult. The general was in a rage. It was the first time he had ever tasted the humiliation of defeat. And Bukavu was more than just a minor defeat. It had been necessary to snuff out the government enclave at Bukavu before he could begin the triumphal march on the biggest prize of all—Léopoldville. But now, after he had failed miserably at Bukavu, Léopoldville seemed farther away than ever.

Who was to blame for the defeat at Bukavu? It was, of course, the Americans. The had supplied the T-28's which had killed so many of his Simbas, *dawa* or no *dawa*. And they had flown in reinforcements for Mulamba aboard the C-130E's. Olenga ached for revenge. Then he remembered Michael Hoyt and the others whom his Simbas were holding as hostages in Stanleyville. He wrote out a message. The radio crackled. Stanleyville acknowledged receipt.

At noon on August 21, just as Hoyt and the others were sitting down to lunch, Patrick Nothomb burst into the American consulate. As soon as Hoyt saw Nothomb, he knew that something terrible had happened.

"Do you have any last messages for your family?" Nothomb asked.

The five Americans stared at Nothomb.

"The Simbas are coming for you," Nothomb said. Tears streamed down the little man's cheeks. "You've got to prepare yourselves for death. They're going to shoot you."

There was a long silence; then Hoyt spoke.

"Isn't there something we can do?" he said.

"I don't think so," said Nothomb. "I'm sorry but I just don't think so."

Nothomb explained that the Simbas had just received a radio message from Olenga. A Belgian radio operator had seen the text and he had notified Nothomb. The message was long and rambling, the first part an attack on "American imperialism." Then Olenga declared: "It is obligatory to arrest all Americans who are in the Congo and take them before a court-martial for judgment without pity."

The words "judgment without pity" were all too clear. To the Simbas, this meant that the men were to be executed.

Commandant Sengha came into the consulate. He was very much upset. I've heard about the message from the general," he said. "This is very, very serious. Maybe I can do something. I don't know. I didn't know when I came here whether I would find you, my dear friends, alive or dead. It's risky for me to be here. But life doesn't mean much to me any more. Did you know that the Simbas killed my nephew?"

Sengha told the men that the Simba authorities had found a copy of one of Hoyt's telegrams in the glove compartment of the nephew's car. It was a telegram that Hoyt had sent earlier to the embassy in Léopoldville concerning the evaluation. Hoyt had given a copy to Sengha. Somehow the nephew obtained it. When the Simbas saw it, they regarded it as proof that the man was an "accomplice" of the Americans. So they killed him.

Several agonizing minutes went by. Then Patrick Nothomb and the others had an idea. "Don't kill them today," Nothomb said. "Let them send a radio message to their ambassador in Léopoldville requesting that the Americans call off their support for the Tshombe government."

Nothomb was at his crafty best at that moment. He knew the Congolese well. He knew that they acted on the impulse of the moment. If something could be delayed for a few days, it would soon be forgotten—even a death sentence.

"That's a good idea," said Sengha.

Nothomb and Sengha raced out to Camp Ketele to talk with Colonel Joseph Opepe, the number two man in the Simba army, who was acting as the military commandant of Stanleyville during Olenga's absence. While they were gone, Hoyt and the others started to resume their lunch, but then pushed their plates aside. Hoyt kept turning the matter over and over in his mind. It seemed impossible that the Simbas would execute foreign diplomats. Yet the Simbas were capable of anything. In any case, they had been ordered to do it by their general—and Hoyt knew that in the past Olenga had had Simbas shot for disobeying his commands.

Soon, Nothomb and Sengha were back with Colonel Opepe, the man who would determine whether they would die that day. Opepe was interested in the proposal that the executions be stayed while a message was sent.

Colonel Opepe was one of the most fascinating of all the Simba officers. Everyone in Stanleyville had strong opinions about him. Some people maintained that Opepe did his best to protect Europeans; others said he was a cold-blooded murderer. Each side would present arguments to back up their case. But perhaps both sides were right. General Olenga may not have been the only man with schizophrenic tendencies.

Opepe was much older than the other Simbas—about fifty. He was a short and fat Batetela tribesman. He dressed roughly—in khaki slacks and shirt. The shirt was unbuttoned most of the time and a bulging belly protruded for all the world to see and admire.

Opepe was a professional soldier, a veteran of the brutal Force Publique, and, later, of the ANC. He enlisted in 1939 and seems to have been something of a behavior problem. There were seventeen entries in his punishment record, for disobedience, lack of respect to officers and deceit. On one occasion, he was reprimanded for using an improper technique in flogging an enlisted man; he gave illegal supplementary lashes on the back stroke. But a little rough stuff never hurt anyone's career in the Force Publique and Opepe quickly rose to corporal, sergeant, first sergeant, then sergeant major. That was as far as a Congolese could go in colonial days; the most important requirement for being an officer was to be white. When independence came, Opepe was jumped in rank to major. For a time he was chief of staff for the ANC in Stanleyville. He retired from the ANC in 1963 and soon after joined the Simbas.

Opepe was a devout Catholic. He drank a lot; indeed, he was drunk much of the time.

But when Opepe showed up at the consulate with Sengha and Nothomb, he was perfectly sober. Speaking in Swahili— Sengha translated his words into French—Opepe asked Hoyt: "Do you really sincerely believe that the United States should stop its assistance to the central government? Do you believe that the Americans are interfering in internal Congolese affairs?"

Hoyt evaded a direct answer. "I'm very willing to send a message," he said.

Sengha said something to Opepe in Swahili. Apparently he embellished the response to indicate that Hoyt was in perfect agreement with the Simba view on American "imperialism." Opepe nodded with satisfaction.

Things were looking up. But then another Simba colonel, a man named Kifakio, burst into the consulate with a platoon of soldiers. Kifakio was a follower of Kinghis and was as volatile as his master. With a show of satisfaction, he announced that he had come to carry out the death sentence. But Opepe outranked him and waved him aside.

Opepe whispered something to Sengha. Sengha whispered to Hoyt that Opepe said that General Olenga frequently gave orders when he was drunk or angry, orders which he later regretted. And so, Opepe said, he would postpone the executions if the Americans sent the cable.

With assistance from Nothomb, Hoyt and Grinwis wrote the following message, addressed to the American Ambassador "for transmission to the Department of State and to President Johnson":

WE REQUEST OF YOU IN THE MOST INSISTENT MANNER TO RECONSIDER AMERICAN MILITARY ASSISTANCE TO THE CENTRAL CONGOLESE GOVERNMENT STOP WE ARE ALL UNTIL NOW IN GOOD HEALTH BUT THE CONTINUATION OF AMERICAN MILITARY AID WOULD PUT

WITHOUT ANY DOUBT IN IMMEDIATE DANGER REPEAT IMMEDIATE DANGER THE LIVES OF THE AMERICANS LIVING IN THE TERRITORY CONTROLLED BY THE PEOPLE'S ARMY OF LIBERATION

Nothomb was counting on the Simbas to forget the entire matter in a day or two. But he was taking no chances. Speaking through Sengha, he told Opepe: "When the Americans receive this message they will immediately stop their aggression because it is a very important message. President Johnson has to see it, so it will take a little time. Within three, four or five days President Johnson himself will answer."

Opepe and Sengha took all five of the Americans to the post office to send the message via commercial telecommunications. Nothomb excused himself. The Americans seemed relatively safe at the moment. Nothomb had another job to do. A Belgian had just been arrested and threatened with death. Nothomb had to go to his aid.

Later on that day, Nothomb ran into troubles of his own. It turned out that not just one, but a great many Belgians, had been arrested. When Nothomb tried to secure their release, he, too, was arrested. He and the others were taken before Kinghis, beaten by Simbas in his presence, then finally released.

After the Americans had sent the message, Opepe took them to Kinghis's office. The homicidal president beamed with pleasure when he saw that the Americans were prisoners again. "You Americans are like children," he exclaimed. "You don't understand the Congolese. You don't understand Africa. You're trying to do things you can't accomplish."

That was probably the only true observation that Kinghis ever made.

On Kinghis's orders, the Americans were taken to the airport at the edge of the city, to be placed under the guard of Major Nasor, the man who had had them beaten at the consulate some days before and who had made them chew on American flags.

A mob of Simbas fell on the Americans when they were brought into the airport terminal. They were kicked and punched for ten minutes, then thrown into the women's washroom. The room was only five feet wide and ten feet long. At one end there were two cubicles, each with a toilet.

The toilets were out of order; they had, quite obviously, been broken down for a long time, perhaps ever since the Belgians left. But that had not prevented anyone from using them. The floor was covered with excreta. The stench was so awful that the Americans gagged and retched.

A short while later, the Simbas opened the door and threw six Congolese civilians into the washroom. From time to time the Simbas opened the door to show the prisoners off to newcomers. There was no knob; they turned the lock with the tips of their bayonets. "Ah, the Americans!" the newcomers whooped. "We're going to kill you." They flourished bayonets and machetes. "We will cut you open." Some Simbas pointed to individual Americans and said, "I want to kill that one."

Then the door banged shut. There was hardly any light in the room. All the while a deafening uproar went on outside. The Simbas had turned in to Radio Stanleyville. A ghastly cacophony of Congolese cha-cha-cha poured out with hypnotic repetition. Then an announcer broke in to read General Olenga's message from Kindu: "It is obligatory to arrest all Americans who are in the Congo and take them before a court martial for judgment without pity."

The announcer read the message over and over, in French, Swahili and Lingala, another native tongue.

The Americans were dragged from the washroom and forced to dance and hop around while the Simbas beat them with their fists and kicked them. Then they were told to sit in a row of chairs. They were given rice and fish and told to eat, but no one could. After that, they were pushed back into the foul-smelling darkness of the washroom. The six Congolese prisoners had appropriated most of the meager floor space. There was only enough room for three Americans to squat. The other two had to stand. They took turns trying to sleep while squatting. But no one got any sleep. The Simbas were having a wild party. They brought out empty fuel barrels and beat them as drums most of the night.

In the morning, the Simbas opened the door continually. Each time they ordered the Americans out of the washroom and subjected them to blows and taunts. As the Simbas became more frenzied, they boasted of how they would devour the men. Then the Americans would be thrust back into the washroom, only to be brought out again a short while later.

But Simba brutality was an off-again, on-again affair. Inexplicably, a Simba officer told Hoyt and Grinwis that it would be all right if they went to the consulate to pick up some food. The two men were driven to the consulate under guard. Hoyt shaved and changed his shirt. His servants whipped up a big lunch and the men dined heartily. Then, bringing with them food for the three radio operators, they were brought back to the airport.

Soon after their return, tension built up among the Simbas. They screamed and shouted at each other. The Simba officers were not there and the soldiers became very menacing toward the Americans. One of the guards tried to keep them at bay, but he was losing control of the situation. He told the Americans to get back into the washroom. He locked the door and whispered for them to keep quiet. The uproar increased outside. Someone rattled the doorknob violently, but the lock held. Eventually the racket died down.

Finally, the door was opened. A white man, his pregnant wife and their two small children were in the terminal. While the Simbas restrained the man, pummeling him all the while, they slapped the woman on the head. Then they shoved the couple and the children into the washroom.

"We're American citizens. I'm going to complain to the American consul about this," the white man said, his voice quivering with helpless indignation.

Hoyt pushed his way through the crowded and darkened room and came close to the man. "I am the American consul," he said.

8

THE PEOPLE'S REPUBLIC

The white man who had just been thrown into the washroom with Hoyt and the others was thirty years old, six feet one inch tall. He had the well-fed, well-scrubbed look of an upper-class American. He spoke with a New England accent and, in happier moments, radiated confidence and charm. He looked every bit an Ivy Leaguer. But Charles E. Davis was a one-time juvenile delinquent who had grown up in the slum jungles of Boston's Roxbury section. As a boy, he stole cars. He was handy with his fists and participated in many a bloody street brawl. In other circumstances, Davis might well have wound up in prison—not a Congolese prison, but an American one. Many of his boyhood friends did.

Davis instead became very religious while still in his teens. By dint of hard labor, he worked his way through college. He was ordained and became a missionary. He knew well the dangers of life in the Congo, but he volunteered to spend his life spreading the gospel there. And he had brought his wife and children with him.

Davis was a most likable man. Quick and bright, he was usually happy and outgoing. He made friends easily, even among those who were skeptical about the fundamentalist doctrines he preached. He had a great sense of humor and he talked easily, almost torrentially. After all, he was a preacher, and a marvelous one at that. When he spoke of sin and Satan, his voice simmered with rage. When he talked of Christ and

Heaven, his words took on a melodic lilt. When he discussed Hell, one could almost hear the Eternal Fires crackling. When he got around to the subject of wickedness, his denunciations were no less than thunderous. And when he told of Judgment Day, one could almost see the sinners creaking up from their coffins to receive the Righteous Sentence.

Although Davis was an unabashed fundamentalist, he had a tolerance for others who did not share his views. That tolerance was perhaps born of a rather intimate acquaintance with man's frailties. As a boy he tangled often with the police, but he was fortunate in one respect: the cops knew his father, who was a poor and honest workingman. As Davis later recalled, "They filled the seat of my pants with shoe leather and sent me home." After one of many such encounters with the law, the family decided he ought to attend church regularly, and packed him off to Boston's Ruggles Street Baptist Church, where, as Davis put it, he "got the call."

After graduation from high school, Davis enrolled in Gordon College of Theology and Missions, near Boston, not particularly to study but rather because he wanted to play basketball for Gordon. He became captain of the team. He worked his way through college with a number of jobs that included teaching crafts, serving as a golf and swimming instructor and collecting garbage. Of this latter employment he once remarked: "You learn a lot of humility that way; it's good for you."

Davis received a bachelor's degree from Gordon, then enrolled in an affiliated seminary as a fellow. He decided to become a missionary. After reading the journals of the explorer Stanley and of the great missionary Livingstone, he became interested in mission work in Africa. He was ordained by the American Baptist Church, then he and his wife, Muriel, moved to Blue Ridge, Virginia, near Roanoke, where he preached for two years in a Southern Baptist Church. Meanwhile he collected pledges of financial support so he could go as a missionary to Africa. A schoolteacher promised $5 a month; a church said it would provide $18.50 a month. Finally he secured twenty-two pledges totalling $290 a month, the minimum he would need to maintain his family in Africa as a teacher with the Africa Inland Mission, an interdenominational group.

The family left for Europe in late 1962. The idea was that he would learn French in Europe before going on to the Congo. For a while he feared that they might have to go to Paris. "There are all sorts of crimes going on there," Davis explained. But the family was able to escape the dangers of Paris and went, instead, to Neuchâtel, Switzerland, where Davis spent fourteen months learning French. Then they flew to Uganda and traveled overland into the northeast Congo. After four months of instruction in Swahili, Davis was ready to go to work. He settled with his family at a mission station in a town called Banjwadi, about forty miles north of Stanleyville.

It was July 27, 1964, when they reached Banjwadi, nine days before Stanleyville fell to the Simbas.

The first few weeks of the Simba occupation went by fairly peacefully. The Simbas took all of the mission vehicles and radio equipment, but no one was harmed. Indeed, the Simbas assured Davis: "We Congolese are having a dispute among ourselves. The white people have nothing to do with it. You are perfectly safe."

On August 22, a Simba officer and two soldiers came to the mission station. "Come with us," they told the Davises. "All Americans are going to be evacuated together with the staff of your consulate." Davis did not know that General Olenga had just ordered that all Americans were to be judged "without pity" and the officer did not tell him that.

Mrs. Davis and the two children, Stephen, four years old, and Beth, twenty months, got into the car with their father. It was a hair-raising ride. The car zoomed along a narrow and winding dirt road at sixty miles an hour. But this was nothing compared to what greeted the Davises when they reached Stanleyville.

The officer took the family directly to Camp Ketele. "An ungodly place!" Davis exclaimed. A crisis seemed to be going on in the camp. Hundreds of Simbas milled around angrily, shouting and cursing at each other.

"Get these white people out of here," the officer told the driver.

When the car neared the gate, a mob of Simbas swirled around it. They were knocking a Simba around. They slammed him against the car, evidently trying to knock him down. But he kept his balance. Then a Simba tripped him and he fell just beside the car. The other Simbas opened fire at his prostrate body. They riddled his body with perhaps fifty shots.

Davis's son, Stephen, became hysterical. "Daddy, they shot that man," the four-year-old wailed. Davis put the boy's head in his lap and tried to soothe him. Mrs. Davis clutched the infant girl.

The soldiers spotted the white people in the car. *"Mateka!"* the shrieked. They thrust guns through the windows of the car. The Davises found themselves looking into the barrels of a dozen weapons that were still hot from the killing of the Simba soldier. Davis and his wife both prayed that if the Simbas opened fire they would kill everyone in the car. They did not want their children to be left alone in that madhouse. But the Simbas did not shoot.

The driver finally succeeded in forcing the car through the Simba mob. As they raced through the streets of Stanleyville, one of the Simbas in the car took the couple's wristwatches as well as Davis's ring. Mrs. Davis managed to hide her ring in her dress. The family was taken to the airport, where, after being pummeled, they were thrown into the women's washroom with Hoyt and the others.

All of the Americans in the washroom were, of course, terrified. But Davis's anguish was all the more acute because he had his wife and infant children with him. Mrs. Davis sobbed. The children clutched her. They were hysterical. Hoyt and the other consular personnel tried to comfort them, but there was little they could say.

The door opened. Major Nasor beckoned to Mrs. Davis and the children. "You come with me," he said. The others were pushed back into the washroom and the door was slammed.

Nasor drove away with Davis's wife and children. Davis had no way of knowing what had happened to them. At times he wept, as times he sat there, mute. And he prayed.

Soon after Mrs. Davis and the children left with Major Nasor, the Simba who had been guarding the Americans in the washroom was pushed aside by some young Simbas who had just been recruited into the movement from the *jeunesse*.

There were no officers present and the *jeunesse* were spoiling for fun. They ordered Davis and the five consular employees out of the washroom.

"Take off your ties," one of the *jeunesse* ordered.

The men complied.

"Your coats and shirts."

The Americans removed their coats and shirts.

"Your trousers . . . shoes . . . socks."

All six men were standing there in their under shorts.

"Dance!" the *jeunesse* said.

The Simbas beat at the feet of the Americans with bayonets, drawing blood, then hit them with rifle butts and punched them with their fists. One of the Simbas dipped a stick into the excreta in the toilet and smeared it on the bodies of some of the men.

The Americans were put back into the washroom. After some time, an officer known as Commandant Yoni opened the door. He had chased away the *jeunesse*. He told the Americans to come out and he gave them back their clothes.

"Things aren't like they are in Belgium, are they?" Yoni said, without being sarcastic. He showed the Americans to some chairs. "Would you like some cigarettes? How about some beer?" he said.

With the exception of Davis, the Americans lighted up Yoni's cigarettes and drank the beer. He brought out another round, then another and yet another. Soon the men were feeling tipsy.

Other Simbas came into the room. They were friendly. As it turned out they, unlike the young thugs who had been locally recruited from the *jeunesse*, were disciplined members of the original hard core of the Simba movement, from the Maniema. They were under tight discipline.

Yoni was drunk when he arrived. Now, after several more beers, he had trouble standing up. Swaying like a palm tree, he declared: "All right, I will fine you each 100,000 francs—is that all right with you?"

One hundred thousand francs is the black-market equivalent of about $300.

"There isn't much I can do about it, so I accept," Hoyt said.

"Gosh," said Davis. "That's an awful lot of money."

"Don't worry; we can raise it," Hoyt assured him.

"Okay, it's settled," said Yoni. He had his men bring out more rounds of beer to conclude the pact.

Yoni said it would be a shame to put the men back into the washroom for the night, so he had the Simbas set up chairs and benches in the corridor. No such consideration was accorded the Congolese prisoners, now eight in number. They were hustled back into the washroom and the door was banged shut.

Next morning tension again built up between the hardcore Simbas and the visiting gangs of *jeunesse*. The regular Simbas appeared to be losing control once more. And so, in mid-afternoon, the Simbas moved the Americans to the Sabena guest house, across the street. They were put into a little bungalow room in which six beds had been placed. There were clean sheets and blankets and a bathroom with running hot water. The men scrubbed the filth from their bodies and felt somewhat better.

All except Charlie Davis. He was frantic over his wife and children. The others tried to console him. Hoyt in particular appreciated the depths of the missionary's anguish, for Hoyt had four children of his own. He was thankful for the fact that they were safe in America. All that Davis knew was that his family was somewhere in Stanleyville at the moment, perhaps the objects of sport at Camp Ketele.

When General Olenga returned to Stanleyville, he burned with anger and suspicion. His fury was not directed against the Americans this time; as Patrick Nothomb had so accurately foreseen, Olenga had forgotten about the death sentences that he had imposed on Hoyt and the other Americans when he ordered that they be judged "without pity."

The general had other things on his mind. He had gained the impression that Alphonse Kinghis, the demented provincial president, and Colonel Kifakio, the number three man in the Simba army, had been conspiring against him during his absence. The two men had heard the erroneous report of Olenga's death in battle. Perhaps they had seen that as an opportunity to step into the master's boots.

The general apparently was angered as well by the executions that Kinghis had been conducting at the Lumumba

Monument. A little slaughter, of course, was not alien to Olenga; he had helped to fill many a graveyard during his career. But he seems to have felt that Kinghis had used the opportunity to settle purely personal scores. Kinghis, as well as the local *jeunesse*, seemed to be slipping from his control, and that was a situation which Olenga could never tolerate.

Olenga fired Kinghis as provincial president. There are those who say that he really wanted Kinghis's blood. But as leader of the fanatic Kitawalist sect, Kinghis was a powerful man in his own right, with a large following in Stanleyville. And so he was only put under house arrest.

As far as Kifakio was concerned, the general may well have felt that it was time to get rid of him anyway. For he alone among the Simba officers had a considerable military reputation of his own and thus stood out as a potential rival. The man's real name was not Kifakio; that was a *nom de guerre* that roughly meant, in Swahili, The One Who Sweeps Clean. Kifakio had led the first Simba columns into both Kindu and Stanleyville. He was the man, too, who had been prevented by Colonel Opepe from carrying out the death sentences at the American consulate.

Now the Sweeper's moment had come. Olenga encountered him in front of the Congo Palace Hotel. There was a wild argument, but it was quickly settled. Olenga whipped out a pistol and, in front of a crowd of people, shot Kifakio dead.

Olenga was no politician. He had no taste for the tedious day-by-day business of running a government. And so, casting about for someone to replace Kinghis, he latched onto two fairly well-known Congolese politicians, a Mutt-and-Jeff team by the names of Christophe Gbenye and Gaston Soumialot.

Late one afternoon, all of Stanleyville snapped to attention as the general's voice boomed over the radio.

"In view of the arbitrary arrests carried out and the disappearance of nationalists, I am forced to take grave measures with regard to both the civilian and military authorities," he said. "The population must now set to work. There is no curfew and no longer any question of nocturnal arrests. My army is not an army of thieves and pilferers. The population must remember this and rejoice in its true independence."

106

Then Olenga whipped off a decree by which he no doubt won over the allegiance of a large share of the population. "All bars," the general declared, "must remain open all night."

On August 28 several thousand Congolese civilians gathered at the Lumumba Monument. They had not come, as in the Kinghis days, to witness human sacrifices at the altar of the great god, but rather to indulge in something more akin to Western politics. As the crowd applauded, a white convertible arrived and a small, thin man with a goatee emerged. Clutching a wreath of flowers, he trudged up the blood-stained walkway and laid the wreath before the photograph of the Congo's first prime minister. The crowd burst into another round of applause. Then, with proper obeisances at the monument, did Gaston Soumialot present himself to Stanleyville.

The newcomer was somewhat better known than others in the Stanleyville government. Even so, foreign correspondents spent a long time trying to discover whether his first name was Gaston or Émile. After diligent research and, perhaps, a toss of the coin, they concluded that his proper handle was Gaston Émile Soumialot. He was a member of the Basonge tribe, who are closely related to the Batetela. For twenty uneventful years he had worked as a clerk in the Léopoldville warehouse of Sedec, a Belgian trading company. One of his proudest possessions, which he carried in his wallet, was a well-worn, much-creased certificate, signed by a Sedec manager, which attested that Gaston Soumialot had put in two decades of loyal service to the company. Pointing to the certificate, Soumialot declared to one visitor: "You see that? *That* is the signature of Monsieur Dupont!"

One of the first things that Soumialot did on arriving in Stanleyville was to visit the Sedec branch. "I have not forgotten Sedec and all that Sedec taught me," he told the startled Belgian manager.

Soumialot's problem was that although he had burning ambitions he was no charismatic fireball. He was a slight, nervous man in his forties—much older than most of his revolutionary colleagues. He was something of a model bureaucrat—modest, prudent and ever ready to listen attentively to a complaint. The Europeans in Stanleyville regarded him as a moderate and, on occasion, he could be quite charming with them. He had an enormous smile which lighted up his entire face. But it was a smile which, though it might win friends, would never move armies into battle.

Soumialot's personal life was a model of middle-class respectability. A Catholic, he attended mass regularly. He had eight sons—a fact in which he took great pride. Indeed, the only thing that seemed out of keeping was that Soumialot often carried a little stick. It was tipped with red feathers. It conferred powerful magic on him.

After retiring from his job with the trading company, Soumialot became an organizer for Lumumba's Mouvement National Congolais. When independence came, Lumumba rewarded him with a cushy job as district commissioner, or chief government agent, in Kindu. But after Lumumba's downfall he was fired. Eventually, along with a number of other politicians who were out of work, he settled in Brazzaville, capital of the ex–French Congo, just across the Congo River from Léopoldville. With money supplied in generous measure by the Chinese Communist embassy there, they set up a Comité National de Libération (CNL)—the National Liberation Committee—which had as its aim the overthrow of the Léopoldville regime and the restoration to public office of the unemployed exiles. Christophe Gbenye was president of the CNL for a time, but then it fell into a disorder that is characteristic of Congolese affairs.

Fed up with the carryings-on in Brazzaville, Soumialot assumed the title of "eastern president" of the CNL and moved to Bujumbura, capital of Burundi, on the eastern borders of the Congo, in early 1964. Bujumbura was relatively close to the Maniema and it gave Soumialot the opportunity to cash in on unrest there. He lived in the Paguidas Hotel, as did members of the staff of the Chinese Communist embassy, and there is reason to believe that they bestowed substantial sums on him once again. Soumialot probably attended the Chinese late-late show in the Paguidas—almost every night the Chinese showed movies on guerrilla warfare to Congolese exiles, disgruntled Burundians and anyone else who wanted handy tips on how to blow up bridges and overthrow governments. Yet, despite Soumialot's associations with the Chinese, there was no evidence that he was a

Communist or even a radical. Like most Congolese politicians, he would take anyone's money.

Operating from Bujumbura, Soumialot exploited a series of tribal revolts in the eastern Congo. In June, Albertville fell in one such revolt. Soumialot moved to Albertville, as did Nicholas Olenga, and attempted to set up a civilian government without too much success. When Olenga set out from Albertville on his march to Stanleyville, Soumialot soon followed, hoping to establish himself as an important official in the new regime.

Soon after his arrival in Stanleyville, Soumialot asked an elderly Belgian priest, Father Paul Van Vereertbrugghen, the dean of Stanleyville's cathedral, to celebrate a requiem mass for everyone who had died during the revolution—not only for the Simbas, but, Soumialot insisted, for the Europeans and even for the ANC soldiers.

It was one of the biggest events held in Stanleyville during the Simba occupation. The cathedral, which overlooks the Congo River, was filled to capacity. Baron Nothomb and all of the other foreign consuls had been summoned—all, that is, except for the Americans, who were imprisoned in the Sabena guest house. The consuls wore suits, white shirts and ties.

Soumialot arrived, dressed in slacks and an open-necked shirt. Ties were, of course, taboo. He carried his little magic stick. General Olenga appeared in similar rough attire and so, too, did Colonel Opepe, the number two man in the Simba army. Soumialot and the Simba officers took the first row of pews. The consuls were directed to the second row. Hundreds of Simbas took up the remaining pews.

The throng was silent. The Mass for the Dead began. Surrounded by white-robed Congolese altar boys, Father Vereertbrugghen prayed in Latin at the candle-lighted altar.

"Grant them eternal rest, O Lord, and let perpetual light shine upon them," he intoned.

The Simbas were kneeling. Soumialot kept his magic stick pointed at the altar.

Singing in Latin, the Congolese choir began the great, dirgelike *Dies Irae*, the Day of Wrath, a litany that has been sung in Catholic churches since the Middle Ages.

That day of wrath, that dreadful day
When heaven and earth shall pass away
Both David and the Sibyl say.

What terror then to us shall fall
When lo, the Judge's steps appall,
About to weigh the deeds of all.

The mighty trumpet's dolorous tone
Shall pierce through each sepulchral stone
And summon men before the throne.

Craning his neck as far as piety permitted, Baron Nothomb discovered that the Simbas all kept their hats on—the usual gorgeous array of military caps, cowboy hats, UN helmets and ladies' bonnets. The reason was apparent: Olenga was not a Catholic and, to show his independence, he kept his cap on. As a result, none dared remove his—none except one. Colonel Opepe, who was a devout Catholic, removed his cap and sat with bowed head.

In suppliant prayer I humbly bend,
My contrite heart like ashes rend;
Regard, O Lord, my final end.

Oh, on that day, that tearful day,
When man to judgment wakes from clay,
Do you the sinner's sentence stay
O spare him, God, we humbly pray.
And grant to all, O Saviour blest,
Who die in you, the saints' sweet rest.

A mournful "Amen" hushed through the cathedral. Many of the Simbas appeared to be moved by the dirge. The Latin words were, of course, incomprehensible. But the awesome message nevertheless seeped through. Colonel Opepe in particular seemed lost in thought.

"Dominus vobiscum"—"The Lord be with you," Father Vereertbrugghen intoned.

On the morning of September 5, thousands of Congolese turned out for another gala reception at the Lumumba Monument. A motorcade roared up and another newcomer alighted and reverently placed a wreath at the altar of the great god. The newcomer was Christophe Gbenye, Soumialot's old pal in the Comité National de Libération in Brazzaville. While the crowd cheered, General Olenga announced that he was forming a "People's Republic of the Congo." Gbenye would serve as president and Soumialot as minister of national defense. But, as everyone knew, the real power remained in the hands of Olenga himself.

The new president was a bizarre figure even by Congolese standards. Heavily bearded, he wore tight blue jeans, with a pistol peeping from a hip holster. One European who knew him well described him as: "A Congolese Clark Gable—you know, riverboat-gambler type: big man, big smile, big teeth, sideburns." Gbenye could be quite ferocious. But if someone started to weep in his presence great tears of sympathy often would roll down the president's face.

Gbenye was an old pro in the Alice-in-Wonderland world of Congo politics. Thirty-seven years old, he was not from the Maniema, but rather was a Babua tribesman from a region near Stanleyville. He had been a clerk in Stanleyville and a union organizer. Then he went into politics, but one suspects that his ideological commitments were never too firm. He served as minister of the interior in Lumumba's government, held the same post in Gizenga's left-leaning secessionist regime in Stanleyville, then appeared as minister of the interior and later as vice-premier in the pro-Western government of Cyrille Adoula in Léopoldville.

Adoula fired him. So Gbenye fled to Brazzaville, rallied other unemployed politicians and became the first president of the CNL. One man who was close to the situation in Brazzaville said: "The reason they picked Gbenye as president was that people felt that since they couldn't find anybody whom everyone trusted, they'd settle for someone whom everybody distrusted."

But Gbenye seemed to have little talent for holding a job. Soon he fell out with the CNL and they sacked him. He tried to make a deal with Tshombe, who by then was staging his political comeback, but nothing came of it. And so Gbenye was stranded, forlorn and unemployed, in Brazzaville.

Just two weeks before his arrival in Stanleyville, Gbenye

had undertaken a secret diplomatic safari to Belgium itself. He had, throughout his stay in Brazzaville, kept in discreet touch with the Belgian embassy there. He wrote letters to Paul-Henri Spaak, the Belgian foreign minister, demanding that Belgium withdraw its support for Tshombe and put its money, instead, on Christophe Gbenye. In one such letter, Gbenye commented that it was difficult to discuss politics by mail. And Spaak replied: "If you want to come to Brussels, I will be glad to talk to you."

Gbenye replied that he was glad to come—except that he was broke. Would the Belgian government pay for an air ticket for him and an associate? The Belgian embassy in Brazzaville forked out the cash and the two of them flew to Brussels, arriving there on August 21. They were put up, at Belgian expense, in the Hotel Métropole. Next morning, Gbenye was driven to Spaak's vacation villa in the Ardennes forest for the first of two long talks. But, as one Belgian official said: "The conversations consisted essentially of an irrational monologue by Mr. Gbenye, attacking everything and everybody, and especially the Americans, and insisting that only he could bring peace and order to the Congo."

Spaak managed to extract a promise from Gbenye that he would use his influence to protect Belgians and other foreigners in rebel-held territories. But the promise was never kept.

Gbenye left Brussels by plane on August 25, bound for Bujumbura. From there he traveled overland to Stanleyville to become General Olenga's new president.

Soon after Gbenye's arrival, the foreign consuls were summoned again to the cathedral, this time for a *Te Deum*, a Hymn of Thanksgiving, to mark the founding of the "People's Republic." Gbenye turned up in blue jeans and pistol as usual. Soumialot arrived with his magic stick. General Olenga, Colonel Opepe and several hundred Simbas were there as well.

The Simbas knelt. Soumialot aimed his magic stick at the altar. Father Vereertbrugghen prayed:

> *Grant, O Lord, to keep us without sin this day.*
> *Have mercy on us, O Lord; have mercy on us.*

After the service, Gbenye spoke briefly with Patrick Nothomb. The president had a woeful expression on his face. "I am really sorry," he said. "No Catholic priest, black or white, has volunteered to be the chaplain of the Simbas. It's a shame! I'm a Catholic and it makes me very sad."

After Charlie Davis and the other Americans had been held four days in the bungalow at the Sabena guest house, they learned that Mrs. Davis and the two Davis children were safe and sound. Davis wept when he heard the news.

What had happened, as they pieced the story together later, was that the Simbas had taken Mrs. Davis and the children outside and had told her to "go home." Mrs. Davis did not speak Swahili and she understood only a little French, but she managed to let them know that she lived at Banjwadi, forty miles away.

"We can't take you there," the Simbas said.

After another linguistic struggle, she managed to ask them to take her to another mission station about five miles from Stanleyville.

"No, we can't go there, either," the Simbas said. "We'll take you to Camp Ketele for the night."

Mrs. Davis winced. She tried to protest, but could not remember the right words in French. Then she remembered the word "Leco." That was the name of a missionary bookstore in downtown Stanleyville, just across from the central prison. Mrs. Davis had only heard the name "Leco" once, when some missionaries had prayed for it, but the name had remained in her mind.

"Can you take me to Leco?" she said.

The Simbas did not know what or where Leco was. They drove down the road, in the direction of Camp Ketele. Then they stopped and asked a passing European about Leco. He shrugged. A Congolese came up. "Leco? It's just up the street at the next corner," he said.

The Simbas dropped Mrs. Davis and the two children at the bookstore and speeded away. She knocked on the door. An elderly English couple, Mr. and Mrs. Herbert Jenkinson, who had been in the Congo as missionaries for more than forty years, took her and the children in.

They were safe, at least for the moment.

*   *   *

Charlie Davis and the five American consular personnel were held prisoner in the Sabena guest house for two weeks. From time to time they were subjected to taunts by visiting Simbas. One afternoon a guard beat several of the Americans, drawing blood from Davis and Parkes. When the officer in charge heard about the beatings, he had the guard flung into solitary confinement.

Dr. Barlovatz visited them and treated Hoyt for a bronchial cough that had developed from heavy smoking. Later on a package arrived from Barlovatz—books, to help them pass the time. The men had cards and they played gin rummy and casino. Charlie Davis had a missionary's distaste for cards, so he spent the time reading a Bible which he always carried in his hip pocket. He also composed a number of thunderous sermons, to be stored up for future use. Davis asked if the others would mind if he said grace at mealtimes. They agreed. Sometimes, when Grinwis felt that the prayer had gone on too long, he would rattle his knife and fork impatiently. Davis would frown. But otherwise things went along smoothly.

The Simbas explained to the Americans that it was necessary to hold them incommunicado because they otherwise would "call their brothers" to come and rescue them. One Simba officer confided to Patrick Nothomb that the Americans were great magicians, that they could conceal radio transmitters even in malaria pills. Another officer explained to Nothomb that he feared the Americans might send a submarine up the Congo River and shell Stanleyville.

"But you know as well as I do that the Americans couldn't bring a submarine up the rapids at Léopoldville," Nothomb said.

"Those Americans are clever—they'd find a way," the Simba replied.

As the days passed by, the Americans spent many hours discussing escape plans. It seemed so easy. Often the Simba guards went away, leaving their loaded weapons in the room. One would only have to pick up a gun and then . . .

But the Americans knew that it was impossible to escape. Every man in Stanleyville thought of nothing else during those days and each of them came to the same conclusion. There were only a few roads leading from the city, and they were blocked every few miles by the Simbas. It was impossible, too, to escape in the jungle; one could never find his way out through that wilderness; death by snakebite or starvation was inevitable. There was, of course, the river. Perhaps the Americans could get a boat, or a canoe? But this, too, was impossible. It was several hundred miles to government-held territory and the Simbas controlled both banks every mile of the way.

Late in the afternoon of September 5, the day that the People's Republic was proclaimed, the Americans received some welcome visitors—Patrick Nothomb and Peter Rombaut, the honorary British consul. They had what seemed to be good news. They had been in touch with Gbenye and he had indicated that it might be possible to move the Americans back into the consulate. In the meantime, Nothomb and Rombaut were to escort Hoyt and Grinwis to a reception that afternoon at which the consular corps would be presented to the new president.

As the two men dressed for the occasion, their spirits rose. If they could establish more or less normal relations with Gbenye, then they, as foreign consuls, would probably be released and allowed to go to Léopoldville. Things were looking up.

The president's palace was only a short drive from the airport. Nothomb chatted airily with them. They got out of the cars, straightened their ties and started into the palace.

Just then General Olenga drove up.

"What's going on?" he said.

"It's a meeting of the consular corps," Rombaut replied.

"Not the Americans!" Olenga screamed. "Take them to prison!" He motioned to his soldiers. They grabbed Hoyt and Grinwis by their collars and propelled them at a run across the lawn, away from the palace, jabbing at them with rifle butts. They flung the two men into a Land-Rover and drove them to the airport, where they also brought Davis and the three radio operators. All six men were knocked about with rifle butts. They were ordered into cars. A little boy of about eight thrust a spear through the car window and tried to stick it into Davis's back, but an older Simba rolled up the window.

With General Olenga leading the procession, the Americans were driven in cars to the central prison. The prison guards took away their belts and shoved them into a filthy cell. No food was offered them; no one informed them as to what Olenga had decreed should be done with them. The men slumped down against the walls of the cell, too shocked, too bruised to talk.

9

THE MEN FROM GENEVA

In Tucson, Arizona, eight thousand miles from Stanleyville, Jo Hoyt picked up a telephone each day and put through a call to the State Department in Washington. After returning to the United States with the children, she had spent a few weeks at the couple's vacation home in Jerome. When the new school term started, she moved to Tucson, where she had relatives, and enrolled the children in local schools. Then she began what was to be a long vigil.

Mrs. Hoyt rang up the State Department even on Sundays for news of her husband, but the department had little to offer. They had been out of direct communication with Hoyt since August 11. They had received Hoyt's message of August 21, but they knew that it had been written under duress. Otherwise they had only fragmentary reports, from roundabout sources. They did know that Hoyt and the others had been held in the Sabena Guest House, at least for a time. And they knew the men were in great danger. But that was about all.

"Why don't you do something to get Michael out?" Mrs. Hoyt would shout.

It was a good question. The honor and prestige of the United States had been sorely damaged. Until the Simba occupation, Hoyt and the others had been ordinary and obscure people. But they will go down in history. For this was the first time that the staff of an American consulate had been beaten, threatened with death, humiliated and thrown into prison.

What should the United States do about it?

In former times, the response would probably have been quick and decisive. One is reminded, for example, of the case of a naturalized American of Greek origin named Ion Perdicaris, who was seized in Morocco in 1904 by a local chieftain named Raisuli. President Theodore Roosevelt sent the fleet to Moroccan waters and fired off an ultimatum: "Perdicaris alive or Raisuli dead." Perdicaris was promptly released.

This time things were different. The American embassy in Léopoldville, with the approval of Washington, had, of course, considered a helicopter rescue of the consular personnel, but the idea was dropped because it would have meant abandoning Ernie Houle and the American missionaries to possible retaliation by the Simbas.

After that various officials in Washington worked on other plans. One idea was to land a group of twenty-five armed men in Stanleyville from planes or helicopters. They would be, one official said, Americans who were "not readily identifiable as Americans"—that is to say, American Negroes. They would be "armed to the teeth" and their job would be to find Hoyt and the others and take them to waiting aircraft.

But the idea was dropped. Intelligence was too fragmentary and American officials were not certain where Hoyt and the others were being held. As one official put it, "We couldn't go around ringing doorbells and asking, 'Is Mr. Hoyt here?' "

All along, many officials in the State Department were reluctant to rescue the Americans by force. In conversations with this writer, they said they were afraid the United States would be criticized by African and other countries for behaving in an "imperialistic" manner.

The attitude of these officials points up the dilemma in which the United States now finds itself. It is the strongest power on earth, the only one with truly worldwide military capabilities. Yet it has become ever more reluctant to use that power because of "world opinion." The most glaring instance was at the Bay of Pigs, but there have been many others as well. United States embassies have been attacked by mobs that have been stirred up by foreign governments.

Property owned by Americans has been confiscated and U.S. citizens have been mistreated. But the United States does little but protest.

It could well be argued that it was too early, during the first few weeks of the Simba occupation, to rescue the Americans by force. To send troops would have been a risky proposition. There was always the possibility that the Americans would be massacred in retaliation minutes before the troops arrived. If the Americans could be freed by negotiations, they at least would come out of Stanleyville alive.

But the fear of offending "public opinion" in various foreign countries nevertheless persisted in Washington.

Soon after the fall of Stanleyville, the U.S. attempted through third parties to negotiate for release of the men. The first efforts were made through the United Nations mission to the Congo. With the approval of Washington and Brussels, the chief of the UN mission, a Mexican citizen named Bibiano Osorio-Tafall, got in touch with the Simba authorities by radio in mid-August and proposed that the UN and the International Committee of the Red Cross be allowed to send a plane to Stanleyville with doctors and medicines for the local population. In later messages, he suggested that the plane be allowed on the return flight to bring out the American consular personnel and other foreigners who wanted to leave.

The Secretary-General of the UN, U Thant, made a similar plea by radio. "Such a gesture on your part would certainly receive worldwide appreciation," he said.

On September 2, a reply was received: "General Olenga is absolutely in accord with a landing in Stanleyville."

The plane was readied. But then, after another flurry of messages, Olenga canceled permission, saying that he lacked confidence in the UN. And so the UN stepped out of the picture.

Acting on instructions of the International Committee of the Red Cross in Geneva, the local ICRC representative radioed Olenga and proposed that the Red Cross, not the UN, send a plane. At first Olenga agreed. But then he sent another message denouncing not only the UN, but the ICRC and the World Health Organization as well, as "spies" and part of an "imperialist plot." No one would be allowed to leave Stanleyville, Olenga said. They would remain as hostages against air attacks. He warned that his Simbas would shoot at any Red Cross or UN plane that approached the city.

But the Red Cross did not give up. Officials in Geneva contacted Jean-Maurice Rubli, a prosperous physician who practices internal medicine in Zurich, and asked him if he would go to Africa to see what could be done. Like many other Swiss citizens, Dr. Rubli had often undertaken missions on behalf of the Red Cross in many parts of the world. He agreed and on September 8 he left for Africa. His first task was to contact officials of other African governments and try to win their support for a mission to Stanleyville.

The ICRC has had a lot of experience in dealing with difficult situations. For more than a century, it has worked quietly and effectively to assist the victims of war and natural disasters. There are eighty-seven national Red Cross societies in the world, but the ICRC, the parent body, remains independent. It is governed by up to twenty-five Swiss citizens. Scrupulously neutral, the representatives of the ICRC, or delegates as they are called, have earned the respect of just about every nation in the world. Even in wartime they have been allowed to circulate freely behind the lines on mercy missions.

Under the aegis of the ICRC, more than one hundred nations have signed the Geneva Conventions of 1949 which lay down rules for the humane treatment during wartime of civilians and of captured enemy soldiers. One of the things that the conventions specifically forbid is the taking of hostages.

Dr. Rubli's quiet diplomacy soon paid off. On September 18, Gbenye, now the president of the People's Republic, radioed permission for a Red Cross plane to land. Rubli returned to Geneva and chartered a DC-4. It was painted white and marked with conspicuous Red Cross emblems. Medicines valued at about seven thousand dollars were loaded onto it. Four Swiss doctors were recruited to assist Rubli. The plane took off from Basle on September 22 and flew to Bangui, the capital of the Central African Republic, which adjoins the northern Congo. They waited three days, then received permission to continue on. In the early morning of September 25, they took off for Stanleyville.

*   *   *

The spirits of the Americans who were being held in the Central Prison had sunk to a new low. They had been beaten and humiliated in front of their fellow diplomats. They had been thrown into a prison filled with common criminals and Simbas who were accused of theft and other offenses. But, even worse, the Americans were now completely isolated, physically as well as psychologically, from other white people in Stanleyville. Soon after their arrival in prison, another white man, a Belgian, was brought in. He apparently had insulted General Olenga. The Americans were eager to talk with him, but he was wary of being seen with them.

The Americans were put into Cell Number One, a filthy, dimly-lighted room that was about twenty-four feet long and ten feet wide. They were given six dirty pallets, thinly filled with straw, to sleep on. They had a foul-smelling latrine and they could wash, or rather make an attempt to do so, under a spigot from which cold water oozed. The cell door was not locked and the Americans could venture into the inner courtyard of the prison. But each time they went out, they were taunted and threatened by the Simba prisoners, and so they stayed in their cell most of the time. The cell had a corrugated metal roof and during the middle of the day the room was stifling.

Life in prison was particularly difficult for Grinwis; he could see hardly anything. He was very near-sighted and ordinarily wore strong contact lenses. But he did not dare wear the contact lenses now because he was afraid that he might be struck in the eyes, which could cause severe injury or even blindness. Hoyt ordinarily wore glasses. These had been stolen by the Simbas weeks before, but he was only slightly myopic and he was able to manage fairly well without them.

Hoyt's servants brought food from the consulate each day. It was fortunate he had the servants as neither the central government nor the Stanleyville regime ever bothered to feed prisoners; they were expected to arrange for their own food, one way or another.

For a while, Hoyt and the others feared that they had been forgotten by the outside world. But Doctor Barlovatz and his wife had not forgotten them. They sent soap, toothbrushes and towels. After some difficulty, Barlovatz managed to get permission to visit them. The elderly doctor gave them what news he had. Then he insisted on giving Grinwis a flu injection.

"But I don't need one," Grinwis said.

"Shh," said Barlovatz. "The Simbas are suspicious about my coming here. I told them I had to treat you, so . . ." The doctor jabbed Grinwis with the needle.

One afternoon a group of Simbas came to visit the Simba prisoners. The visitors were fascinated by the American prisoners. They made them line up and run around the prison compound while being beaten and shoved. A Simba officer who was himself a prisoner complained to the guards. They broke it up. On another occasion, the Americans were forced to dance about in their cell and sing "I love Lumumba" in French. But otherwise there was no rough stuff. There was, instead, only the utter boredom and futility of prison life, mixed with dread.

One morning General Olenga came to the prison. The Americans were made to line up outside the cell door at attention. Olenga proceeded to pass sentence on various Simba prisoners. Anxiety arose among the Americans—perhaps Olenga was going to judge them as well. But the general ignored them until he started to leave. Then he said: "We have captured 108 American mercenaries near Bukavu. We did not kill them. We are going to bring them to Stanleyville. Then we will have proof that you Americans are fighting us."

None of the Americans said anything, and Olenga left.

Three days later Olenga paid another visit to the prison. The Americans were forced to line up at attention outside the cell door. As he was leaving, he harangued them again about "American mercenaries." Then he said: "I'm told that one of you is a missionary—which one is that?"

Charlie Davis stepped forward.

"It was a mistake to arrest you," Olenga said. "Missionaries enjoy a special status in the People's Republic. Lumumba gave you this special status because missionaries are good people. You can go."

Davis hurried to Leco, the missionary bookstore in which his wife and two children had taken refuge earlier. They had by this time moved to the regional headquarters of the Unevangelized Fields Mission, at a crossroads known as Kilometer Eight outside the city. Davis spent the night at Leco, then joined his wife at Kilometer Eight.

One day General Olenga's car roared up in front of the bookstore. But it was not the general who had come. A kindly Congolese matron stepped out. It was Olenga's wife. She had attended a Protestant mission school and now she wanted to know if Leco could find a teacher for the Olenga children. The teacher was found. Mrs. Olenga was delighted.

On September 15, after Hoyt and the other American consular officials had been in prison for ten days, they received a distinguished visitor: Gaston Soumialot, the minister of defense. His eyes darting about nervously, the little man lectured the men on American policies in the Congo. But then he promised to discuss their case with Gbenye.

At nine o'clock that evening one of Soumialot's aides arrived at the prison and announced that the Americans were going to be placed, instead, under house arrest. The men were taken back to the Sabena Guest House. Their old guards greeted them warmly. Nothing in their room had been touched during their absence. The Americans had baths—the first time in ten days that they had managed to get really clean—and shaved off their beards. The guards brought beer and they and the Americans sat around until late in the night, drinking and talking. Great friends were they.

The next day, September 16, an American missionary named William Scholten died in a Simba prison at Aketi, a town 180 air miles north of Stanleyville. Scholten had been critically ill with malaria, filariasis and dysentery. The Simbas dragged him from his sickbed. They accused him of being a "spy" and said they were going to put him in prison. Scholten asked that he be allowed to take a blanket with him, but the Simbas refused. He died in his cell three days later from exposure and lack of medical attention. He was the first American casualty in the northwest Congo.

Scholten was thirty-three years old and came from Johnson City, Tennessee. Together with his wife and five small children, he had been in the Congo for nearly two years as a missionary with the Unevangelized Fields Mission, which has its headquarters in Bala Cynwyd, Pennsylvania. He was an instructor in a teacher-training school and spent a great deal of time working with Congolese youth.

When Scholten was taken to prison by the Simbas, his parting words to his wife and Congolese converts were: "I'll see you in Heaven." Mrs. Scholten and the children were rescued eventually by government troops.

For Michael Hoyt and the other four Americans, life at the Sabena Guest House was, if nothing else, somewhat more pleasant than it had been in prison. Dr. Barlovatz brought them books and cards.

From time to time Simbas who were ambulatory patients from a nearby hospital visited the guest house and made the Americans stand at attention while they taunted them. Several times Hoyt and Grinwis asked them how they could have been wounded in view of the fact that they possessed powerful *dawa* which made them immune to bullets. "It was my fault because I looked to one side when I should have been looking straight ahead," one man said. Another explained: "I made a mistake; when I heard the airplane I looked up at it." Their faith in the *dawa* that Olenga's sorcerers had administered remained unshaken.

The Simbas were unpredictable. Although some taunted the Americans and threatened to kill them, others paid friendly visits and gave them gifts of beer and cigarettes.

Hoyt's servants continued to bring them food, but supplies were running low. For days on end, the men had nothing but sardines and rice, flavored with ketchup, mustard, garlic and salt.

After they had been held in the guest house for eight days, they were visited by Soumialot and by Francois Sabiti, the minister of public works. Soumialot extended his hand to Hoyt. Hoyt hesitated; he knew that the Simbas considered it taboo to touch a white man.

"I'm just an ordinary person," Soumialot said, his face wreathed in his enormous grin.

Hoyt shook his hand. It was the first time he had ever shaken hands with a Simba.

"Do you have the keys to your consulate?" Soumialot said, bubbling over with his customary nervous energy.

Hoyt said the servants had the keys.

"Will you come with me to the consulate?" Soumialot said.

Hoyt got into a car with Soumialot and Sabiti. As they rode along, Soumialot said, almost casually: "The Red Cross wants to know if you want to leave Stanleyville."

Hoyt kept control of his emotions and, very cautiously, he replied: "Yes, we would like to leave."

"We'll see what we can do," Soumialot remarked.

The consulate looked the same as it had when Hoyt and the others had been arrested a month earlier. The windows had not been repaired—they still were shattered from the machine-gun attack—and walls and furniture were full of bullet holes. But the consulate had not been looted and the servants had kept the place fairly tidy while the Americans were gone.

"Yes, this will be my office," Soumialot said, pointing to Hoyt's office. "And I'll live over there," he added, pointing to the consul's residence next door.

The consulate was, of course, U.S. property. But Hoyt knew it was useless to resist.

Hoyt found some gin and he and Soumialot and Sabiti drank gin and water. Soumialot seemed more reasonable and intelligent than the other Simbas and Hoyt took the opportunity to complain about the beatings and other humiliations the men had endured.

Soumialot looked at Hoyt with mournful sympathy. "General Olenga is a military man; he does not understand how diplomats and consuls should be treated," Soumialot said. "But things will improve, I can assure you of that. However, you must realize that the people are angry because American troops are fighting against us."

"There are no American troops fighting you," Hoyt said.

"Would you stake your life on that?" Soumialot said.

Hoyt made no reply.

With Sabiti in tow, Hoyt and Soumialot went to a home that Soumialot had been occupying temporarily. Five or six attractive Congolese women were sitting in the living room. People wandered in and out. Soumialot's servants served beer. Soumialot introduced Hoyt to several of the visitors. "This is Monsieur Hoyt, the American consul," Soumialot said, radiating his great smile, as he presented his friends to

Hoyt. To Hoyt's surprise, each shook hands warmly with him.

But nothing concrete emerged from Hoyt's outing with Soumialot. The minister evaded any direct replies when Hoyt asked if the Americans could leave on the Red Cross plane. And, although he promised to have the men moved to their apartments in the Immoquateur, Hoyt instead was taken back to the Sabena Guest House and locked up once more.

Two days later, at 11:20 A.M. on September 25, Hoyt looked out the window of his bungalow-prison and saw a white plane, emblazoned with Red Cross emblems, landing at the airport just across the road.

The Red Cross plane came in low and fast; the pilot feared that it might be fired upon. After the plane had come to a stop, the pilot kept the motors running, just in case.

But the Simbas were not hostile. Colonel Opepe, the number two man in the army, came up to the plane. He shook hands politely and introduced the Swiss visitors to his officers, each of whom shook hands in turn. Only one officer, a captain, was alarmed about losing his *dawa;* when Rubli touched his arm, he started to tremble violently.

Soumialot was waiting at the edge of the field. He greeted the Red Cross doctors courteously. But as they were leaving the field in cars about a hundred young thugs, members of the *jeunesse*, rushed out across the field toward the plane. Rubli insisted that Soumialot send an officer back to make sure that the *jeunesse* did not molest the crew. Soumialot sent Colonel Opepe, who ordered the *jeunesse* to leave.

Rubli and the other members of the delegation were taken directly to Gbenye's office for the first of ten hours of talks that continued for two days. Both Gbenye and Soumialot said they did not know what the International Committee of the Red Cross was. When told about the Geneva Conventions and particularly the ban on holding people as hostages, they said they had not heard about that, either. In any case, they added, they did not consider themselves as bound by the Geneva rules. The conventions, they scoffed, were "written by whites."

Gbenye and Soumialot told the Red Cross delegates that they intended to keep the white population as hostages to prevent any bombing of Stanleyville by Tshombe's planes. They pointed out that soon after a partial evacuation of Europeans from Albertville, the city had been attacked from the air.

The delegates asked if the members of the American consulate could leave. Gbenye said no. "Are you at war with America?" someone asked. The president thought for a moment. "To my knowledge, no," he replied.

Rubli asked if children and sick persons could leave on the return flight. Among the children were thirty Belgian youngsters who had come to Stanleyville to visit their parents during the summer holiday from school in Belgium and who had been stranded in the city when it fell to the Simbas. Gbenye replied that he could not allow even the children and sick people to leave. "My people wouldn't understand," he said. "If I authorize you to evacuate anyone right now I could not ensure your security—or mine—or that of my government."

At that very moment, four of Gbenye's children were at school in Europe—in Geneva, where they were being cared for by a lawyer friend of his.

The Red Cross delegates saw that it was hopeless to plead with Gbenye and Soumialot. They gained the impression that neither man had any real authority. One man made the major decision in Stanleyville and that was Nicolas Olenga. Olenga was not in the city; he had gone to Kindu to prepare a second major assault on Bukavu.

Rubli ordered the medicines unloaded from the plane. He did manage to wring one minor concession from Gbenye. The president agreed that the Red Cross could return with messages from the hostages to their relatives in the outside world.

The Red Cross delegates spent the night under guard in a hotel. They were not allowed to circulate in the city and talk with people on the streets. The elderly Doctor Barlovatz did manage, however, to speak briefly to one of the delegates in a bar. He told the delegate about the mistreatment of the Americans and urged him to try to do something to get the men out of Stanleyville.

At noon on September 26, two Simba officers arrived at the Sabena Guest House with Red Cross forms. They said the

Americans should each write a twenty-five-word message to their families, messages which would be taken out on the Red Cross plane.

"What do you think?" Hoyt asked Vice-Consul Grinwis.

"I think we should refuse," Grinwis answered.

The men decided to defy the Simbas this time. They had submitted to much suffering at the hands of their captors, but it was too much, they felt, to expect them to write "I am well" messages to their families when a plane was standing by, just across the road, which could take them to safety if the Simbas only gave a nod. The two officers argued and threatened. But the Americans refused to write the messages. The officers left in a huff.

Rubli had one last talk with Gbenye that morning. But the president, who was decked out in tight blue jeans and a T-shirt, was adamant. He promised to allow an evacuation of certain foreigners, for "humanitarian reasons," later on. But the Red Cross plane should leave Stanleyville at once. They could carry on further discussions in radio messages.

At 1:45 that afternoon, Hoyt and the other Americans saw, from their windows, a motorcade approach the airport. They could not see the plane, but they heard the engines start up. The white plane taxied into view and went to the far end of the field. The pilot revved up the four engines and the plane took off, bound for Bangui.

Hoyt and the other four men lay on their cots for an hour and a half. No one said a word.

In the weeks that followed, the Red Cross delegates sent message after message to Gbenye, asking that they be allowed to carry through the partial evacuation that he had promised. But either they got no reply, or they were told: "Mr. Gbenye will deal with the matter when he returns to Stanleyville."

For once, the Red Cross had failed.

10

EMPLOYMENT WITH A DIFFERENCE

Soon after Moise Tshombe was sworn in as the Congo's new premier, a group of tough-looking white men checked into the Memling Hotel in downtown Léopoldville. They hung around day after day waiting, it seemed, for something. The men were close-lipped, but hardly anything remains a secret very long in the Congo. Soon the word was out: they were South Africans, Rhodesians and others who had fought as mercenaries for Tshombe during the Katanga wars. Now Tshombe had another job for them.

Nothing happened for several weeks. The men sat in the Memling bar, drinking beer and staring vacantly at the antics of a pair of caged monkeys. The men were not the sort who would be interested in international negotiations. Yet they were the objects of a great deal of high-level anguish and delicate diplomatic scuffling which was going on behind the scenes.

Tshombe was, if nothing else, a hard-headed realist. He knew that the ANC was powerless to halt the advance of the Simbas, much less push them back. And he knew that unless substantial military victories were forthcoming soon. he would be finished politically. He needed outside help—and the mercenaries were only too willing to supply it. But there were political difficulties.

The two countries on which Tshombe relied chiefly for the support of his regime—the United States and Belgium—

were fearful of the repercussions elsewhere in Africa over the use of the mercenaries. The reason was that South Africa and Rhodesia are citadels of "white supremacy" and are hated passionately by black Africans of all political persuasions. To invite mercenaries from those countries to come to the Congo would be, in their view, the same as if an Israeli prime minister asked the Gestapo to help put down disturbances in the Jewish homeland.

The United States and Belgium cast about for an alternative. Washington reportedly proposed that Belgium send troops. But the Belgian government, fearful of reprisals against Belgian citizens in Simba territories, rejected the idea. The United States had an election coming up and thus had no desire to send troops. At the prompting of the United States and Belgium, Tshombe appealed to five moderate African countries for soldiers. The United States let it be known that it might pay a large share of the costs. But the other African countries were suspicious of Tshombe and, in any case, had few troops to spare. Nothing came of that idea.

And so Tshombe turned to the white mercenaries. This was particularly embarrassing for the United States as it had, a few years before, joined the African countries in denouncing Tshombe for using the same men in Katanga. The Congo, it seemed, has a way of confounding everyone.

After waiting several weeks, a small, blond-haired man with an autocratic bearing was summoned from the Memling for a meeting with Tshombe. He was Michael Hoare, a forty-four-year-old former British officer who had been born in Ireland and who served with the Chindits in Burma during World War II. Hoare worked as an accountant in London after the war, then moved to Durban, South Africa, where he established an accounting firm and an auto agency. But life as an adder-up of figures was too humdrum for Hoare. He had served as an officer in Katanga and now he was back, at Tshombe's invitation, for another job.

Tshombe's instructions to Hoare were simple—raise an army of white mercenaries *immediately*; objective: *Stanleyville*. Hoare was a no-nonsense British officer of the old school— used to giving orders, used to having them obeyed at once. He made a number of enemies among other whites in the Congo. But even his critics conceded that he got the job done.

After the meeting with Tshombe—Tshombe made him a Congolese major, later upped to lieutenant colonel—Hoare sent messages. Within days, recruiting offices were opened in Johannesburg and Salisbury, the capital of Rhodesia. Mysterious advertisements appeared in newspapers: "Any fit young man looking for employment with a difference at a salary well in excess of £100 ($280) a month should telephone [a number was given] during business hours. Employment is initially offered for six months, immediate start."

On August 23, the first planeload of recruits from South Africa touched down at Kamina, a huge military base 260 air miles northwest of Tshombe's old capital of Elisabethville, in the Katanga. They were soon followed by several more planeloads. Thus was born the mercenary army. Or, as some liked to call it, the Congo Foreign Legion. Or, as others termed it, Tshombe's Praetorian Guard.

The mercenary army was one of the most preposterous military forces that has ever been assembled. Men came from all over Europe and Africa. They included, in addition to the South Africans and Rhodesians, Belgians, Germans, Italians, Frenchmen and men of many other nationalities. Some of them had had prior military experience, but many had never fired a shot in anger. Quite a few seemed to have unsavory backgrounds, but, as with other foreign legions, no questions were asked. They got only rudimentary training—or none at all—and then were thrust into action. They were poorly equipped and utterly undisciplined. There were never more than a few hundred in action at any one time. Yet they turned the tide in the Congo. Without them, Léopoldville would in all likelihood have become General Olenga's capital.

The mercenaries were a tough bunch. Many had been born in Africa and, in many respects, were not much different from the Congolese. In another age, they would have found their calling on the Spanish Main. They would have fitted well into the ranks of the *condottieri*, the hired soldiers who fought in Renaissance Europe. And they would have done themselves proud as gunfighters in the American Wild West.

Some of the mercenaries were psychopathic killers. They relished their work. One young man had an incurable cancer

131

of the stomach; he came to the Congo hoping that it would hasten his end. Some signed up for the pay. Some were out for loot—and loot there was, in abundance. But others were ordinary young men from the farms and factories of southern Africa who were looking for adventure. And they found plenty of that, too.

When you asked the mercenaries why they were in the Congo, they often would look at you with a straight face and say: "To fight Communism." Then they would burst into laughter.

If there was a common denominator about the mercenaries, it was that they found it a bit difficult to settle down to routine life. "I made a lousy civilian," a former British soldier said, and many echoed his words. Most were of the laboring class, with only a limited amount of education. They were older than most soldiers—the average age seemed to be around thirty. They tended to be deferential toward white men with more education and a higher social status.

There was a tremendous weeding-out process in the mercenary army. Those with a weak stomach, or, perhaps, a strong conscience, broke their contracts and went home. Some left because of hardships and danger. Many were dismissed and sent home because of perversions, alcoholism and excessive indiscipline.

The mercenaries operated in a cruel and merciless world. It could not be dignified as war, if war can be dignified; it was, instead, just slaughter. The world of the mercenaries was the absolute negation of civilization, of learning, of religion and of everything else to which man aspires. It was the world of the jungle, kill or be killed, the survival of the fittest. Mercy and compassion were virtually unknown. Only death meant anything, and it meant a lot; it was ever close at hand.

Neither the mercenaries nor the Simbas ever surrendered. If the mercenaries came upon wounded Simbas who could not flee, they usually shot them. One mercenary sergeant made a specialty of cutting the throats of Simba wounded. An officer estimated that the sergeant cut two hundred throats in all. "He just went berserk the first time he went into action," the officer said. "He had a beautiful knife—an American knife—what do you call it, a Bowie?"

Bowie Knife

Yet, in the demented world of the Congo, the mercenaries were showing mercy of a sort when they shot prisoners or slashed their throats. If they let the ANC get them, the ANC would dispose of them in the Congolese way. One method was to shoot a man in the wrists and ankles, then, much later, in the knees and elbows and then, much, much later, in the heart. Another technique was to tie the victim with strips of wet rawhide and leave him in the sun. As the rawhide constricted, it would cut through to the bones.

Even ordinary young men with no liking for slaughter were brutalized by seeing the maimed bodies of Europeans killed by the Simbas. "They call me a sadist," one young man said. "After what I've seen, they can call me anything they want." He said he personally had killed thirty-seven Simbas.

One mercenary cracked under the strain and ran amok in a crowded room, firing an automatic weapon at the other mercenaries. "Kill him, kill him," an officer screamed as bullets whizzed around. The others brought the man down with a bullet in the chest. As he lay on the floor, the officer leaned over and said, "I hope you die, you bastard, you."

The mercenaries carried sidearms or grenades. These were seldom used in battle—the mercenaries preferred automatic weapons, which are of course much more efficient. The sidearms and grenades were for use on themselves, if capture by the Simbas seemed inevitable.

Ordinary mercenaries were paid $420 a month, half of it deposited in banks back home, half paid in Congolese currency. They got, in addition, $12.60 a day extra in combat zones. But all this was only a part of their incomes. Whenever the mercenaries went into action, they carried boxes of dynamite. The ostensible purpose of the dynamite was to blow up trees that had been felled across jungle roads. But, more often, the mercenaries used it to blow open safes in banks and business firms of "liberated" towns.

Some of the mercenaries amassed small fortunes in the Congo and went home with tens of thousands of dollars. Along with cash, they took ivory, gold, diamonds, jewelry, tape recorders, radios, anything and everything of value. Even if the object was nailed down, it made no difference: they pried it or blew it loose.

One mercenary shot and killed a rebel who was carrying a brief case. He picked up the case, opened it and gasped. It was stuffed with two million Congolese francs. The mercenary closed the case quietly and walked off with it. No need to share it. Later he traded the francs for four thousand American dollars.

Although many of the mercenaries looted with unabashed enthusiasm, others made an attempt to justify it on the grounds that the ANC would steal the items anyway. That may not have been a convincing moral argument, but it was true enough. The ANC similarly made off with anything it could get its hands on. The ANC's problem was that most of them were too cowardly to travel at the head of a column. They let the white men get out in front and they brought up the rear—usually miles behind. This meant that the whites had the first crack at loot.

Money was the only thing of value in the mercenaries' world. On one occasion, a boatload of mercenaries crossed a river to attack Simba positions on the far shore. A sergeant, armed with an automatic rifle, jumped overboard when the boat ran aground a few yards from the bank. Holding his weapon aloft, he waded through chest-deep water. Then he realized to his horror that he had a check for $300 in his hip pocket. He flung the rifle aside, pulled the check out of his pocket and, holding it in the air, stormed ashore. While bullets whizzed past his ears, he found a rock, spread the check out and blew on it while waiting for it to dry in the sun. Fortunately for him, his fellow mercenaries took care of the Simbas.

Hoare and at least some of his officers gave strict orders against looting, but they could not be everywhere at once. The mercenaries, for their part, were outraged at attempts to make them stop looting. One of them complained: "The lieutenant would not let us rob anything. It's funny—he's a mercenary, but he just wouldn't let us blow a bank. I don't understand that man."

The mercenaries were well-paid cannon fodder. They had virtually no training. Speed was of the essence; they had to be thrown into the battle at once. They were often short of arms and ammunition, and frequently the Simbas had better equipment. The mercenaries had few armored vehicles. Most of the time they traveled along jungle roads in jeeps and trucks, never knowing if a machine gun was trained on their heads from the impenetrable thickets a few yards away.

Although Hoare tried hard to whip together a real army, he was handicapped by the bureaucratic corruption and incompetence that surrounds just about everything in the Congo. The mercenaries went unpaid for months. They had to scrounge their uniforms. As a result, no two mercenaries were dressed alike. Often there were no rations for them; they were forced to forage for food. One group, stranded in a remote jungle village for weeks, lived on local chickens—chickens which had fattened themselves by picking at Simba corpses. There were no doctors with the mercenary columns. They came down by the score with malaria, dysentery and strange fevers. One man died of gangrene from a minor wound—there was no one to care for him.

The attitude toward the mercenary casualties seems to have been that of Ko-Ko, the Lord High Executioner in *The Mikado*—"But it really doesn't matter whom you put upon the list, for they'd none of 'em be missed, they'd none of 'em be missed."

The mercenaries had little discipline. If they didn't like the cut of an officer's trousers, they told him so—provided, of course, they were bigger or stronger than the officer. One officer, a thin and wiry man who was a karate expert, kept his men in line by practicing his chops on the disrespectful ones. It worked. They admired him greatly.

Sometimes Hoare would put recalcitrant mercenaries into a local Congolese jail—no mean punishment. Otherwise, all he could do was send the worst ones home.

When the mercenaries went on leave from the killing, they headed for Léopoldville. There they lived it up with frenzied drinking in cheap bars and heroic fist fights. Many of the men picked up Congolese prostitutes. Back home in South Africa, they would have been flogged for that. Each morning there were monumental hangovers. And then the mercenaries would go back to the front, perhaps to die an anonymous death in the jungle.

The mercenaries had few friends. The United States refused to allow the mercenaries to ride on the C-130E's. That, it was felt, would be damaging to the American "image" in the rest of Africa. The mercenaries, however, did manage to sneak rides on the big planes from time to time.

The Simbas were convinced that the mercenaries were Americans. What made this all the more ironic was that the U.S. State Department had gone out of its way to make sure that no Americans served in the mercenary army. The department acted under a federal law that provides that an American can lose his citizenship if he serves in the armed forces of a foreign country without the consent of the U.S. government. A few Americans made inquiries about joining the mercenaries, but they decided not to pursue the matter after the embassy warned them that they would lose their citizenship. One American joined anyway after renouncing his citizenship.

The only admirers the mercenaries really had were, of all people, the Catholic and Protestant missionaries. The mercenaries made countless trips, despite great risks, to mission stations deep in the jungles to rescue missionaries and their families from what would have been, in many cases, death by torture. Curiously enough, even the most brutal mercenaries volunteered readily for these missions. They took great satisfaction in saving the missionaries' lives.

No one worried about the mercenaries' lives. They were, after all, hired soldiers or hired killers, depending on the point of view—persons who were not, in any case, considered worthy of sympathy. The Congolese government did not even provide burial facilities. The mercenaries had to buy coffins for those who died, and either dig the graves themselves or hire Congolese to do it.

The mercenaries had a tender regard for their dead. On one occasion, the body of a sergeant was accidentally left behind during an ambush. When they realized the body was still there, they fought their way back for thirty-five miles to retrieve it. Decomposition comes swiftly in the Congo and the body was hideously bloated. But the mercenaries nevertheless brought it back, fighting all the way. They held a funeral service, then found that the body was too big for the coffin. They wrapped it in canvas and tried to put it into the grave, but it was too big for the hole. Retching from the stench, they enlarged the grave, then lowered their comrade to his eternal rest.

An American airman who was a folk singer tinkered with, "The Ballad of Roger Young." The mercenaries made a tape recording of his guitar-strumming version. Whenever they played the recording, they got tears in their eyes. It went:

> *To the everlasting glory of the mercenaries,*
> *Stands the name of Walter Smith.*
> *Walter Smith, Walter Smith,*
> *To the everlasting glory of the mercenaries,*
> *Stands the name of Walter Smith.*

The first operation of the mercenaries—the attack on Albertville—was not the sort that will go down in military annals as a brilliant operation. It was, instead, something that might have been staged by the Marx Brothers.

With about twenty men, Major Hoare set out from Baudouinville, on Lake Tanganyika, and marched north. But the men had come from the temperate climate of southern Africa; they were not used to the tropical heat and humidity and, in any case, they were not in peak physical condition. After marching eight miles, they halted and had a swim.

While they were resting, a band of rebels attacked. The mercenaries opened fire with their FN's—automatic rifles—and killed more than twenty. Only a few escaped. So far, so good—from the mercenaries' point of view.

Emboldened, they boarded several small boats that had been brought up. Each boat had an outboard motor, but the men had only enough gasoline to operate one. So they set out with that boat towing the others. They arrived off Albertville in the middle of the night and were greeted with heavy gunfire from the beach. The mercenaries turned their boats around and put-putted away.

Two days later, they attacked again. By now they had no gasoline at all. They even tried Congolese whiskey as fuel, but it did not work; they had to row the boats for nine hours. They arrived at Albertville in the middle of the night and went ashore. The rebels attacked, killing two mercenaries and seriously wounding two others. The bodies were later displayed by the Simbas as trophies.

The rest of the mercenaries retreated to their boats and started to row back south. When morning came a brisk wind started to blow and big waves built up. They tried rowing into the waves, but could make little headway. Albertville remained in sight all day. The mercenaries became seasick. Their hands were raw from pulling at the oars. Night came; the lake calmed down and the men rested. In the morning, there were waves again. The mercenaries battled the miniature tempest all day. Albertville was still in sight. The men were faint with hunger that night. On the third day, they finally managed to row out of rebel territory.

In the meantime, an ANC column took Albertville on August 30. It was the first important city to be taken back from the rebels and the victory bolstered Tshombe's prestige greatly. Among those who rejoiced in the city's capture were twenty-eight Europeans. They had been imprisoned by the rebels and were to be executed in reprisal for an air attack on the town. Two other whites were not so lucky. They were killed several days earlier.

The mercenaries learned a lesson from the debacle at Albertville. They realized that although the Congolese rebels were not particularly formidable as soldiers, they were not pushovers. Hoare returned to Kamina, where more recruits were waiting. He trained them and got them more equipment. Soon they were ready for a second try.

The first successful campaign was conducted in the jungles of the northwest Congo. It was a weird type of warfare. The mercenaries never ventured into the thickets—neither, for that matter, did the Simbas. The mercenaries kept to the roads, riding in jeeps and trucks. Frequently they were ambushed, but most of the time they never saw their attackers. It was a nerve-racking operation. The mercenaries never knew where or when a machine gun might open up on them. Even worse were Simba snipers a hundred feet up in huge trees. Because of the dense foliage, it was all but impossible to spot them. And so, as they rode along, the mercenaries fired thousands of rounds wildly at bushes, trees and anything else that suggested a hidden ambush.

Jeeps and trucks broke down under the pounding they received from the rutted roads and many were abandoned. One mercenary column had thirteen vehicles, but of these seven had to be pushed to get them started in the morning. At times the men were soaked to the skin by furious tropical downpours. Vehicles slithered helplessly in mud. Then the blazing sun would return and soon the road would be filled with great clouds of fine, choking dust.

The mercenaries saw marvelous sights. One column came across a herd of nearly fifty elephants. Monkeys leaped through the trees as the columns passed by. All day long, tropical birds warbled and trilled overhead. But the jungle had its horrors. Often the men were besieged by clouds of mosquitos and biting gnats. One man plunged into a muddy river for a swim and was bitten on the hand by something—a crocodile or a snake, no one knew. The hand swelled horribly. All the while, the mercenaries were enveloped in oppressive greenery, and in debilitating heat and humidity. They could seldom see more than a few yards to either side of the road. Some felt they were being suffocated slowly. They drank beer, gin, brandy, whisky—anything they could lay their hands on—to steady their nerves.

On September 15, the mercenaries brought off their first victory. A column known as 5/1 commando, led by Lieutenant Garry Wilson, a twenty-five-year-old former British army officer and a graduate of Sandhurst, stormed the town of Lisala, a port on the Congo River about three hundred miles downstream from Stanleyville. Wilson had forty-two white mercenaries, plus a supporting company of Katangese troops. But only fifteen of the mercenaries had ever had any previous military experience and that only in peacetime. Wilson himself had served in Cyprus during the terrorist days.

Lisala was defended by about four hundred Simbas. They opened fire as the commando neared. Immediately the Katangese bolted into the jungle. Wilson quickly took stock of the situation. He was reluctant to expose the inexperienced mercenaries to fire, so he sent them to the rear. Then, with the fifteen men who had had peacetime training, he attacked the Simbas.

The Simbas were grouped on a hill, about two hundred yards away. They made no attempt to take cover. They were much better armed than the white men—they had machine guns and a bazooka. And they had magic on their side. Sorcerers hopped up and down and waved palm branches, chanting, "*Mai, mai*," to ensure that the mercenaries' bullets would turn to water.

The fifteen mercenaries had only automatic rifles, but they walked slowly up the hill toward the Simbas, firing as they went. They killed an estimated 160 Simbas. The rest fled. "It was like a shooting gallery," said Wilson. He himself stopped counting after he had killed thirteen men. The mercenaries suffered only one casualty—one man was wounded slightly.

The mercenaries made some extraordinary friends in the northwest Congo. One commando of thirty-nine white men, accompanied by sixty-five ANC troops, was on the outskirts of Yakoma, getting ready to attack, when the ANC told the mercenary officer that some local tribesmen wanted to join them in the battle. The officer blinked incredulously when he saw the volunteers. They consisted of about twenty-five little men, only about five feet tall, dressed in bits and pieces of European clothing. Each carried a little bow, about twenty-four inches long, and a quiver of small arrows.

The volunteers were half-wild Gwaka tribesmen. They were not pygmies, but they were much smaller than other Congolese. Despite their size, they were greatly feared by their neighbors. They were ferocious fighters; their little arrows were tipped with a deadly poison. And they were cannibals.

For some reason or other, the Gwakas were violently anti-Simba. They were itching for a fight and were in a jolly mood over the arrival of the mercenaries. The mercenaries welcomed them, and so the white men, the ANC troops and the little men all trooped off for Yakoma.

Yakoma was defended by an estimated nine hundred Simbas. They opened fire when the column entered the town. The ANC bolted in panic, but the Gwakas charged into town, whooping with glee. One Gwaka, a fifteen-year-old whose name was Pierre and who seemed to be their leader, won the admiration of the mercenaries. When a rebel darted across a road, Pierre whipped out an arrow and shot the man through the neck at fifty yards. He toppled over dead.

When the battle was over, Pierre and the others announced that they would have a banquet that evening. Pierre confided that his favorite dish was heart. But the officer put his foot down. "Anyone caught eating anyone else will be shot," he declared.

The officer interrogated twelve prisoners. One after another, they fell over dead. The officer was not concerned over their demise—he himself had sent plenty of men to the eternal rest. But he was puzzled. In a moment, however, the puzzle was solved. Pierre had walked along behind the row of prisoners and had scratched each of them with a poisoned arrow.

Pierre attached himself to the officer and announced that he would be his bodyguard. He followed him everywhere, like a faithful dog. Later, when the mercenaries were ordered to leave for another assignment, Pierre followed them to the airstrip and broke down and wept. It was tragic to lose such good friends.

Some of the mercenaries were appalled at the slaughter. One man, a rough and tough South African, fifty years old, recalled that he and his comrades shot and badly wounded a young Simba near Yakoma. The mercenaries stood next to him, wondering what they should do. The South African continued: "I saw plain murder. I tell you, I saw plain murder. One of our Congolese soldiers came up with a dagger and put five stab wounds in the chest. Finished off by cutting his throat. And then wiping the dagger on the boy's leg."

The mercenary advance continued. Not long afterward, Lieutenant Wilson's commando roared into Bumba, another Congo River port, at sixty miles an hour, firing wildly as they came. The Simbas fled in disorder. There were fourteen white people in Bumba. They wept when they saw Wilson. The Simbas were going to execute them at 1 P.M. that day. Wilson arrived at 12:40 P.M. Bumba was just 225 miles from Stanleyville.

Wilson's men came across a Simba in Bumba whose foot had been shot off. He had been a medic in the ANC for fifteen years and now he was performing the same task for the Simbas. He even wore a Red Cross armband. An ANC sergeant demanded that the mercenaries hand the Simba over to him. But Wilson refused; he knew only too well what the Congolese would do. Wilson drew his pistol and aimed it at the man's head. It was, after all, only like putting a wounded animal out of his misery. Wilson counted to ten. Then he put the gun down. He could not do it. He walked away, tears in his eyes.

It was easier for a twenty-one-year-old Rhodesian nicknamed "Ugly." Without hesitation, Ugly stepped up to the man and pumped six slugs into him. Ugly walked away, muttering, "It's mass murder; it's mass murder."

Wilson had no heart for the war. He was a different sort of man from the others. He had been taught at Sandhurst that wars were to be conducted in a more gentlemanly fashion. He brooded long over the Simba medic with the Red Cross armband. And then he left the mercenary army.

There were others, too, who had problems. One, Lieutenant Douglas Day, also a former British officer, led a com-

Ilyushin-18

mando for twelve hundred miles through the jungle. His armored jeep was attacked continually by villagers, armed only with spears and the protective *dawa*. "They were extraordinarily brave," Day said. "They're the kind of people a country needs. We should never have killed them. We should have knocked them on the head with a long pole and left them there on the side of the road to wake up and then go home."

He, too, left the mercenary army. But there were others, of course, to take their place.

Slowly but surely, General Olenga was being squeezed back. In late September, he made a second attempt to take Bukavu, the highland city on the shores of Lake Kivu. But this time Colonel Mulamba had, in addition to his own men, a platoon of white mercenaries. They stopped the Simbas nine miles from the city, inflicted heavy casualties and put Olenga and the rest in full retreat. It was the last time Olenga would take the offensive.

On October 7, the general suffered an even worse setback. Forty South Africans, together with twenty truckloads of ANC troops, stormed into Uvira, at the north end of Lake Tanganyika. With the capture of Uvira, the central government cut the Simbas off from contact with the Chinese Communist embassy in nearby Bujumbura, the capital of Burundi.

The Simbas were on the defensive but they were far from defeated. In late October, a Soviet-built Ilyushin-18 turboprop plane, believed to have originated in Algeria, flew to Arua, in northwestern Uganda, bringing the first of many air shipments of Communist-made arms to the Simbas. The Simbas, moreover, learned more effective techniques. They no longer staged mass attacks, led by witch doctors, which had, all too often, made it possible for the government forces to mow them down. Now they set up careful ambushes. Initially they often felled a tree across a road at an ambush point. But they learned that this was a mistake—the government forces would see the tree from a distance and realize that the Simbas were waiting for them. Now they let the first vehicles pass before opening fire. The Simbas even made armored cars for themselves, by welding steel plates to vehicles.

Despite the stiffened resistance of the Simbas, the mercenaries boasted that they would be in Stanleyville any day. But a lot of things would happen first.

11

PLEASE KILL ONE FOREIGNER

To Michael Hoyt and the four other Americans who were imprisoned in the Sabena Guest House, life had become an incredible mixture of boredom and suspense. During the first days of their imprisonment, they had entertained faint hopes that they would be allowed to leave Stanleyville—somehow. But even these had been shattered by the departure of the empty Red Cross plane. Now there was nothing to do but wait out the days, wait to learn what the Simbas were going to do with them.

Like a spring that is being compressed ever more tightly, the danger to their lives grew each day. The Simbas, driven back by the mercenaries and the ANC, were becoming increasingly desperate. The anti-American outbursts from Radio Stanleyville and the newspaper *Le Martyr* had reached an insane crescendo. Propaganda is a potent weapon when used against civilized people, but in the Congo it is truly explosive. There was a growing danger that the civilian populace might attack the Americans. There was a danger that the Simbas or *jeunesse* might do it. And there was a danger that General Olenga might order the men executed. He had done so once before—when he failed to take Bukavu—and he might do it again at any time.

The American embassy in Léopoldville had been urging Washington to send American troops to the rescue. Some officials in Washington were thinking along the same lines.

One was W. Averell Harriman, then Under Secretary of State for Political Affairs. Harriman had several meetings in September and October with General Earle G. Wheeler, chairman of the Joint Chiefs of Staff and, at Harriman's urging, Wheeler's aides drew up plans for sending American forces to Stanleyville.

But others in Washington were reluctant to take military action. Many State Department officials were afraid of the political consequences. They knew that American influence in Africa would suffer from a military intervention, even one that was carried out for humanitarian purposes. Most African countries have been independent of white rule for only a few years. Resentment over European domination in the past still runs high. The State Department officials knew that many if not most Africans would respond emotionally; they would ignore the humanitarian side of a rescue operation and view it, instead, as old-fashioned "gunboat" domination.

Other people thought the government had an obligation to go to the rescue of its nationals in such a circumstance. To do otherwise would be to acquiesce in face of piracy and blackmail. It was, in this view, regrettable that the Africans would misunderstand the motives for the rescue; but the U.S. government's obligation to its citizens was more important than any political difficulties that the operation might cause.

There was another consideration which may have figured into Washington's attitude. A presidential election campaign was under way. There had been criticism in Congress and in the newspapers about the American involvement in the Congo. The critics had asked if the Congo was becoming another Vietnam. Although no one in a policy position in Washington would say so publicly, some officials said privately that they felt the government was reluctant to commit troops to the Congo at that time because it might lose votes in the November election.

And so, for one reason or another, the State Department continued to work through diplomatic channels in an effort to secure the release of the Americans in Stanleyville. The Red Cross had failed, but now the State Department turned to the Organization of African Unity (OAU), which is the African equivalent of the western hemisphere's Organization of American States.

The OAU was not particularly concerned about the white hostages in Stanleyville, but it was eager to promote a general political solution to the Congo crisis. And so it might be argued that the OAU was as good a place as any on which to pin one's diplomatic hopes.

The OAU held a special meeting in Addis Ababa, the capital of Ethiopia, in early September to discuss the Congo in general. Delegates from thirty-four African countries attended the session—including Tshombe. But the Congo premier remained an outcast; most other African delegates still viewed him as a "white man's puppet." They were particularly irked by the fact that he had hired white mercenaries. But Tshombe would bargain: he said he would dismiss the whites if other African countries would send troops to help him put down the rebellion. Some moderate countries were interested in the proposal, but the majority voted down his plea for African troops. Then, for good measure, they adopted a resolution demanding that he send the mercenaries home anyway.

Before the Addis Ababa conference ended, the delegates set up a ten-nation Congo Reconciliation Commission, headed by Jomo Kenyatta, the prime minister and later president of Kenya. The commission met in Nairobi, Kenya's capital, from September 18 to 22. It took a curiously one-sided view of the Congo crisis. First, it offended Tshombe greatly by granting a hearing to four rebel leaders who were, of course, bent on his destruction. Then, to the astonishment of Washington, it demanded that the United States withdraw all of its planes and other military equipment, as well as its military personnel, from the Congo. The commission made no mention of Communist China, which was supporting the rebels. Then the commission appointed a five-nation delegation which was to go to Washington and present the demand to President Johnson.

President Johnson refused to see them.

Later on, American diplomats succeeded in getting Kenyatta to send a radio appeal to Gbenye, urging that foreigners be protected and that the Red Cross be allowed to return to Stanleyville. Gbenye was not in the city when the

147

message arrived, and on October 19 Soumialot broadcast an evasive reply. The lives of foreigners were "not in danger," Soumialot said. "We will always facilitate Red Cross activities and are still prepared to study with it all matters relating to its humanitarian mission. . . . Our revolution is not racist and we will not attack white people."

But the Red Cross was never allowed to return to Stanleyville. Eventually it became plain to Washington and to Brussels that the OAU was not going to be any more successful than the Red Cross had been in rescuing Stanleyville's sixteen hundred white and Asian hostages.

After the Americans had been held nearly two weeks in the Sabena Guest House, Hoyt and Grinwis were taken to see Soumialot, the minister of defense. The nervous little man informed them that he would take over the American consulate as his office and home. There was nothing Hoyt and Grinwis could do about this new humiliation to them and their country. But Soumialot was a stickler for doing things properly. He wanted to conclude a formal agreement with the Americans.

By this time, Hoyt was bone-weary from the endless, inane discussions with Simba authorities. But he mustered what diplomatic spunk still remained and made one more effort to secure the release of the Americans from Stanleyville.

"You can take over the consulate if you allow us to be evacuated," Hoyt said.

"Certainly, certainly," Soumialot said, his face wreathed in his habitual enormous smile.

Soumialot was a methodical man, a former warehouse clerk. What they ought to do, he told Hoyt, was draw up an inventory of all the furnishings in the consulate. And so Hoyt and Grinwis got into a car with Soumialot and were driven to the consulate to arrange for the inventory.

The consulate was locked and the servants had gone off with the keys. Time is not very important in Africa and Soumialot and the men waited two hours for the servants to return. Soumialot was considerably brighter than the other Simba authorities, and he had some knowledge of, and interest in, what was going on in the outside world. As he chatted with Hoyt and Grinwis, he suddenly said: "When do you think people have the right to revolt?"

Grinwis saw this as a possible opportunity to establish some rapport. And so he replied: "Well, you know there is a very famous American author by the name of Thoreau who wrote an essay on civil disobedience in which he said that when a government grows intolerable it is the duty of the citizens to refuse to collaborate with it—in other words, to revolt."

"Marvelous!" Soumialot exclaimed.

"Did you know that the United States was a colony once itself?" Grinwis said.

"Really!" Soumialot replied. His face blazed with astonishment.

Grinwis broached other topics, but Soumialot had by then exhausted his intellectual curiosity. He told the men that he would send for them again soon. Then he had them taken back to the Sabena Guest House. Next day, Soumialot moved into the consulate. He never kept his part of the bargain, however. Hoyt and the other Americans were not allowed to leave Stanleyville. They remained prisoners in the Sabena Guest House.

With Soumialot presiding, the American consulate took on the disorderly atmosphere of the court of an African chief. While the great man sat at Hoyt's desk, signing decrees and firing off dispatches, dozens of people wandered in and out of the room. They came beseeching favors or making complaints. Sometimes the noise was so great that it was difficult for the visitor to make himself heard.

One day a Belgian named Jacques Prevost, who was the Stanleyville manager for Sedec, visited Soumialot. The minister was composing diatribes against the American government to be broadcast by Radio Stanleyville. He greeted Prevost cordially and reminisced about his days with the company. While they were talking, a woman pushed her way through the milling throng and said to Soumialot: "Give me five thousand francs to buy some cloth."

"Be quiet," Soumialot said. "You're bothering me."

"No, give me the money," she said.

Soumialot turned to Prevost. "Mr. Prevost—she's asking me for five thousand francs. That's ridiculous, isn't it?"

Soumialot asked Prevost what he would like to drink. Prevost asked for grenadine. Soumialot was aghast. "Grenadine! Oh, no. You'd better have beer or some alcohol."

Prevost settled for a glass of beer. Soumialot took a cognac. Soumialot was much more fastidious than the other Simba leaders. They guzzled beer; he sipped liqueurs.

Among the hangers-on in Soumialot's office was a fat, squat ex-boxer named Bubu, who was a major in the Simba army. Bubu was unable to speak properly, but emitted animal-like grunts and snarls and made wild, disjointed gestures with his hands. (Bubu means "mute" in Swahili.) Soumialot was fascinated with Bubu; he kept the man with him all the time as a pet. Or perhaps Bubu was a fetish. While Prevost was talking with Soumialot, Bubu broke in frequently with a series of excited grunts. Each time, Soumialot burst into laughter.

"Mr. Prevost—isn't that the funniest thing you've ever heard?" Soumialot said.

On other occasions, Soumialot was anything but amused. On October 3, for example, he summoned Hoyt and Grinwis to the consulate. Exploding in rage, he said that the Stanleyville airport control tower had overheard a radio message from the Léopoldville control tower clearing the flight plan of an American plane which was to overfly Kindu. Soumialot interpreted this to mean that the plane would bomb the city. He told Hoyt to write a radio message to the American embassy in Léopoldville. The message, he said, should state that if the plane attacked Kindu it would "provoke grave incidents" against Hoyt and the other Americans. The implication, of course, was that they would be executed. Hoyt wrote the message, then returned to the Sabena Guest House.

Two days later, Soumialot spoke over Radio Stanleyville. "I inform the American government that I can safeguard peace and also the property of Congolese and foreigners," he said. "I am very surprised that the Americans are continuing from time to time to kill women and children and also patients in hospitals. If the Americans do not stop dropping bombs on towns already liberated, then their brothers who are killing people will be killed when found in these towns.

"I have never killed Americans and I do not like to kill, but if this bombing goes on we will be compelled to take action against these Americans in the Congo. If they continue killing men, women and children, then I inform them that if one Congolese is killed, he will be buried in his grave together with twelve Americans."

The Simbas were becoming ever more desperate. On October 7—several hours after Uvira was captured by the central government—General Olenga sent a message by radio from Kindu, addressed to Gbenye, Soumialot and Colonel Opepe. The message, which was in Swahili, said: "I give you official order. If NATO aircraft bomb and kill Congolese civilian population, please kill one foreigner for each Congolese of your region. Only chance which remains for us is to die with foreigners inhabiting liberated zones. If no bombing, please treat foreigners as honored guests in accordance with Bantu custom. Give them food and drink."

The message was repeated at intervals. Radio Stanleyville rebroadcast it and upped the ante. The station reported that Olenga had ordered the Simbas to kill *two* foreigners for each Congolese.

One morning Hoyt and the other consular personnel were taken to see Christophe Gbenye, the "Congolese Clark Gable" who had become the president of the People's Republic. It was their first meeting with him. Seated at a desk, the burly and bearded Gbenye engaged in a long monologue. He droned on and on, almost hypnotically. He made no apologies for the incident three weeks earlier when Hoyt and Grinwis were beaten by the Simbas after they came to his residence for the diplomatic reception. He assured them that they would be evacuated from Stanleyville later on—when "normal air communications" were established. But it had been impossible for them to leave in the Red Cross plane. That would have had a "bad psychological effect" on the local populace. No one, in fact, could leave the city now. Perhaps, the president mused, whites would be allowed to go in the future if they abandoned their property. He would see. Gbenye added that he was aware that the American consular personnel should not be executed. "You are diplomats," Gbenye said.

Hoyt made a few attempts to break into the monologue, but Gbenye kept droning away, his beard bobbing up and down rhythmically as he spoke. Hoyt gave up. He realized

151

that Gbenye was not interested in their plight. They were objects to be used—nothing more.

A few days later, Hoyt and Grinwis saw Gbenye again. They told him that they were at the end of their strength. They pleaded that he have them moved to quarters where they would be safe from attacks by unruly Simbas or the *jeunesse*. Gbenye said he would think about it.

On another occasion, Hoyt and Grinwis had a chat with one of Soumialot's top aides. "Perhaps we will lose this war, but sooner or later we nationalists will triumph in the Congo," the man said. The two Americans were astonished at his words. It was the first time that any of the Simba leaders had ever talked of defeat. Although the prospect of a Simba defeat was good news in a sense, it was ominous in another way. It increased the possibility that the Simbas would execute the Americans in a final act of desperation and defiance.

Late in the afternoon of October 4, several Simba officers appeared at the guest house and told the Americans to pack their things. They were ordered into a bus. A mob of Simbas, many of them ambulatory patients from the nearby hospital, gathered around the vehicle, pounded on it with their fists and shouted that the Americans should be killed. The five Americans waited half an hour. All the while, the mood of the mob became uglier. The Simba officers got into the bus, but it would not start. Everyone got out and pushed. Finally it started. Hoyt and the others now were sick with a new fear. They were afraid that the bus would break down in the town and that they would be set upon by the civilian mob. And they were afraid that they were being taken to Camp Ketele, perhaps to be executed.

But the Simbas took them to the Congo Palace, a brand-new seven-story hotel in the heart of the city. The Americans were registered as guests and taken to the second floor, where each was given a room. Two guards were assigned to the floor, but the Americans were free to circulate to each other's rooms.

They were still prisoners, but now they were incarcerated in a gilded cage. The telephones were removed from their rooms, but otherwise the men reveled in luxury. The rooms were air conditioned. Each man had a double bed and a private bath. All day long, dreamy music was piped into the rooms. They were told they could order beer from the hotel bar if they wished, and they took advantage of that golden opportunity.

The men were isolated from the rest of Stanleyville's white community. It was as if they had ceased to exist. On one occasion Dr. Barlovatz tried to visit them, but he was turned away by the guards. Hoyt and the others spent hours gazing out the windows. They saw Europeans walking along the streets, seemingly little affected by life under the Simbas. They saw European children troop off for school, then return home, shouting and laughing. Stanleyville, as seen from their windows, was as seductively beautiful as ever. The coconut palms swayed in the balmy breezes. Birds sang and flowers bloomed. The days were sunny, soft and languid. At night a golden moon glowed gently in a velvet sky.

Up until that time, Baron Patrick Nothomb and the other Belgians had managed fairly well under the Simbas. The Simbas had reserved their wrath for the Americans, who, the Simbas maintained, were fighting against them. What made this all the more ironic was that there were no American troops fighting the Simbas, but Belgians very definitely were involved. Belgian officers were serving on loan with the ANC as advisers. Large numbers of individual Belgians were joining the mercenary army. The Belgian involvement was no secret. It was widely reported on international radio broadcasts which could be heard in Stanleyville. But the Simbas paid scant attention to that. They had made up their minds that American troops were fighting them and that was that.

On October 7, however, the situation changed. That was the day when Uvira was captured by forty South African mercenaries and a column of ANC troops. A West German radio station, in a shortwave broadcast, reported that the mercenaries had freed Belgian and Italian hostages. The Simba authorities heard the broadcast and took it to mean that Uvira had been taken by Belgian and Italian troops. Gbenye sent for Nothomb.

"The Belgians and Italians are fighting us now," Gbenye shouted, in a rage. "I'm going to arrest you and the Italian consul."

Nothomb protested that he had heard the same radio

broadcast and that Gbenye had misunderstood it. The Belgian civilians in Stanleyville were, in any case, neutral in the Congolese war, Nothomb added. He argued with Gbenye for an hour, explaining over and over again that he had misunderstood the news report.

There comes a time when even a tough man like Nothomb begins to weaken. In arguing with Gbenye he felt as if he were talking to a stone wall. Finally, in frustration, he burst into tears.

"What's the matter?" Gbenye asked.

Nothomb sobbed.

Gbenye sniffled. Nothomb looked up. Tears were streaming down the president's face. Nothomb had heard it said that Gbenye often wept in sympathy, but he could scarcely believe it. Nothomb was so surprised that he stopped weeping. Gbenye, however, kept on sobbing. Finally the president dried his tears and blew his nose. "All right," he said, "I won't arrest you."

But the cancer had set in. From then on, Gbenye and the others were convinced that Belgian troops were fighting them. If nothing else, they needed more scapegoats to account for the mounting defeats they were suffering. Now their hatred was directed not only against the Americans, but against the Belgians as well—the Italians having been forgotten in the welter of newly-found passions.

When Stanleyville's Belgians ventured onto the streets, they were frequently taunted and threatened by Simbas and by the young roughnecks in the *jeunesse*. The African capacity for self-delusion is such that soon the Simbas were vowing that they had seen thousands of Belgian soldiers in action against them. And Radio Stanleyville and the newspaper *Le Martyr* whipped up anti-Belgian feelings still further.

For the Belgians, it was the beginning of a nightmare akin to that which the Americans had been going through for two months.

At 6:30 P.M. on October 9, a group of Simbas burst into the Congo Palace Hotel and told Hoyt and the four other Americans to pack their belongings.

"Where are you taking us?" Hoyt said.

"To prison," the Simbas replied.

The men were hustled downstairs and told to climb into the back of a truck. Simbas milled around the vehicle and shouted that the Americans were going to be executed that evening. The men were taken to the Central Prison. Then they were put into Cell Number Eight. The door was banged shut and locked.

Later the men learned that General Olenga had returned from Kindu that morning. He had flown into a rage when he learned that the Americans were living in comparative luxury in the Congo Palace. It was on his orders that they were taken back to prison.

It was the third time the men had been put into the Central Prison. The first time they had been held for only a few hours, the second time for ten days. Now, however, it would be a long, long time before they would get out.

Cell Number Eight was fairly large—about thirty feet long and fifteen feet wide, but it was incredibly filthy. Some bare planks were laid between low ledges so as to keep them off the floor; the men would sleep on them. They slumped down on the planks, too exhausted emotionally to talk. But in a moment everyone was on his feet again. The planks, they discovered, were crawling with vermin.

Next morning the Americans settled into what would become their daily routine for a long time to come. The cell door was unlocked at six each morning so that the men could go into an inner courtyard and use the latrines. The Americans were let out ahead of the Congolese prisoners, so as to keep them from being beaten or otherwise mistreated. The cell door was left open until 6:30 P.M. but the men were told not to venture out except to use the latrines.

As the morning wore on, a new and grave worry arose. Up until a few days previously, Hoyt's servants had brought them food from the consulate each day. But then Soumialot, the new master of the consulate, ordered the servants not to take any more food to the Americans. Hoyt and the others wondered whom they could turn to.

Almost providentially, Hoyt was called to the prison office that morning and presented with a box of food. It was supplied by Herbert and Alice Jenkinson, the elderly British missionaries who ran the Leco bookstore across the street from the prison, and by Alexander Barlovatz and his wife

Lucy. Food supplies were getting scarce in Stanleyville by then—the city had been cut off from the outside world for more than two months. But the Jenkinsons and the Barlovatzes nevertheless shared what they had with the five Americans.

Each morning, the Jenkinsons' servant brought a box filled with sandwiches and thermos jugs that contained coffee and cold boiled water. The boiled water was particularly appreciated; the men knew that if they drank the tap water in the prison they might come down with diarrhea or with such diseases as amoebic dysentery. And then, each afternoon, the servant appeared with another box, containing warm stew, meat and vegetables, or, perhaps, a rice dish. Usually there was dessert or cookies as well.

The Americans owed their survival to the two couples. The Barlovatzes also sent insecticides, for coping with the vermin, and blankets and pillows. The Jenkinsons arranged to have their laundry done regularly. And Dr. Barlovatz sent over a steady stream of books from his library. The elderly physician had a pixyish sense of humor: among the volumes which he chose was *My Six Convicts*, a story of prison life in the United States.

Late that first afternoon, the Americans received a final humiliation from General Olenga. On the general's orders, the guards dressed the men in convict uniforms—sleeveless sweaters with yellow and blue prison stripes, and skimpy blue cotton shorts. The men were allowed to keep their undershorts, but these stuck out from beneath the outer shorts, much to the amusement of the Simbas.

Now there was no longer any pretense that the Americans were being held in protective custody. They were dressed like the prison's convicted criminals and presumably they were to be treated the same way.

Although the Americans were terrified over what the Simbas might do with them, they had by now reached a psychological turning point. They resolved that they would never again ask the Simba authorities for anything. No matter how badly they were treated, they would not lower themselves to complain or to plead for mercy. The Simbas, of course, could not have cared less whether the Americans complained or not. But the decision was of great psychological importance. It gave the Americans a feeling of moral

156

superiority over the Simbas. It gave them a secret inner strength and pride which would carry them through the horrors that lay ahead.

From time to time, one man or another grew irritable. Tempers flared. The strain was particularly great on Parkes and Stauffer because they did not know French. Frequently the Simbas screamed at Hoyt and Grinwis in French. Or there would be long conversations in that language. Parkes and Stauffer would listen in terror, never knowing if a death sentence had been announced. Sometimes the strain of waiting for a translation became unbearable and they flared into impatient anger.

Nights were the worst. Dangling from the ceiling, a bare electric light bulb burned brightly throughout the night, making it difficult to sleep. Often the men heard the scurrying of little feet. Great lean and nervous rats had entered the cell. In an instant, every man leaped up and threw shoes and other objects at them. They killed a few, but most darted out under the cell door, only to reappear a short while later.

Almost every night, the tomblike stillness of the prison was shattered by wild cries and screams that were only remotely human. The prison doubled as an insane asylum; about twenty-five lunatics were confined in a courtyard just beyond the window of the Americans' cell. From time to time, something would upset them and they would all begin to shriek. Then they would settle into a cadenced chant in Lingala.

For a long time, Hoyt and the others did not know what the madmen were chanting. But then someone explained that they had picked up the mood of the times. They were chanting, "Kill the Americans, *kill the Americans!*"

All five Americans nevertheless bore up remarkably well on the whole. They themselves were on the brink of insanity and it was as if an instinct now came to the fore. The instinct told them that they would have to keep their emotions under control or else they might topple over the edge. One after another, the men had fits of depression. But each time the others cheered him up and pulled him gently back from the abyss.

Hoyt and Grinwis made some unexpected friends in prison. Among the Congolese who were being held were several young radical "intellectuals" who had been influenced by the Chinese Communists. At first they were afraid to be seen with the Americans, but eventually they visited them in their cell and carried on long political discussions.

Among these was a Simba officer in his early twenties named Henri Bablon. He was a member of the Lokele tribe, a small group of people who live near Stanleyville and who have advanced far more than most Congolese. Bablon had a high-school education. He was vaguely pro-Communist in his views. Before the Simba conquest, he had been the leader of a radical youth group in Stanleyville. Like the other young radicals, he had welcomed the Simbas and they made him an officer. Bablon and the others felt that the Simbas would carry out radical reforms. But the Simbas had no real ideology or political program. The Simba uprising was, instead, a revolt of discontented and unemployed tribesmen in the Maniema. Bablon and his associates soon became disillusioned. And, inasmuch as the Simbas viewed people with even a few years of schooling with suspicion, Bablon and some of the others eventually wound up in jail.

Now, sitting on the planks that served as beds for the Americans, Bablon said that all of the young radicals in Stanleyville were opposed to the Simba regime. They were only waiting for the proper time to carry out a counter-revolution. The revolution had been betrayed by Olenga, Gbenye and Soumialot. Bablon was especially bitter about the latter two, whom he described as "old, discredited politicians." And he added that he was shocked that the American diplomats had been imprisoned. Once the counter-revolution was successful, Bablon said, American and other foreign diplomats would be accorded the respect and immunities to which they were entitled by international law.

Life in Stanleyville was full of surprises, but this topped most. Hoyt and Grinwis, the representatives of "American imperialism," were now the political confidants of Stanleyville's pro-Communist radicals. And the radicals, moreover, promised to rescue them once they came to power.

The imprisonment of Bablon and the others served to emphasize the truth of the old maxim that revolutions always "eat their own children"—meaning that people who help start revolutions are often destroyed by them later on. The maxim originated in Europe, where any eating that might be done would be purely figurative. Naturally, the maxim took on added pungency in the Congo.

Among the other prisoners was Commandant Oscar Sengha, the man who had helped save the lives of the Americans when they were to be executed on August 21 and who had befriended them on several other occasions. Sengha had been too friendly for his own good and the suspicious Simba authorities had thrown him into prison.

After the Americans had been in prison four days, a tall, husky young white man with a magnificent flowing beard was thrust into their cell. He was an Englishman by the name of Jack Siggins who worked in Peter Rombaut's tobacco factory. The Simbas had caught him working on a radio receiver. Despite his protests, they declared that it was a transmitter and, on Soumialot's orders, he was taken to the prison.

The five Americans greeted Siggins warmly. It was the first time they had had contact with someone from the outside world. Siggins was a hearty man and the Americans quickly became friends with him. They talked, played cards and exchanged jokes. Siggins was high-spirited and effusive and in his presence the five Americans were able to forget, for a little while, the anguish which gnawed at them.

A few days later, Soumialot arrived to judge the Simba and civilian prisoners. The wispy little defense minister sat at a table near the main door of the prison. One after another, the prisoners were brought out for "trial."

Soumialot sent for Siggins. The Englishman did not understand French, so Hoyt went along as an interpreter. Soumialot told Siggins that he was free to leave. Then Soumialot took a long look at Hoyt. He was obviously shocked to see him in prison uniform.

Soumialot turned to an aide. "Why are they in prison uniform?" he asked. The man mumbled something, but Hoyt was unable to catch it.

"This is a military matter, your being in prison," Soumialot said. "When the general comes back, we'll look into your case."

While Hoyt watched, Soumialot resumed judging the Congolese prisoners. Soumialot had the power of life and death over them. One word from him and a man would be taken away to be executed. The little ex-clerk seemed to relish his new role. For twenty years he had scrupulously carried out orders that others had given him. But now he was no longer humble; now it was he who ordered men about—and even to death.

When one man was brought before him, Soumialot ordered the Simbas to put him into the *cachot*, the solitary-confinement cell.

"Beat him first," Soumialot ordered.

The Simbas fell on the man with rifle butts and clubs, then dragged him off, bruised and bleeding, to the *cachot*. Soumialot grinned hugely. Another man was brought forth.

"To the *cachot*," the defense minister said.

The man knew that he, too, would be beaten, so he ran to the *cachot*, hoping to escape some of the blows. But it did no good; the Simbas caught him and worked him over with rifle butts. Soumialot beamed.

But those two men got off lightly. Soumialot decreed that some of the others should be taken to Osio, a prison on the left bank of the river. Osio was a dreaded word in Stanleyville. It was a prison from which no one returned. It was said that each day the condemned men were given fifty lashes with a *kiboko*, a hippopotamus-hide whip.

The men who had been condemned to Osio said nothing. There was not a ripple of emotion on their faces. Africans have an extraordinary fatalism; when death is coming, they accept the fact calmly and without protest.

Although Soumialot could be brutal, he also had some notion of civilized proprieties. He told the guards to allow the Americans to change back into their regular clothes.

Several days after Siggins's departure from prison, he managed to have a note sent back about a problem that was worrying the five Americans.

"St. Louis over the Yankees, four to three," the note said.

The days blurred past. Then, one afternoon, a silence came over the prison. Looking out the cell door, the Americans could see that the Congolese prisoners were rigid with fear. It was like a motion picture that stops at one particular frame, freezing everyone into a paralyzed pose. A group of guards had come from Osio to take away the men Soumialot had condemned. The guards carried their hippo-hide whips. The condemned men were brought out of their cells. Then the Americans saw with horror that the Osio guards were coming into their own cell.

"Ah, the Americans," one of the guards said, caressing the whip with his fingers. "You don't know it, but this is a paradise compared with Osio."

The Americans too were frozen with terror.

"We're waiting for you to come to Osio," the man said. A smile curled about his lips.

The guards rounded up twenty men. All of them had been active in a moderate political party under the Adoula regime. Among them was Bonaventure Zambiti, a newspaper editor and nephew of Victor Nendaka, the chief of the secret police in the Léopoldville government. Weeks later, when Stanleyville was finally liberated, the bodies of Zambiti and the other men were found in Osio. They had been beaten to death.

One day a Belgian businessman was put briefly in the cell with the Americans. He had electrifying news. The Simbas, he said, were suffering one defeat after another. It appeared that even the Simba authorities feared that Stanleyville might fall. Rumor had it that Soumialot and Gbenye kept autos under guard, ready for a quick escape. But, again, although this was good news in a sense, it only increased the possibility that the Americans might be slaughtered in reprisal just before the city fell. It was becoming ever more difficult to see how it all would end.

During the afternoon of October 23, as the men were dozing on their plank beds, another white man was put into the cell. He was a thin man of medium height. He looked a bit absurd—he carried a pith helmet filled with bananas. Although cartoonists are convinced that white men always wear pith helmets in Africa, they have virtually disappeared; only a few elderly missionaries still wear them. But this man was fairly young; he seemed to be in his late thirties. He was wearing a white shirt and khaki trousers. And he had two suitcases which were so battered that the contents were spilling out.

Hoyt thought that the man was a Belgian. "*Bon jour, monsieur.*" Hoyt said to him.

The man started to reply in French, then took a second look at Hoyt. "Are you an American?" he said in English.

Hoyt introduced himself.

"My name is Paul Carlson," the man said. "I'm an American, too—a missionary. Gee, it's great to meet some Americans again."

Hoyt gave Carlson a drink of water. Carlson asked if Hoyt had any candy; he was dying, he said, for something sweet. Hoyt found a jelly sandwich for him.

At that time, Paul Carlson was an obscure medical missionary. In a matter of weeks, however, his name would be in headlines around the world.

Paul Earle Carlson was a highly trained surgeon. If he had remained in the United States, he would in time have become a wealthy man. But Carlson gave up a promising medical practice. With his wife and two children, he journeyed halfway around the world to spend his life ministering to primitive people, some of them grateful and some of them not, in the green hell of the Congo's rain forest.

Until he was arrested by the Simbas, the thirty-six-year-old doctor operated a mission hospital in a tiny village called Wasolo, in the northern Congo, not far from the frontier of the Central African Republic. Belgian colonial officials used to call Wasolo *"le coin perdu"*—the lost corner. The name was apt. Wasolo was little more than a wide place in a winding jungle track, a cluster of grass huts and a mission hospital, hundreds of miles from a town of any consequence.

Carlson was the only doctor in a region that had a population of 100,000. His Congolese patients called him *Monganga* Paul—Dr. Paul. They came from all over the province to seek aid from him, trudging along jungle paths or coming down the rivers in dugout canoes.

The health problems of the region, as in many other areas of Africa, were enough to stagger most men. Perhaps half of all newborn infants died before they reached the age of two. Virtually everyone had chronic malaria and intestinal parasites. In some villages, perhaps 10 percent of the population was blind. In other villages, most of the people had hideous goiters. Tuberculosis was widespread. So, too, was elephantiasis, a disease of the lymphatic system which gets its name from the fact that in some cases the victim's legs swell until they begin to resemble the legs of a young elephant. And, along with everything else, the ancient scourge of leprosy was rampant.

For thousands of years, tropical Africa has been riven with these diseases. Millions of people have been robbed of their energies and sent to early deaths. African tribes have traditionally accepted these afflictions fatalistically: they represented God's will, or, perhaps, the work of angry spirits. In any case, there was nothing that ordinary mortals could do about them.

But then men like Paul Carlson came along. There was so much to do that he was busy for up to eighteen hours a day. On a typical day, two hundred people would turn up at the hospital. Carlson had up to eighty bed patients to look after. Most days he performed surgery. Often he was confronted with exceptionally difficult cases. But there was no opportunity to call in a specialist. Carlson would pore over his medical books for guidance, then perform the job himself. If the sun went down before the operation was completed, Carlson finished up while a Congolese assistant illuminated the incision with a flashlight.

Twice a week, Carlson trudged along jungle paths with his assistants to visit a leper colony that he maintained. The lepers would walk, hobble or crawl out of their huts to receive their regular injections of sulfone. Many were without fingers, hands or feet. The extremities of lepers tend to shrivel up; the patient loses all sensation in them and often accidentally loses fingers or hands in cooking fires without being aware of it.

Carlson operated a baby clinic, where he taught hygiene to Congolese mothers. He maintained four outlying dispensaries. He handled the distribution of surplus American food. When he made house calls, he often rode a motorbike. Or he went by canoe.

Other men might have gone wild from boredom, or from a claustrophobic feeling of being enveloped in the dripping jungle. But Carlson delighted in his work, and in his letters back home told with amusement of the absurdities of life in the Congo. He remarked once how odd it seemed when he and his Congolese assistants sang Christmas carols as they trudged along jungle trails. He talked about his new diet—bananas, papayas, pineapples, goats, chickens and occasionally a small antelope that a native killed. "So life goes," he said in his letters.

Carlson was an evangelist as well as a physician, preaching doctrines of compassion and hope in a savage land that had known little but warfare, cannibalism and ritualistic murder. He was a member of the Evangelical Covenant Church, an offshoot of Swedish Lutheranism, and it was that church which was sponsoring his work in Wasolo.

Much has been written about the motives of men who spend their lives as missionaries in remote areas of the world. The missionaries themselves feel that they are only obeying God's will. Critics have accused many of them of being hypocrites—overseas versions of Elmer Gantry—bores and prudes. The interesting thing about Paul Carlson is that he won the admiration and respect of even the skeptics who met him in the Congo. He was no righteous zealot, but rather a man who was unassuming to the point of being humble. The world would never have beaten a path to his mission station. No one ever heard of Wasolo, no one cared. Wasolo was not even on the standard maps of the Congo.

Carlson loved life. He laughed and joked continually. He was an ordinary American in appearance; he would be lost in the crowd at a baseball game in Chicago, on a subway in New York or at a county fair in Nebraska. And he was so stoical martyr. When death seemed near, he worried greatly about it, anguish written on his face. But it was characteristic of the man that if someone needed medical attention he would interrupt his broodings and he would even apologize. And then, mustering some cheer, he would go to work.

Carlson was born in Culver City, California, a suburb of Los Angeles. His father, a Swedish immigrant, was a machinist. Paul joined the Evangelical Covenant Church at the age of seventeen, taught Sunday-school classes and participated in other church activities. When he was eighteen, he enlisted in the navy and served two years as a seaman. He attended North Park College, a church-sponsored institution in Chicago, then received a degree in anthropology from Stanford University. In 1950 he married the former Lois Lindblom, a nurse. The couple moved to Washington, where Carlson enrolled in the medical school of George Washington University. Lois worked as a nurse to meet expenses and Paul did part-time jobs. Even so, he managed to find time for church activities. He did volunteer work among derelicts at a gospel mission not far from the Capitol. He collected drug samples from faculty members and set up a pharmacy at the mission. On one occasion a semester was scheduled in which, one morning a week, there was no eight-o'clock class. So Carlson promptly organized a weekly religious service for that hour.

After graduating with distinction from George Washington, Carlson put in five arduous years, first as an intern, then as a surgical resident at Harbor General Hospital in Torrance, California. Finally, in 1960, at the age of thirty-two, he was ready to earn money. But instead he volunteered for a five-month tour of the Congo with the Congo Protestant Relief Agency. Part of that time was spent in Wasolo. Back in Alhambra, California, Carlson went into private practice and soon was earning $12,000 a year—not a lordly sum for a doctor, but one which would surely have increased considerably in a short while. Carlson, however, longed to return to the Congo. As he told his wife: "It does something to you to work out there."

In mid-1962 Carlson made a decision: he would return to Wasolo. He turned his practice over to other physicians. Then he set out to acquire new skills that would make him even more useful in Wasolo. First he spent four months in England, studying tropical medicine at the University of Liverpool. His family joined him there, then they all went to Paris, where Carlson and his wife spent six months learning French. And then they went to Wasolo to spend the rest of their lives with the Congolese.

When the Simbas neared Wasolo, Carlson was faced with a difficult decision. The Congolese leaders in his church urged him to remain. On September 4, he took his wife and two children—Wayne, nine years old, and Lynette, seven—to safety in Bangui. Then he returned to Wasolo. At first he was not mistreated. The Simbas gave him a Red Cross armband and allowed him to circulate freely. Carlson treated, along with everyone else, the Simba wounded.

The Simbas discovered a radio transmitter—one which Carlson used to keep in touch with other mission stations. They accused Carlson of being in contact with "American imperialists." He was thrown in the back of a truck and beaten severely, particularly on the head. Then he was taken to Aketi. It was a long ride, during which Carlson's bruised body was bumped painfully along on jungle roads. On reaching Aketi, he was put into the same prison in which missionary William Scholten had died a few days earlier. The Simbas gave Carlson a knife that had no handle and forced him to cut grass. His surgeon's hands soon were raw and bleeding from being forced to hold the sharp edge of the implement. Next he was ordered to clean the gutters of the prison.

Two days later, the mission doctor was put into a truck and taken to the town of Buta. There the Simbas put him under house arrest in a Catholic mission. The priests fed him and cared for him until his injuries healed. A month passed. Carlson thought that the Simbas had forgotten about him.

On October 20, everyone in Buta turned out to welcome a distinguished visitor—a local boy who had made good. The native son was Christophe Gbenye, the blue-jeaned president of the People's Republic, who was making a tour of outlying towns. The local Simbas informed Gbenye that they were holding an American. An idea seems to have taken shape in Gbenye's mind at that time. He ordered the American taken in the back of a truck to Stanleyville. The priests gave Carlson the pith helmet to shelter his head from the midday sun. Although Carlson later joined the others in laughing about his old-fashioned pith helmet, he was glad to have it during the long ride to Stanleyville, as the day was particularly hot.

A few days after Carlson's arrival in Central Prison, this announcement appeared in the newspaper *Le Martyr:* "The President of the People's Republic of the Congo informed the public that Mr. Paul Carlson, a major of American nationality, was captured on the 20th of September, 1964, during the battle which took place at Yakoma. Mr. Carlson is in good health. A military tribunal will study his dossier before he appears in front of a court of justice."

It was a deliberate lie on Gbenye's part to accuse Carlson of being a major. Gbenye knew as well as everyone else that he was a mission doctor. When Carlson arrived in Stanleyville, one of the Simbas, who had known him in Wasolo, interceded with Gbenye on his behalf. The Simba told Gbenye that

Carlson was a "good man" and that he had saved the life of the Simba's father.

But Gbenye was not interested in truth or justice. All along, he and Olenga had attempted to blame the Simba defeats on the fact that they were opposed by "thousands of American troops." All along they declared that they had captured American soldiers and that these soldiers would be brought to Stanleyville as proof. But they had nothing to show until Gbenye had the good fortune to come across Carlson during the visit to his home town.

Gbenye's announcement in *Le Martyr* was followed by a communiqué read over Radio Stanleyville. Warming up, the president declared that Carlson was not only a major, but a "spy" as well. Thus the unassuming medical missionary from California was being prepared as a human sacrifice to the waning fortunes of the Simba regime.

12

PRISONERS OF WAR

"Dreadful!" Patrick Nothomb said as he shoved his plate back. He and the thirteen other Belgians with whom he shared his meals in his Immoquateur apartment had just finished lunch. But was it really a lunch? The jaunty young baron was, among other things, a gourmet. He had in his time dined in the great restaurants of Europe. His waistline proclaimed the fact that he was no ordinary eater. But now, as supplies continued to dwindle in Stanleyville, his table was graced—or cursed—only with such things as sardines, corned beef and plain bread. *"C'est la guerre,"* he told his dining companions in a brave but unconvincing attempt to make a joke of it.

Nothomb was interrupted by someone banging on the door. Opening it, he saw a group of Simbas in the hallway. "You're under arrest," they said. Nothomb shrugged. He had long ago given up protesting that he was supposed to have diplomatic immunity. It was October 27, the last day that the Belgian consul would remain at liberty in Simba-ruled Stanleyville.

The Simbas took Nothomb to Gbenye's office. The president was fuming. There were no sympathetic tears this time. The Simbas had suffered a major defeat two days earlier near Beni, a town in the eastern Congo that is situated almost in the shadow of the fabled, snow-covered Mountains of the Moon. The Simbas needed an excuse for this new setback

168

and, their capacity for self-delusion being what it was, they soon had one.

"The whole Belgian army attacked us at Beni," Gbenye screamed. "Therefore I must revise my policy toward the Belgians. Yes, my patience has run out. I am obliged to arrest all of you Belgians."

Nothomb was like a cat who always lands on his feet. He remembered the day, more than two months previously, when he had saved the lives of Hoyt and the other Americans by urging the Simbas to postpone the executions so that Hoyt could send a message to President Johnson, urging an end to American military support for Tshombe. The trick worked that time—the Simbas promptly forgot about the death sentences. Perhaps, Nothomb thought, he could use the same trick again to keep the Belgians from being arrested. And so, beaming with innocence, he said:

"Let's send a message first to the Belgian government, asking them to withdraw their soldiers."

Gbenye was glum. "I have already sent many messages to the king of Belgium," he muttered. His voice took on a touch of petulance. "He didn't answer me!"

Nothomb suppressed a smile. He grabbed around in his mind for another idea. Then he had one. "What about General de Gaulle?" he said. "If we send a message to him, maybe he will speak to the Belgian government and make it change its mind."

The suggestion was preposterous, but Nothomb knew what he was doing. De Gaulle enjoys a fantastic degree of popularity in Africa. One reason is that he personifies everything that an African thinks ought to be embodied in a ruler: tall, imperious, haughty, a mighty warrior, a wearer of gorgeous plumes, a man who brooks no discussion, no dissent.

Gbenye was interested. "You can try if you want," he said.

Nothomb went to the home of the acting French consular agent, a man named Joseph Guerlach, who ran a photo studio, and together they wrote a message to the great chief of Paris. Guerlach took the message to Gbenye's office. Nothomb started back to the Immoquateur on foot. But now his luck had run out. As he passed the Hôtel des Chutes, an old and somewhat decrepit hostelry near the banks of the river, he was grabbed by the Simbas. They put him in the hotel dining room. There were thirty Belgians in the room; they, like Nothomb, had been seized when they walked past the Hôtel des Chutes.

All afternoon, the Simbas raced around Stanleyville in trucks, arresting all the Belgians they could find, men, women and children. The captives were brought to the hotel dining room. By evening the number of prisoners had risen to three hundred. The dining room was fairly large, but with that many people in it there was no room for many of them to sit down.

The captives included many priests and nuns. They had been seized in their churches, convents and mission schools, loaded into trucks and brought to the Hôtel des Chutes with the civilians. There were about sixty children, some of them infants, in the crowd. The children wailed in terror. The parents tried to comfort them, but the noise was so great that one could hardly be heard.

Colonel Joseph Opepe, the portly number two man in the Simba army, lived in Room 109 of the hotel and it was he who took charge of the captives. Opepe was the former ANC officer who was a pious Catholic. It was he who was the object of so much controversy among the Europeans. Some said he tried to protect them; some said otherwise.

Opepe was drunk that afternoon and evening. From time to time, he shouted and swore at the Belgians. He had a powerful voice, which he had used in former times as a sergeant in the Force Publique to put the fear of God into the troops. The Belgians in the hotel dining room were similarly cowed by the bellowing voice. But some among them thought that Opepe was putting on a performance for the other Simbas. By that time it had become dangerous—even suicidal—for a Simba to show any kindness to whites. The Simbas may have become doubtful about Opepe's loyalties; he had a reputation, all along, of being friendly to Belgians. Now, it seemed, he may have been trying to show that he could be just as ferocious as the others.

Opepe sat at the door of the dining room, dressed in khaki slacks and a sport shirt that was unbuttoned to the waist. His enormous belly bulged forth. He looked, some said, like a Congolese Buddha. As each European was brought into the room, Opepe examined his papers to make sure that he was a Belgian. Only Belgians were being arrested.

A Spanish nun was brought before Opepe. He studied her papers. "Where's Spain?" he said to his aides.

The Simbas were stumped.

"Oh, let her go," Opepe said.

The Spanish nun, along with several other non-Belgian nuns, was put into Opepe's car to be taken back to their mission school. On the way, one of the nuns told the driver: "Don't turn at this corner—that isn't the way."

"Shh—we know the way," the Simba driver said. "The colonel told us to detour around so we won't run into the general."

But Opepe was not so considerate with the Belgians. He bluntly informed them that all would die if Stanleyville were attacked.

Patrick Nothomb was becoming desperate. As the Belgian consul, he was responsible for the well-being of his nationals. Some three hundred people were jammed into the dining room. There was no food. Nor were there any mattresses or beds. Some of the Belgians, who had been arrested in their homes, brought blankets with them. They gave these to the children and tried to make them as comfortable as possible. But it did little good; the children were frightened and hungry. They screamed. The adults became frantic. To make matters worse, there was only one toilet for all three hundred people. It quickly overflowed.

Nothomb and some of the other men hit upon an idea. They pushed through the crowd to where Opepe was sitting.

"We offer ourselves as hostages," Nothomb told Opepe. "Put us in prison—but, please, let the rest of these people go home."

Opepe jumped up and screamed at Nothomb in Swahili, which Nothomb did not understand. He stood there, smiling benignly at Opepe, while the colonel delivered the tirade. Many of the other Belgians knew Swahili and they were aghast at Opepe's words. Opepe said that Nothomb would be eaten—eaten after being covered with a sauce which he, Opepe, would provide. Nobody knew what the sauce was; Opepe never explained. Nothomb, who understood none of the tirade, stood there smiling. Opepe paused. He looked incredulously at the baron, not realizing that Nothomb spoke no Swahili. He interpreted the little man's attitude as one of immense courage. Opepe was impressed—and disarmed. He sat down and said nothing for two hours.

At 8:30 that evening several boxes were brought into the room. When the Belgians opened them, they gasped with surprise. The boxes contained food—cans of corned beef and sardines, as well as bread. For once Nothomb did not turn up his gourmet's nose at the offering.

The food was sent to the captives by those of Stanleyville's foreigners who had not been arrested—most Indians, Pakistanis and Greeks. Nothomb and the other Belgians were deeply touched. But that was only the beginning of the generosity of the other foreigners; each day they kept the Belgian captives supplied with food. As time went on, it became ever more difficult. Yet the other foreigners always managed to find enough to keep the Belgians alive and more or less well. The Belgians organized mess facilities. Women cooked the food and the men saw to it that it was shared equally by everyone in the room.

Throughout the first evening, Opepe sat next to the door, brooding. Opepe was a rough soldier, but he apparently had no heart for guarding women and children. At eleven o'clock, he stood up and told the nuns to go upstairs and spend the night in the hotel bedrooms. Then he told the women who had children to take whatever rooms remained. Opepe's rage was passed; he spoke gently.

The nuns and the women with children departed. Now there was room to stretch out on the floor, yet no one did so. The Belgians milled around. Then a curious reaction came over them. They became almost jovial, as if they had gathered for a party.

Among the captives was Théo Papazoglakis, the Belgian of Greek origin who had gone for a stroll near the Lumumba Monument and who had been told by an elderly Congolese friend that a dog had snatched up a piece of human meat that the old man had intended for his own consumption. Papazoglakis was a happy-go-lucky man and now he and his brother Antoine, who was twenty-seven, amused their fellow captives by performing card tricks.

As Colonel Opepe watched the two brothers, his eyes widened. "What sorcery!" he exclaimed.

At 3 A.M., a Belgian got out a phonograph and played records. Colonel Opepe, too, was in a jovial mood now. He shared a bottle of Cinzano with the captives. The Belgian who owned the phonograph selected a very special record of a French popular song and played it over and over again at full volume.

"*Non rien de rien; je ne regrette rien,*" the song went. "No nothing, no nothing; I regret nothing."

The captives roared with laughter each time it was played.

In the morning, the mood was that of a hangover. Sixty-five more Belgians were brought to the hotel, bringing the total to 365. Anxieties rose. Nothomb managed to extract some concessions from Opepe; the colonel agreed that all of the women could sleep upstairs, as well as the old men—some were over seventy—and those who were sick. Opepe, moreover, assigned four bathrooms for the men who remained in the dining room. But no one could leave the hotel.

There were about 135 other Belgians in Stanleyville. They were never arrested, but life for them was scarcely any better than it was for the 365 who had been grabbed. They spent their days hiding in cellars, attics and cupboards in their homes. Some spent the day in elevators that were stopped between floors, as they had nearly three months earlier when the Simbas attacked the Immoquateur. They came out only at night.

The third day the Belgians were held at the Hôtel des Chutes began on a pleasant note. Colonel Opepe appeared at the door of the dining room and asked for Nothomb. Opepe was quite sober—it was too early in the day for serious drinking—and he radiated good cheer. When Nothomb appeared, he presented him with a melon—a traditional Congolese gesture of friendship.

Nothomb was a friendly and sentimental man. He was touched by the gesture. For a moment, he forgot about his troubles. But the mood did not last long. One of the Simba guards told the Belgians that General Olenga was furious. "You Belgians have dropped an atomic bomb on Beni," the guard said. "You have killed 100,000 of our Congolese brothers."

Tension rose. Nothomb felt that something was about to happen.

Then it was noon, high noon in Stanleyville. The wail of a siren was heard. From the dining-room window, Nothomb saw a car arrive in front of the hotel, followed by others. Nothomb knew that General Olenga was coming—when he traveled about the city, he was always preceded by a car with a siren.

Some twenty Simbas jumped from the cars, each pointing a submachine gun at the hotel. Olenga got out of his car—a new Olenga. This was not the victorious warrior whom Nothomb had met at Camp Ketele in August, the man who, dressed in a general's uniform and carrying a sword, had radiated confidence and magnanimity. Olenga now was dressed in a dirty shirt and slacks. The expression on his face was one of rage and frustration—the face of a cornered animal.

"Where's the Belgian consul?" he shouted.

"Here," Nothomb called. He had no desire to go near the general.

"Come here," Olenga commanded.

While the 364 other Belgians watched in silence, the little baron trudged toward him.

Olenga punched Nothomb in the nose with all his strength. Nothomb reeled back. Then, to keep from falling, he bent forward slightly, trying, all the while, to clear his head.

Olenga punched him in the nose again. Nothomb struggled to keep his balance.

"Read this," Olenga shouted, thrusting a piece of paper at Nothomb.

Nothomb started to read, but Olenga punched him in the nose again. Somehow Nothomb managed to read the message: "The Belgians have dropped an atomic bomb on Beni. They have killed 100,000 people."

Olenga punched the Belgian in the nose for a fourth time. One of the general's aides rained several other blows on Nothomb's head and shoulders.

Colonel Opepe looked astonished. Then, apparently taking a cue from his master, he bellowed threats at Nothomb. But he did not touch him.

The Belgians in the hotel watched with rising anger. The Simbas kept their submachine guns trained on them. Nothomb was afraid that the Belgians might try to come to his aid. If they did, Nothomb knew, they would be gunned down. One man lost his head, but the other Belgians held him back.

The Belgians muttered angrily. "Silence, silence," one of them shouted at the others. They looked at him and fell silent.

Olenga and another officer kept on punching Nothomb. Now there was no longer any pretense that one would lose his *dawa*, his protection from bullets, if he touched a European.

Blood was spurting from Nothomb's nose. One of the Simbas wrenched Nothomb's watch from his wrist. Another taboo fell by the wayside.

Olenga sent for Paul Duqué, the Belgian vice-consul. A Simba who had a ring on his finger slapped Duqué in the face until his face was covered with blood.

On Olenga's orders, the two men were taken into the street and told to stand there. The two men were convinced that they would be executed in a few moments. They prayed. But they accepted the idea that they were going to die. They had no thought of running. There was, of course, no place to run to. But they did not want to run. They surrendered in face of what seemed to be the inevitable.

Olenga came up. He ordered them into a Volkswagen. "To the monument," he told the driver—meaning the Lumumba Monument.

Nothomb and Duqué had been reprieved, but only for the moment. Now it seemed that the general wanted them killed at the altar of the god Lumumba. As they rode through the streets to the monument, a change came over the two men. Now they wanted, very intensely, to live. Their fatalistic acceptance of death was gone. They were, after all, too young for that to last any length of time.

The cars stopped in front of the monument. Nothomb found Duqué's hand and squeezed it. The Simbas cocked their automatic weapons.

"No," said Olenga. "Put down your guns."

Olenga may have been a madman, but he was clever enough not to throw away his best trump cards. He knew that Nothomb and Duqué had value—value as hostages, value in bargaining.

"Take them to the radio station," he said. "They will broadcast a message to their government."

Nothomb and Duqué knew that they were saved—at least for the time being. Emotion flooded back. Nothomb was not sure whether he wanted to laugh, cry or scream.

At the radio station, Nothomb was forced, under the direction of a Simba officer, to make a tape-recorded statement which later was broadcast to the outside world. In it, Nothomb said that Stanleyville's Belgians and Americans were being held hostage. They would be released only if the U.S. and Belgian governments withdrew military support for the Tshombe regime. "I have seen with my own eyes the most irrefutable proof of Belgian aggression in the Congo," Nothomb said in his gun-point speech.

The idea of using civilians as hostages to secure political concessions was, of course, contrary to the Geneva Conventions and to international law and civilized behavior. But Nothomb knew that his government would realize that he had made the appeal under duress. And he was, in any case, glad to make it as he felt that this would alert the outside world to the plight of Stanleyville's Belgians and Americans.

Nothomb had, by now, gotten over his brush with death. He was back in orbit once more. Beaming with innocence, he suggested to the Simbas that he include a sentence in the message saying that the hostages were in danger of death. "If I say that, Mr. Spaak will surely change his policy," Nothomb explained.

"Good idea," said the Simba officer. "Put that in."

The Simba did not realize what Nothomb was up to. Nothomb wanted to make sure that the outside world realized in full measure the danger the hostages were in. It was, in effect, a cry of alarm, a cry for help. But the Simbas were not aware of it.

While Nothomb was making his radio statement, General Olenga stood by in silence. He seemed to be in a daze. Finally, in a quiet and almost forlorn voice, he said: "I was a friend of the Belgian consul. I thought he would be my friend and now I am very disappointed."

Nothomb said nothing aloud. But under his breath he muttered, "And I am very disappointed with *you*."

Soon after, Nothomb and Duqué were taken in a jeep to

the Central Prison. They were put in a cell with Michael Hoyt, Dr. Paul Carlson and the other Americans.

Nothomb was astonished at the appearance of the Americans. They had been in prison for twenty days and had not shaved in that time. The men had long beards and their hair had grown down to their necks.

Hoyt put his arms around Nothomb's shoulders and greeted him warmly. "Nice to see you, Patrick," he said. "Sorry, though, that it has to be in prison."

"What's the difference whether we're here or outside—all of Stanleyville is a prison," Nothomb replied.

Paul Carlson examined Nothomb's nose and told him that fortunately it had not been broken.

At the Hôtel des Chutes Colonel Opepe was busy getting drunk. He sat by the door of the dining room as he drank. He seemed to be brooding. The Belgians watched him apprehensively.

Suddenly Opepe stood up. He ordered the nuns and priests to come forward. "Take off your clothes," he shouted.

The priests and nuns thought they had not heard him correctly. Opepe was, after all, supposed to be a devout Catholic. He attended mass regularly.

"Take off your clothes," he bellowed. No one moved. He shouted the order again.

The priests removed their outer robes. The nuns began to sob. One of them had a birthday that day—she was seventy. Slowly the nuns took off their headgear. "Off with your robes," Opepe said. The nuns took off their outer garments. "Take off the rest," he said. Each removed another robe, leaving a sort of skirt underneath.

The nuns were herded into the street. One nun fingered a crucifix and said aloud: "My Lord, if you demand this sacrifice of me, I will gladly go through with it."

Another Simba officer appeared. He seemed to be embarrassed. He ordered the nuns to return to the hotel and put their clothes on. Colonel Opepe made no objection. He continued drinking. Then he had another idea. He told his Simbas to take the children away from their mothers and give them to the nuns. The women shrieked as they were separated from their children. The children howled. The men milled around in great agitation. Opepe bellowed oaths at everyone.

But, soon after, Opepe called it off. The children were allowed to go back to their parents.

Not long afterward, Opepe visited Monsignor Augustin Fataki, a Congolese prelate in Stanleyville. "I have acted in a bad way toward the Belgians," Opepe told the startled monsignor. "I am ashamed of myself. I hope that the Belgians will forgive me."

Interestingly enough, many of them did.

In the evening of the same day, a truckload of Simbas arrived at the hotel with a new prisoner. The prisoner was Clifford Schaub, a short and chunky American missionary. Schaub, who was thirty-six years old and who came from the Pittsburgh area, had been in the Congo for ten years as an evangelist with the African Christian Mission, which has its headquarters in Cincinnati. With his wife and two sons, he lived on the outskirts of Stanleyville and preached in mission churches in the native quarters of the city.

Opepe studied Schaub's identity papers. "So you're an American," he said.

"That's right," said Schaub, who spoke fluent Swahili.

Opepe chatted pleasantly with Schaub. Then the Simbas who had arrested Schaub came into the hotel, carrying a camera, radio and typewriter that they had taken from Schaub's home.

Opepe exploded. "You thieves—what are you doing with those things?" he shouted. "I didn't tell you to bring them here. Take them back!"

The Simbas quailed before the terrible voice.

Opepe turned back to Schaub. "Do you have a family?" he asked. His manner was most pleasant.

"Yes, I have a wife and two children—they're at the house now," said Schaub. "And there's another American lady there, too—she's a missionary."

Schaub was referring to Miss Phyllis Rine, twenty-five years old, of Bangs, Ohio, near Mount Vernon. She was a plain, heavy-set young woman who wore glasses and who was exceptionally quiet and modest. As a student in the Cincinnati Bible Seminary, she had done church work with Negro children. She volunteered for the Congo after hearing Schaub speak at the seminary during one of his home visits. In her application, she said she wanted to serve in the Congo because, while working in Cincinnati, "I came to know and love the Negro people." Miss Rine had been in the Congo two years. She conducted Bible classes for Congolese children and taught domestic arts and hygiene to Congolese women. And she lived with the Schaubs.

After Schaub told Opepe about the women and children, the colonel turned to the Simbas. "Why didn't you bring them in?" he said.

"That man's an American—we're afraid of him," a Simba said. "We didn't know what we were supposed to do."

"Go get them," Opepe growled.

The Simbas left. Schaub became worried. "What are you going to do with the women and children?" he asked Opepe.

"They'll stay here—they'll be all right," the colonel replied.

"Here? In the hotel?" said Schaub.

"Come along," said Opepe. He led Schaub to the dining room. "They'll stay here," Opepe said.

The Greeks and Asians had sent over a load of blankets that evening and the Belgians were passing them out.

Schaub followed Opepe back into the corridor. "Will the women and children be treated well here?" he said, with a quiver in his voice.

Opepe frowned. Without a word, he got up and disappeared. Schaub waited. Then Opepe returned with an armload of blankets.

"The blankets are going fast," he said. "I was afraid that you wouldn't get any. Here—that's plenty for you and your family."

Soon after, Schaub's wife, Helen, and their two sons, Timmy, eight years old, and Mark, six, arrived, together with Miss Rine. The women and children were sent to sleep in the hotel bedrooms upstairs. Schaub spent the night on the dining-room floor.

The Simba authorities, all the while, were becoming even more frantic. They dispatched one appeal after another for aid from leftist African countries. But, although they did receive a planeload of arms, believed to have come from Algeria, in late October, and although the leftist countries favored the Simba cause, none of them sent troops. And none of these countries extended diplomatic recognition to the Simba regime.

Even at his best, Gbenye was not particularly rational. Now, he directed his anger at the leftist African countries who, he felt, had let him down. And so, on October 29, he delivered a tirade over Radio Stanleyville in which he handed down an "ultimatum" to the leftist presidents of Egypt, Algeria, Ghana, Guinea and Mali.

"I inform your excellencies that the responsibility for the loss of Africa is shared between you and me," Gbenye said. "I have done that which I could to safeguard the honor of Africa and you have left me alone under the American and Belgian bombardments.

"I ask you in a final appeal, in the name of Lumumba, if you do not intervene within a few hours, I will adopt a scorched-earth policy and thus the Americans and Belgians will find only a desert."

Colonel Opepe also was jittery over the future. He had a series of furtive talks with Belgian business leaders who were among the captives in the Hôtel des Chutes. They told him that, if he would protect them, they, in turn, would use all their influence to see that he was spared the wrath of the ANC should Stanleyville fall. Opepe made no commitments, but he was interested in the offer.

He remained utterly unpredictable. One afternoon he appeared in the hotel with a bow and arrow. He waved them angrily at the captives. "Here is what we fight with while the others have atomic weapons," he said.

On the evening of October 30, after the Belgians had been held three days in the Hôtel des Chutes, the men were separated into four groups. They were taken in trucks to Camp Ketele and other military installations scattered around the city, to be held as hostages against air attacks. The women and children remained at the Hôtel des Chutes. Single women and married women who had no children were sent to the Congo Palace Hotel.

That night, Simba soldiers broke into the upstairs rooms at the Hôtel des Chutes and raped four Belgian women.

One group of forty Belgian men spent a harrowing night in an outlying military camp. The men were locked in a small room with no space to lie down. There was no food, no water, no toilet facilities. The men relieved themselves on the floor. The stench soon was unbearable. A group of Simbas gathered outside the door. They were smoking hemp. They shouted that they were going to kill the men in the morning. Over and over, they said: "We don't have much ammunition left so we're not going to kill you with bullets, but with spears and knives. This will be better; you'll suffer more that way."

Throughout the night, the Simbas thrust pieces of burning wood into the room. Some of the Belgians cracked under the strain. One man screamed: "I'm going to stand next to the door. They're going to kill us in the morning. I'd rather go first; it will be faster that way."

Another Belgian tried to calm him down. "I'll bet you two bottles of champagne, which I'll collect from you in Brussels, that nothing will happen," he said.

But the other man remained inconsolable. As it turned out, he lost the bet. He lived. But his wife was machine-gunned by the Simbas.

The Simba authorities began to worry that they could not control the troops at that camp. They moved the forty Belgians to Camp Ketele, where thirty-eight other Belgians and one American—Clifford Schaub—were being held.

There were a few incidents—but not many—at Camp Ketele. The captives were forced on one occasion to dance the cha-cha-cha, to the amusement of the Simbas. They were told to get rid of their eyeglasses—the Simbas were convinced that these were magical devices that could attract planes. On one occasion, too, the Simbas threatened to make "corned beef" of the hostages. The Simbas felt that corned beef was really human meat. Years before, a Belgian trading firm had sold cans of corned beef that had a picture of a cowboy on the label. The Congolese assumed that the picture indicated that the contents were human meat, cowboy meat. They have always been convinced that Europeans eat human meat—after all, there is nothing wrong with that from the Congolese point of view.

Schaub and the seventy-eight Belgians were kept in the chapel at Camp Ketele. Each day the Greek and Asian communities sent food for the men. They gave them foam-rubber mattresses and blankets. The Simbas cadged food and cigarettes from their prisoners—a variation, as it were, of foreign aid. The Belgians had learned from previous experiences to hide their wristwatches in their breast pockets when arrest was imminent. "It's strange," a Simba officer declared one day. "Not a single European has a watch any more."

Within a few days the Simba authorities realized that Stanleyville's faltering economy had come to a complete halt owing to the fact that most Belgians were imprisoned. The Simbas released eighty-five persons—all of the priests and nuns as well as some laymen. Several dozen others were allowed to leave the detention centers at eight o'clock each morning to go to their business firms, with orders to return at noon. But no one did any work. Those who were freed in the mornings simply went home, had a bath, slept in a comfortable bed, then reported back at noon.

Clifford Schaub received a visit at Camp Ketele from a Simba officer whom he had previously known. The Simba asked if he could take over Schaub's house. Schaub shrugged; there was nothing he could do about it. Schaub had learned that his house had been looted during his absence and that three bicycles, two radios and Phyllis Rine's sewing machine had been taken.

A few days later, the Simba officer appeared, riding one of the bicycles that had been stolen. "Look what I found," the officer said. He had let it be known among the civilians that he wanted the stolen goods returned and they, fearful of his wrath, had sent back most of them.

The officer's wife paid Schaub a visit. "We found another one of your bicycles and your sewing machine and a typewriter," she said.

One day the officer pedaled up to the chapel-prison on one of the bicycles. He was carrying three little cakes. "I just bought them at a bakery—if I gave them to you, would you eat them?" the Simba said.

"Sure," said Schaub.

"You are really my friend," the officer said.

The foreigners who kept the men supplied with food brought Schaub notes from his wife, who was being held, along with their two children, in the Hôtel des Chutes. She had not been harmed. Mrs. Schaub and Phyllis Rine were the only non-Belgian women who were being held.

Miss Rine, along with the other childless women, was put into the Congo Palace Hotel. The first few nights, Simbas came to their rooms, eager, apparently, to have sexual relations with the women. But the Simbas did not force themselves on the women. General Olenga lived in the hotel and thus there was discipline among the troops. The women complained to the general about the nocturnal visits. Olenga said vaguely that the women might be freed if they would sleep with the Simbas. There were no volunteers and Olenga put a stop to the visits.

On two occasions, Miss Rine, the shy and plain-looking schoolteacher, was summoned to the general's presence. "You're an American—maybe you can explain something to me," he said. "Why are the Americans coming over to kill us? Are the Americans people of God or people of the devil?"

"I don't know," Miss Rine said. She was frightened. In any case, she knew nothing about the war. She was only a teacher of Congolese children.

The Simbas continued to comb the Stanleyville region for Belgians and Americans. On Sunday, November 1, they appeared at the headquarters of the Unevangelized Fields Mission at Kilometer Eight, just outside the city. Kilometer Eight was ordinarily the office and home of Alfred Larson, a thirty-six-year-old missionary from Brooklyn, New York, who served as the field secretary for all UFM activities in the northeast Congo. But other missionaries had taken refuge there as well, including Charles Davis, who had been imprisoned briefly with Hoyt and the other consular personnel in September. As a result, there were twenty-eight white people at Kilometer Eight when the Simbas arrived—five men, nine women and fourteen children.

The Simbas wanted to arrest everyone, but there was not enough room in the vehicles for all of them. So they took Larson and Davis and the three other men: Delbert Carper, thirty-nine, of Kansas City, Missouri; Hector McMillan, forty-nine, a Canadian citizen from Avonmore, Ontario; and Robert McAlister, an Irishman. When they reached the Hôtel des Chutes, the men were taken before Colonel Opepe. Opepe noticed that Carper was wearing a hearing aid.

"What's that?" he said.

Carper had had no end of trouble with the Simbas for

weeks over his hearing aid. They suspected, as usual, that it was a radio transmitter. With much weariness, he tried to explain to the colonel that it was only a gadget to improve his hearing. Carper even produced a letter from Doctor Barlovatz which attested solemnly that the hearing aid was not a transmitter.

Opepe was not convinced. His aides grew excited. Everyone talked at once. Then one officer reached over and tweaked Carper's nose.

"Our colonel is not a fool!" the man said.

Another Simba spoke up. "You are in contact with Léopoldville. You are telling lies about us. We are going to bury any transmitters we find—and the owner with it."

Carper, who was fluent in Lingala, managed to convince them in their own language that it was not a radio. But the Simbas were not going to take any chances: they took the hearing aid away from him. From then on, Carper lived in a world of semi-silence. He could hear only if someone shouted.

The five men were not moved to Camp Ketele or the other places where the Belgian men were being held. Rather they were put into a small two-bed room in the Hôtel des Chutes. After a week, Peter Rombaut, the honorary British consul who operated the tobacco factory, managed to convince Opepe that McMillan, the Canadian, and McAlister, the Irishman, were not Americans. They were released. They went back to Kilometer Eight to look after the twenty-three women and children.

Larson, Davis and Carper remained in the room. Their meals were brought to them by the Greeks, Asians and other foreigners who remained at liberty. Several other white men were also put in the room, including two physicians, one a Hungarian and one an Italian. Soon there were ten men living twenty-four hours a day in a tiny room. In addition to the two beds, they had extra mattresses on the floor. But there was hardly any room in which to move around. Fortunately, they had a private bathroom.

The three missionaries held prayer meetings each day. They studied their Bibles. Herbert Jenkinson, the elderly British missionary who operated the Leco bookstore, sent them religious tracts in French, Swahili and Lingala. From time to time, Simba officers dropped into the room for a visit.

The missionaries, ever eager to save another soul, passed out the tracts to Belgians and Simbas alike. One Simba, a major named François, came to Larson one day and said he wanted to confess his sins. The two men sat on the edge of the bed. They prayed and read the Bible together.

All was not rosy, however, from an evangelistic point of view. Some of the Belgians with whom the missionaries shared the room were openly skeptical about religion in general and missionary work in particular. "You have failed," they said. "Look at the Congolese—they're as savage as ever." And the missionaries replied that although some of their converts had renounced Christianity, many of them remained as dedicated as ever. "We haven't made the impact we'd like to make," said Larson, "but we've done a lot."

Neither the Belgians nor the missionaries convinced each other.

The Central Prison, meanwhile, was taking on the air of a Grand Hotel. Baron Nothomb and his vice-consul, Paul Duqué were there. So, too, were Dr. Carlson and the five American consular personnel. Two other Americans had also been brought to the prison. They were Gene Bergman, twenty-one, of Paso Robles, California, and Jon Snyder, twenty-three, of Canby, Oregon. Bergman and Snyder were conscientious objectors, members of the Mennonite Church. They had been allowed to come to the Congo for two years of volunteer work in lieu of military service. Both men worked at the fledgling University of Stanleyville—Bergman as a building artisan and Snyder as a bookkeeper. The Simbas arrested them at the university and brought them to prison, but they were not harmed physically.

Soon the cell became crowded. Two other men were brought in. They were Raoul Massacesi, a construction superintendent who was the honorary Italian consul in Stanleyville, and Gleb Makaroff, the Stanleyville manager for a company that handled river and rail transportation for the upper Congo. Massacesi was jailed because the Simbas captured an improvised armored car from the ANC which they said was of Italian manufacture. Massacesi protested that he knew nothing about it and that he, in any case, was only a builder. But the Simbas were never sticklers for detailed evidence. They were convinced that the Italians had teamed up with the American and Belgian "imperialists." And so in Massacesi went.

Makaroff was arrested after a plane strafed a river boat. "*You* called the American plane!" the Simbas declared. Makaroff protested: "Why would I do that? It would ruin my company and myself." But the Simbas had it all figured out.

"Everybody knows perfectly well that after the war the millionaires will give you money to buy new boats," they said.

All day and all night, there was a gnawing fear in the back of each man's mind, the fear that they would be executed if and when a rescue column neared the city. But they nevertheless found time to joke. The irrepressible Patrick Nothomb, for example, announced that he was going to look for a paintbrush and a sign board. He wanted to put up a notice on the door that read:

CONSULATE OF BELGIUM, CONSULATE OF THE UNITED STATES OF AMERICA, HONORARY CONSULATE OF ITALY.
BY APPOINTMENT ONLY

One day Nothomb took Hoyt aside. "Did you make a will or take any other measures for your family?" he asked. "You understand that you and I are threatened more than the others. If they kill anyone, they'll start with us."

Hoyt looked at his friend and smiled blandly. "We have nothing to fear. Don't you realize, Patrick, that we have diplomatic immunity?"

On November 4, the Americans learned through the prison grapevine that Lyndon Johnson had won the election the day before.

Paul Carlson was particularly worried because he knew that he was supposed to be tried soon before a military court on Gbenye's absurd charge that he was an American major and a spy. The others did their best to cheer him up. Hoyt kept telling Carlson that he was, in a sense, Gbenye's last trump card and that Gbenye was not likely to play it. But no one could really predict with any confidence what the Simbas would do.

Carlson made friends with all of his fellow prisoners. All of them, Belgians and Americans, admired him greatly for his courage and composure in the face of possible death. Some of them sought him out to discuss religion and each day he prayed with one man or another. But Carlson was no zealot. He never forced his religious views on the others; indeed, he never brought the subject up except when asked. He joined the others in playing gin rummy and casino.

Time dragged past. For hours, the men lay on their plank bunks. Most of the Americans were bachelors. But Hoyt and Carlson had families and they spent many a forlorn hour wondering if they would ever see their wives and children again. Nothomb, too, had a family—his wife and two children were in Léopoldville—and he, too, wondered if he would ever again see the people in this world whom he loved best. Carlson spent many hours each day quietly reading his Bible. Among the other books which the men had was one entitled *A Death in the Family*. But no one wanted to read it.

One evening the men managed to get a bottle of whisky smuggled into the prison. They sang, laughed and joked. But then, in the morning, there was only the grim reality of the prison.

Although the men got along exceptionally well, tension mounted. Some of them resented the fact that Hoyt had long conversations with Simba officers who visited the prison. Hoyt was, of course, completely justified in talking with the Simbas. He was the American consul and it was his duty to maintain whatever contacts he could with the authorities to determine the situation. He hoped thereby to make plans, however futile they might be, for saving the lives of his people. Some of the men who objected to Hoyt's conversations knew little or no French and thus were ignorant of what was being said. But, although they were being unfair to Hoyt, their attitudes were understandable. They were terrified that they would be killed any day. They felt that Hoyt might make the Simbas angry and thus precipitate their deaths. The men were not diplomats; the only thing they could think of to do was to say nothing.

The Simba regime, meanwhile, seemed to be coming apart at the seams. One day Soumialot's personal staff was put in prison. The Americans were told by the prison grapevine that Olenga had ordered them arrested because Soumialot had fled from Stanleyville. But the next day Soumialot was back in Stanleyville and his staff was released. Soumialot visited the prison himself that day. He laughed continually; some thought he was on the verge of hysteria.

Late one night, eleven Congolese prisoners were taken from solitary confinement, sewn into sacks and thrown into the waterfall at the Tshopo bridge. The next night, two more Congolese prisoners met a similar fate.

The Simbas held in the prison became ever more hostile to the whites. Things got to the point where the Belgians and Americans were glad that the guards locked them into their cell at night. At least they were safe from the Simba prisoners.

By early November, there were eight Americans in the prison. Eight others were being held in hotels or at Camp Ketele. About 280 Belgians, including Patrick Nothomb, were under arrest. And one Italian.

On November 5, Christophe Gbenye declared over Radio Stanleyville that all of the Belgians and Americans in rebel territories were "prisoners of war." The idea that helpless civilians could be termed prisoners of war was nonsense of a barbaric nature. But Gbenye had plans for them. He intended to use their lives to make a deal to call off the advance of government forces on Stanleyville. Even a temporary cease-fire would be to Gbenye's advantage—he was expecting new shipments of Communist-made weapons any day.

The "People's Government," Gbenye said in the radio talk, would "negotiate" with the Organization of African Unity on the fate of the Belgians and Americans.

The same day, in an issue of the newspaper *Le Martyr*, Gbenye said that "Belgian and American soldiers" were massing at the Kamina military base in Katanga. He added: "We must warn that any clash between the People's Army of Liberation and the foreign forces that may be coming from Kamina will set fire to the belongings and will plunge in a blood bath the people whom we have to this date always protected."

13

REMEMBER, REMEMBER,
THE FIFTH OF NOVEMBER

On Sunday morning, November 1, villagers living near the town of Kongolo were jolted from their slumbers by an ominous rumbling noise. Gradually it grew louder and more insistent. It sounded like an enormous swarm of angry bees, or, worse still, a host of irate spirits. Squinting into the distance the villagers saw great clouds of dust rising. The dust hung motionless in the still air. Something was coming up the road from Kongolo, something big, something that probably was dangerous. The villagers fled into the jungle.

The thing that was coming changed the course of history in the Congo. The noise and dust emanated from what was known as Lima One, a ragtag motorized column of white mercenaries and ANC troops that had set out from Kongolo that morning, bound for Stanleyville, some 470 miles to the north. After four weeks of hasty preparations, the Tshombe government was starting its big push on the Simba capital. The outside world watched the progress of the column with intense interest and apprehension. If it could strike swiftly through to Stanleyville, it might be able to rescue the city's sixteen hundred foreign hostages.

Premier Tshombe was similarly eager to see the hostages liberated, but he had other things on his mind as well. Tshombe had staked his political career on an early recapture of the city. It was a risky gamble, but he had no choice. If

Ferret Armored Car

Stanleyville remained in Simba hands, Tshombe's own re-gime would, in all likelihood, soon crumble.

From an orthodox military point of view, Lima One was a joke. It consisted of fifty trucks and other vehicles, on which there rode about 100 English-speaking mercenaries, commanded by Michael Hoare, and about 150 Katangese who made no secret of the fact that they would much rather have been back in Katanga. There were also about 20 other mercenaries sprinkled through the column—Belgians, French-men, Italians and others. The whole effort was commanded by a short, rotund and white-haired man named Commandant Albert Liégeois, a professional Belgian officer on loan to the Congo government. Liégeois had adopted Lima One as the code name for the column because his name starts with the letter L and "Lima" is the word for that letter in the international phonetic alphabet.

Lima One had precisely four armored vehicles, all of which had been acquired from a junkyard for the outing. The column was led by a Ferret, a British-made reconnaissance car that had a .30-calibre machine gun in the turret. Next came three Swedish-built Scania-Vabis armored cars, with twin .30's mounted in front and a third machine gun in the rear. The English-speaking mercenaries could never pronounce Scania-Vabis properly and so they nicknamed them the Sons of Bitches. Everyone agreed that the nickname was appropriate. The vehicles looked like huge bathtubs on wheels, and weighed eight tons each. They were so cumbersome that it was difficult to maneuver them on jungle roads. They were so heavy that they sank to their axles in mud. Their armor was so fragile that a new hole often appeared when they were shot at.

The Ferret and the Sons of Bitches had been brought to the Congo originally by the UN troops and were used in the wars against Tshombe in Katanga. But such are the quirks of fate in the Congo that Tshombe, having acquired them from the UN, was now using them to maintain himself in power as the premier of the entire Congo.

The rest of the Lima One column consisted of jeeps and trucks, each of them heavily laden with weapons, ammunition, food, gasoline, spare parts, white mercenaries and reluctant Katangese warriors. The column crept along at an average of ten miles an hour. They had to keep bunched together for mutual protection, and besides it is difficult to travel much faster on jungle roads.

Lima One's assignment—to take Stanleyville—seemed preposterous. They would have to fight their way for some 470 miles over jungle roads that often were scarcely any wider than a vehicle. The route was guarded by thousands of Simba soldiers, as well as thousands of armed *jeunesse* and local tribesmen who sided with the Simbas. Most of the route lay in the Maniema, the homeland of the Simbas. The terrain was such that the defenders could set up ambushes every few hundred yards. In other circumstances, it would have been suicide to attempt the operation. A handful of determined men, well trained in the techniques of modern warfare and armed with machine guns and bazookas, could have annihilated the column.

But Commandant Liégeois was no fool. A veteran of nearly thirty years in the Belgian Army—he had come up through the ranks—Liégeois had spent many years in the Congo with the Force Publique in colonial times. He reckoned that the Simbas, like the ANC, had no heart for determined and sustained combat—and particularly against white troops. For one reason or another, black Africans have never stood up against white troops.* In early 1963, for example, a handful of British troops arrested and disarmed the mutinous armies of Kenya, Uganda and what is now Tanzania without a single British casualty. Liégeois was further encouraged by the fact that other mercenary columns had been bringing off one victory after another, despite overwhelming odds.

But, on the other side of the ledger, there was always the possibility that the Simbas would stage a determined, last-ditch defense in the Maniema and particularly around Stanleyville. And there was an even greater fear that Communist China or other foreign countries would send in "volunteers" to bolster the Simba defenses.

Commandant Liégeois, who was forty-eight years old, was a shy and unassuming little man with a timid voice. He normally was stationed in Belgium, with the Troisième Chasseurs Ardennais, an infantry unit. Early in September, he was sent to the Congo to help reorganize the ANC for the final drive on Stanleyville. Liégeois went to the big military base in Kamina, where, with other Belgian officers similarly on loan to the Congolese government, he helped organize the influx of arms, ammunition, vehicles and other supplies.

Late in September, an ANC unit, unaided by mercenaries, brought off a real victory: they took back the town of Kongolo, which is on the left bank of the Lualaba, as the upper portion of the Congo River is called. Liégeois moved to Kongolo and spent four weeks hastily recruiting and training a new ANC unit from among a group of Katangese who had fought, more or less, as gendarmes for Tshombe in the Katanga wars.

---

*The disastrous defeat on January 22, 1879 of British troops at Isandhlwana by a Zulu army is the first exception to this "rule" that comes to mind.

The original plan was to have three hundred Europeans, 1,800 Congolese and two hundred vehicles in the column. But the operation was plagued with problems from the start. Some of Hoare's English-speaking mercenaries were scattered elsewhere in the Congo. When he arrived at Kongolo on October 31, he had only about one hundred men. Liégeois, moreover, was able to acquire only fifty vehicles, and he had recruited only 500 Katangese soldiers. But there was room in the trucks for only 150 of them—the rest were left behind.

And so it was under the most inauspicious circumstances that Lima One rolled out of Kongolo on November 1, heading down the left bank of the Lualaba River over a road that roughly paralleled the Albertville-to-Kindu railway. The column made no attempt to catch the Simbas by surprise. That would have been impossible in any case because of the roar of the engines and the clouds of dust. The column traveled instead in what was known as "Belgian style." This was a technique developed by the Belgians in carrying out punitive raids in colonial times. The column fired thousands of rounds of ammunition each day, killing a few and scattering many. The noise could be heard for miles. The aim was to strike fear into the hearts of the Simba defenders.

The Ferret and Sons of Bitches led the way. In the Ferret were two men—a white mercenary named Frenchie, who operated the .30-calibre machine gun, and a Congolese driver. Frenchie was a Frenchman in his early forties who had worked in South Africa's gold mines for many years. He was immensely popular with the Congolese troops as he was a warrior in the old African style. Frenchie gave no quarter to anyone in his gunsights. He fired without hesitation at suspicious clumps of trees, abandoned vehicles, huts and, now and then, people. All the while, his Congolese driver was grinning hugely.

Soon after leaving Kongolo, Lima One came to the Mulongoie River, a tributary of the Lualaba. The Simbas had destroyed the bridge sometime previously. But this posed no problem; Liégeois had sent an ANC engineering platoon, led by two Belgian noncommissioned officers, to the Mulongoie two days earlier and they had constructed a temporary span.

Soon after, Lima One halted for the night. The men piled out of the trucks, covered with dust and bone-weary from bumping along the potholed jungle roads all day. They had a meal of cold C-rations, then stretched out in the backs of the trucks and on the ground. Most people would be horrified at the thought of sleeping on the ground in Africa at night. The jungle abounds in poisonous snakes and insects of all kinds. But many of the mercenaries had, like the Katangese troops, been born in Africa and they thought nothing of it.

The column was under way again soon after dawn. Now what had seemed to be an outing became more of an ordeal. The sun burned fiercely overhead. Clothes were soaked with perspiration. A fine, red, choking dust, thrown up by the wheels of the trucks, penetrated layers of clothing and caked on the skin. Some of the men had bottles of water that had been purified by chemicals, but it became too hot to drink. Obsessions formed. Some of the men could think of nothing but a cold beer or a dish of ice cream. Whenever the column halted, the men threw caution to the winds and drank from streams and ponds along the road. Soon some were seized with cramps that signal the onset of diarrhea.

The mercenaries were, of course, expendable. No one had bothered to issue them insect repellents. Their bodies were covered with so many mosquito and gnat bites that it looked as if they had measles. Some units had malaria suppressant tablets; others did not. But most of the men were too tired at the end of the day to go and get a tablet, even if one were available. Some of the men began to run fevers; the eyes hurt, the heads ached. That was the onset of malaria. There was no doctor in the column. Medical supplies consisted only of first-aid items.

Nerves were soon frayed. The Katangese were sick with fright and the white men were not much better off. Whenever a shot was fired, scores of men would open up with their automatic weapons, spraying blindly into the jungle. But they never knew where the enemy was. A man in the jungle was invisible even a dozen yards from the road.

There was a lot of ill will between the English-speaking mercenaries and the Belgian mercenaries. The English-speaking mercenaries felt that the Belgians were trying to undercut them. The Belgians regarded the Congo as their domain and resented the presence and influence of other foreigners. At one time, Belgian animosity was directed at the Americans.

Now it had shifted to the South Africans and Rhodesians, who, the Belgians felt, were trying to supplant them in the Congo. The South Africans and Rhodesians complained that Belgian military advisers had held back on arms, ammunition and other supplies for the English-speaking commandos.

From time to time, rivalries between the two groups of mercenaries would explode into fistfights. On some occasions, shots were exchanged, but no one seems to have been hit.

Soon after leaving Kongolo, the column entered the Maniema. Most of the men had never been there before, yet in a historical sense they were not really strangers. The history of the Maniema was written in blood. It was the region in which entire tribes were decimated by the Arab slavers and their African allies. The Maniema later on had been ravaged by the mutinous Force Publique troops of the Batetela tribe. Now the Maniema would see some more bloodshed.

The second day after leaving Kongolo, the column reached the town of Samba—Soumialot's home town. The Simbas had abandoned it without a fight. Next day they reached the Lufubu River, another tributary of the Lualaba. The bridge was still up, but the Simbas had destroyed the approaches. The men built a raft and took their vehicles across, one by one.

On the afternoon of November 4, Lima One reached Kibombo. The Simbas made a half-hearted attempt to defend the town and the mercenaries traded fire with snipers for several minutes, killing many and putting the rest to flight.

After the shooting had died down, Lieutenant Alan Stevens, a young Rhodesian, was sitting on the front of the Ferret talking with Frenchie, when an ANC soldier came up and said, "Come with me." The Congolese led them a short distance, then pointed ahead. Going closer, the two men saw a white man lying in the road. Part of his head and face had been blown off by a shotgun blast. The man was still alive.

Stevens sent for a doctor. The ANC soldier pointed to the verandah of a nearby home. Three elderly white men seemed to be sitting motionless in deck chairs. When Stevens went near, he saw that each had been killed by point-blank shotgun blasts. Two had been hit in the stomach, one in the chest. The young lieutenant stared at the bodies for several moments. "Christ!" he said. He had seen violent death before— with the British army in Cyprus—but one never really gets used to it.

A young doctor arrived to treat the wounded man. He turned the man over, looked incredulously at his ruined face and gasped. The doctor raised his eyes to the sky and gritted his teeth. Then he attempted to do something for the man. But everyone knew it was hopeless.

Kibombo was the first town up the route from Kongolo where the Simbas had executed white hostages in revenge for their mounting defeats. But it would not be the last.

Commandant Liégeois was summoned. The wounded man managed to tell the Belgian officer that the Simbas were holding about 125 European hostages in Kindu, seventy-five miles to the north. Then the man died. Liégeois was alarmed. He ordered his men to get ready to move out at once; they might be able to reach Kindu in time to avert more killings.

Just before Lima One left Kibombo, they found a Portuguese who had managed to hide from the Simbas. He was the only European left in town. Liégeois took him along.

Just after dark, the column encountered the first of the Simbas' improvised armored cars. They had welded steel plates to the vehicle and had mounted a .50-calibre machine gun on it. But Frenchie was quicker than the Simbas. He opened fire from the Ferret and knocked out the armored car, killing two men in it. The column was ambushed several times that evening. Some Simbas fired at them from the jungle. Others sniped from high up in the trees where it was almost impossible to spot them. Miraculously no one was hit by the Simba fire.

At midafternoon the next day, Lima One was at the outskirts of Kindu. The men felt that the Simbas would surely make a determined stand in that city. Kindu was, after all, the capital of the Maniema, the province in which the Simbas enjoyed their greatest popular support. Before Lima One staged the attack, they waited until B-26 fighter-bombers, piloted by Cuban mercenaries, had strafed the Simba positions with rockets and machine guns.

The English-speaking mercenaries in the column noted with wry humor that it was the fifth of November—Guy

Fawkes Day—in England. The British celebrate the day with fireworks and bonfires. It marks the anniversary of the discovery of a plot, in 1605, to blow up the British Parliament. "Remember, remember, the fifth of November," an old saying goes. General Olenga would never forget that fifth of November in Kindu.

After the B-26's had finished their work, Lima One roared into Kindu at top speed. "Don't stop," Liégeois had told the men. "Go straight through to the river, to the ferry and the railway station. Then turn around, come back through the town and mop up."

The Simbas opened up with heavy fire. The trucks roared straight at them, with the mercenaries and Katangese troops blazing away with automatic weapons. It was, one mercenary said, like a Wild West show. The Simbas were mowed down by the dozens. Simba trucks exploded and burst into flames. Other Simbas retreated, firing back as they went.

"I had a vision of intense color," Lieutenant Stevens said. "I had been told by old soldiers that when you're really excited and scared and you're firing madly all the colors around you are magnified. The burning trucks were brilliantly red and the houses were brilliantly brown. The noise was just incredible—it was invigorating."

The mercenaries fought their way toward the ferry landing at the Lualaba. As they did, several carloads of Simbas raced to the landing. The Simbas jumped out of the cars and onto the ferry and other boats. They pushed out into the Lualaba, which is about half a mile wide at that point. When the mercenaries reached the landing, they opened up on the ferry and the other boats, raking them from stem to stern. They killed more than 250 Simbas. The warm, muddy brown waters of the Lualaba took on, some said, a reddish tint.

The mercenaries raced around the town, still firing wildly, searching for the European hostages. Fear rose that they had been killed, but finally they were found, safe but thoroughly terrified. In another few minutes, there would have been a massacre.

The Simbas had selected twenty-four of the local European men. They were stripped to their shorts and lined up outside a house for execution. A group of Congolese children, some of them only eight or ten years old, were told to think up ways to kill the men. "Cut that one's ear off and make him eat it," a child piped up. "Put his eyes out," another suggested. But, before the slaughter could start, the Simbas heard shooting in the distance. They ordered the Europeans into the house. The Simbas came back a few minutes later and told the hostages to come out. But the men barricaded themselves in the house and stayed there until the mercenaries arrived.

Sten Gun

There were, in all, about 125 Europeans in Kindu, mostly Belgians and Greeks. They had been held prisoner since July 22. During that time, the rebels had killed four Europeans. One Belgian woman lost her husband and two sons—the *jeunesse* speared and knifed the men to death before her eyes. The murders had been committed three months earlier, but the woman was still crazed with grief.

The Simbas were even more barbaric toward Congolese "intellectuals" and people who had been associated in one way or another with the old regime. During the three and a half months that they held Kindu, they killed more than eight hundred Congolese at the local Lumumba Monument. Many were drenched with gasoline, then set afire. The pavement around the monument was blackened and cracked by the flames.

One of the first things that Lima One did after taking Kindu was to blow up the monument.

While fighting was still going on in town, cargo planes were circling overhead, waiting to land. One mercenary column was sent to take the airfield. The Simbas

198

tried to defend it with a machine gun, but the mercenaries killed the defenders and captured the weapon. The Simbas had covered the landing strip with barrels to keep planes from landing, but the mercenaries quickly rolled them aside.

The Simbas suffered terrible casualties in Kindu. Some men who were in the Lima One column said hundreds were killed. Others insisted that the toll ran into the thousands. No one kept track. One mercenary sergeant, a fellow with a troublesome conscience, said: "After the air strike by the B-26's, the carnage was let loose. We shot everything and everybody. Now I am the first one to confess that many people were killed in Kindu who need not necessarily have been killed. But these are very, very difficult things. We found so many times that we didn't shoot somebody and later on he shot one of our men. So we just cleaned everthing that we could see. I should imagine in Kindu we must have shot at least three thousand people. I'll be honest with you: most of them unnecessarily. But it was necessary to do it because we didn't know that it was not necessary."

When it came to deliberate slaughter, no one could surpass the ANC. The ANC troops had no heart for a real fight; they brought up the rear. But, after Kindu had been secured, the ANC commenced the *ratissage*, the raking up. One mercenary, who was no angel himself, said: "The only difference between the ANC and the rebels was that they fought for different causes—that's all. Otherwise they're the same people. They have a different conception of war than we. The ANC's idea is that all civilians in a rebel area are rebels. Finish. End. They should all be annihilated."

One group of mercenaries piled several Simba bodies in a canoe, intending to shove it out into the current and let it float downstream. A Simba appeared and tried to shoot them with a Sten submachine gun, but the Sten jammed. The mercenaries took the weapon away from him and told him to get into the canoe. He did so without a flicker of emotion, unbuttoned his shirt and turned his bare chest to the mercenaries. They shot him in the chest. He fell over into the dead heap. The mercenaries shoved off the canoe. In a moment, it was gone.

The mercenaries had won Kindu. But they had missed an important prize. One of the few Simbas who managed to

C-124 Globemaster

get away alive across the Lualaba was Nicolas Olenga. The mercenaries found Olenga's Mercedes car and chauffeur. Olenga was said to have taken off his uniform and put it on the chauffeur and then to have fled in civilian dress.

The day after Kindu fell, Michael Hoare and his English-speaking mercenaries went out on a special mission to the tin-mining town of Kalima, forty miles to the east. It was not a mission for loot or glory, but rather to rescue ninety-seven Europeans who were being held hostage in that town. Even those who were most critical of the mercenaries had to concede that they displayed heroism in volunteering for missions of that sort.

When Hoare's column reached Kalima, they found the hostages huddled in a church. They had been beaten and threatened with death, but none had been killed. Hoare had brought up trucks for their evacuation. The Belgians pushed and jostled as each tried to get on the trucks first. Some demanded that they be allowed to pack their belongings. But Hoare had to get the hostages back to Kindu quickly before the Simbas could counter-attack. The Belgians argued and shouted. Hoare lost his temper. "Get on those trucks—leave your bloody goods behind," he bellowed. Muttering angrily, the Belgians climbed aboard.

Some twenty dogs that had been pets of the Belgians milled around the trucks. "Go ahead—take your dogs on the trucks," Hoare said. But no one responded. The trucks started off to Kindu. The dogs ran along behind, looking up at their masters. Soon their tongues were hanging out. One after another, they dropped in the road from exhaustion. The English-speaking mercenaries, who had the British fondness for dogs, were horrified. "I felt like crying and I almost did," said one young man who has killed so many Simbas and Congolese in general that he has long since lost track of the count. It was, the mercenaries declared, no way to treat a dog.

Soon after the capture of Kindu, one of Hoare's units was sent to hold a river bridge seventeen miles north of the city. The mercenaries dug in on the south bank of the river. The day after their arrival, they were attacked by about sixty pro-Simba villagers, armed with spears, machetes, bows and arrows and a few rifles. The villagers had a sublime faith in their witch doctors. They marched smartly across the bridge chanting, *"Mai, mai."* The mercenaries killed every one of them.

The mercenaries became cocksure. There was no need, they felt, to take up defensive positions at the bridge. They figured it was a waste of time to dig foxholes. They simply camped in the open, as if it were a holiday outing. Each morning the men went through a standard British army routine. The men were awakened at 5 A.M. At 5:15, there would be a "stand-to." Each man would take up his assigned position on the camp perimeter. Then, at 5:45, a whistle would be blown to "stand-down." The men would shave, wash and brew tea for breakfast.

The Simbas were watching, hidden in the trees on the other side of the river, two hundred yards away. They were not simple villagers like those who had staged the suicidal attack on the mercenaries a few days earlier. They were, instead, elite Simba troops who had just come down from Stanleyville in twelve trucks. There were 156 of them. They watched the mercenaries for several days until they knew every detail of the white men's routine. They knew, for example, that just after the 5:45 "stand-down," the men would be totally unprepared to resist an attack.

And so, a few moments after 5:45 one morning, when the mercenaries had their faces lathered, a tremendous explosion suddenly shook the camp. The men were astonished. They looked around. Then one, more experienced in such matters than the rest, shouted, "Mortar!" The mercenaries fell flat on their faces. More mortar shells came arching across the river. Each time there was a swishing sound, followed by a ground-shaking explosion. Next the Simbas opened up with a .50-calibre machine-gun and two .30's.

One man was killed—the unit's commanding officer, Lieutenant Jeremy Spencer, an upper-class Englishman, who had come to the Congo to seek adventure. Spencer was sitting in a deck chair when he was killed. He had been waving a captured Simba sword, with the indifference to danger that men of his class are taught to assume.

The rest of the mercenaries lay on the ground, cursing their negligence in not digging foxholes. They had mortars of their own, but could not use them; the charges had gotten wet during the night. They thought of radioing for air support, but then remembered that Kindu would not come on the air until seven o'clock. They lay there for an hour, then, at seven o'clock, sent word to Kindu.

It was all over in a very short time. A Cuban-piloted B-26 roared in at tree-top level and let loose four rockets which slammed into the Simba positions. Then another mercenary unit, which had been sent up from Kindu by road, charged across the bridge and routed the remaining Simbas. A pay list, giving the names of 156 Simbas, was found on the body of an officer.

It was the only big attack that the Simbas staged on the road to Stanleyville.

The mercenaries stayed at the bridge for several more days, waiting for Lima One and Lima Two to form up for the final push. But in the meantime, there was a little problem. There were sixty-three bodies around the far end of the bridge—as well as forty others in the jungle beyond. And, as a mercenary officer related: "These bodies were sprawled all over the place and to tidy things up, because they do smell, you know—after two days they stink—we piled those bodies in a bloody great big heap—just like a pyramid—with the intention of burning them. They were fresh; we don't mind carting fresh bodies around. We piled them into this large pile, poured diesel oil over them and set light to them. But of course this didn't destroy them. What we should have done was immediately to throw them into the river. But we didn't."

White men who go to Africa to kill animals—elephant, rhino, lion and other such creatures—customarily have their photographs taken sitting atop the lifeless carcass of the victim. So it was with the mercenaries; several of them climbed to the top of their little pyramid and had themselves photographed.

14

PHANTOMS IN RED HATS

At 2 A.M. on November 18, a huge C-130E transport plane of the U.S. Air Force landed at a Strategic Air Command base near Morón de la Frontera, in southern Spain, not far from Seville. It was followed, at intervals, by fourteen other C-130E's. The four-engine turboprop planes had touched down at Morón to refuel. Only a few top officers at the base knew where they had come from and where they were going. To the others, it was a mystery.

An American major disembarked to supervise the refueling. He made sure that the doors of the planes remained closed so the ground crews could not see what was in them. But someone opened the rear door of one of the planes to get fresh air, and an airman from one of the ground crews peeked in.

The airman was astonished. Turning to the major, he said: "Who are those guys in red hats?"

"What guys in red hats?" the major replied.

"*Them* guys in red hats!"

"*What* guys in red hats?"

The airman took a second look. Officers, after all, are always supposed to be right. But, sure enough, the plane was filled with men who were wearing red headgear—men who, moreover, were jabbering in a strange tongue.

"Them guys, major—right there in the plane," the airman said.

C-97

The major closed the door. "There's nobody in there with red hats," he said.

As soon as the planes were refueled, they taxied out to the runway. Then they took off and disappeared into the night sky, taking with them the phantoms in red hats.

Ten days earlier, on Sunday, November 8, a limousine pulled up in front of 3038 N Street, in the fashionable George-town area of Washington, D.C. From it stepped a big, bald, bespectacled man—Paul-Henri Spaak, the sixty-five-year-old foreign minister of Belgium. Spaak had come to lunch with an old friend, W. Averell Harriman, the seventy-two-year-old statesman who ranked number three at the time in the State Department hierarchy. Spaak and Harriman had known each other well since the early postwar years in Europe when they worked together on the Marshall Plan.

The two men talked at length about the plight of the white hostages in the Congo. Next day, they resumed their talks with Secretary of State Dean Rusk, in Rusk's office on the seventh floor of the State Department building.

Spaak and the Americans were greatly worried over the safety of the hostages. They knew that the European population of Kindu had been saved from a massacre only by the sudden arrival of the ANC and the mercenaries. And they knew, from radio-monitoring facilities, of Gbenye's statement that all Americans and Belgians in Stanleyville were "prisoners of war."

Harriman had for some time favored the idea of sending American troops to Stanleyville, if necessary, to rescue the hostages. Now Spaak proposed that the two countries intervene jointly if diplomatic moves should fail. Said one high ranking official of the State Department: "Everyone except for Harriman was very cool to Spaak's idea. But Spaak twisted their arms and they didn't refuse."

Spaak proposed that Belgian troops be used, should military intervention be decided upon. The American official agreed. The advantage was that Belgian troops spoke French and many had had experience in the Congo. Belgian troops, moreover, were widely respected—or, feared—in the Congo. Belgium, however, did not have the necessary long-range military aircraft. The United States would supply the planes.

Neither Spaak nor the Americans abandoned the hope that they could get the hostages out of Stanleyville by means of diplomatic moves, particularly through the Organization of African Unity. There was always a hope, albeit a faint one, that the Simba authorities might allow the Red Cross to arrange an evacuation. But the situation was critical. In order to be ready for anything that might develop orders were given for Belgian and American military officers to draw up contingency plans for rescuing the white hostages in Stanleyville.

It was 10 P.M. on Tuesday, November 10, in Paris—P.M. Washington time. Russell Dougherty, a forty-four-year-old brigadier general in the U.S. Air Force, arrived with his wife at the Continental Hotel at 3 Rue Castiglione in Paris for a U.S. marine ball. As they were checking their coats, Dougherty was called aside by another officer and told: "Call your boss right away; there may be a job for you."

Dougherty got in touch with his superior officer, Major General Arthur W. Oberbeck, of the U.S. European Command at Camp des Loges, just outside Paris. Oberbeck told Dougherty to stand by for important orders that were on their way from Washington. Dougherty danced with his wife for a while, but he was too curious about the forthcoming orders to enjoy the ball. The couple left just after midnight and returned to their home in La Celle St. Cloud, a suburb of Paris.

At 5:30 A.M., Dougherty saw a courier arrive at Oberbeck's house, which was next door. Dougherty went over. A message had just come in from the Joint Chiefs of Staff in Washington, ordering that an officer be sent to Brussels to meet with Belgian officers and draw up contingency plans for a rescue mission to Stanleyville.

"It looks like I've got a job to do," said Dougherty.

"Yes—like right now," General Oberbeck replied.

Dougherty changed into civilian clothes. The operation was top secret and he was told not to draw attention to himself by wearing his uniform. The weather was too bad for flying that morning, so Dougherty had an airman drive him to Brussels. By now it was the morning of the 11th—Armistice Day—and the roads were relatively free of traffic. Dougherty had been up all night and he slept in the back seat most of the way. He reached Brussels at noon, after a four-hour drive.

Other American officers, similarly dressed in civilian clothes, were also arriving at Brussels. One, Lieutenant Colonel James Dunn, came from Washington as a representative of the Joint Chiefs of Staff. Another, Lieutenant Colonel James Gray, came from Lindsay Air Station, in Wiesbaden, Germany, representing the U.S. air force in Europe.

The officers conferred with officials of the American embassy and with representatives of the Belgian foreign ministry. They knew that the ANC-mercenary column was at Kindu, but that it would not reach Stanleyville until late in the month. There was every chance that the column would take Stanleyville, but it might be stalled on the edge of the city by heavy resistance; the Simbas would, in the meantime, seek their revenge on the helpless hostages.

"There's a good chance of mass murder," one official said.

On Thursday, the 12th, General Dougherty and the others were taken to the Belgian ministry of national defense, which is housed in a cold, damp and rather decrepit building at No. 2 Rue de la Loi, in downtown Brussels. There they were introduced to several Belgian officers, including the man who would lead the rescue operation at Stanleyville— Colonel Charles Laurent.

Colonel Laurent, who was fifty-one years old, was a short but sturdily built man. He was nearly bald and wore glasses when reading. When not in uniform, he could easily be taken for a schoolteacher or obscure civil servant. Laurent had been a professional soldier for nearly thirty years. He had made more than three hundred parachute jumps, and had been a prisoner of war for five years in Germany during World War II. On one occasion, he rode a motorcycle from Belgium to Katanga—a trip that took two months. He was no stranger to Stanleyville, either; in 1950, he made a practice jump on the airport. And, in 1960, he led the Belgian paratroopers who seized the Léopoldville airport from mutinous Congolese soldiers.

Laurent was now the commanding officer of the Para-commando Regiment, Belgium's elite military unit. He had already decided that if he were ordered to Stanleyville he would use one of his three battalions—the First Parachutist Battalion. That unit had been formed in England during World War II among Belgians who had fled across the channel to carry on the fight against the Germans. It was then a part of the British Special Air Service. The battalion landed in Normandy with allied forces and fought as well in the Ardennes, Holland, Germany and Denmark. Today, the battalion still uses the motto, in English, of the SAS—"Who Dares Wins"—and it continues to wear the Pegasus emblem of British airborne forces. And the men wear red hats—or, more properly, red berets.

Colonel Laurent and General Dougherty, together with their aides, drew up plans for a rescue operation. Monday, November 23, was set as a tentative target date. The Americans agreed to put twelve C-130E's at the disposal of the Belgians for carrying troops. There would be three other C-130Es in the armada, a maintenance plane, a communications plane and one spare aircraft. The plan was that five of the planes would come in over Stanleyville airport just as dawn was breaking. They would fly at a very low altitude— only seven hundred feet—and drop 320 paratroopers. If they could secure the field and clear it of obstacles, seven more planes would land with 225 other paratroopers aboard. Then the men would race into the city to rescue the hostages.

From a military point of view, the operation would be risky. A handful of well-trained Simba machine gunners—or foreign "advisers"—could create great havoc as the planes came over the airport. The planes, which would approach Stanleyville at 230 knots, would have to slow down to 125 knots when they came over the field so that the paratroopers could jump without dispersing themselves too widely. The planes would, as a result, be highly vulnerable to ground fire for the forty-two seconds that each would be over the field.

But Colonel Laurent and the other Belgians were confident that they could take the airfield with few if any casualties. They knew from intelligence reports that the Simbas had .50-calibre machine-guns, but they reckoned that the guns would not be manned, or, even if they were manned, that they would not be fired with any precision. They were fairly certain that there were no Chinese Communists or other foreign military "advisers" in Stanleyville.

"What code name will we give to the operation?" one officer asked.

They thought a moment, then Laurent said, "Why don't we call it the 'Dragon'? Stanleyville will be the Dragon Rouge— the Red Dragon. If there are other operations, we can give them different colors."

"Fine," said an American officer. "How do you spell *rouge*?"

The officers knew that the planes would not be given permission to overfly African countries en route to the Congo. After the British government gave its consent, plans were made to fly to Ascension Island, a British possession in the South Atlantic, seven hundred miles off the coast of Africa. From Ascension, the planes would continue to Kamina in the Congo.

General Dougherty and the American officers went to the American embassy after the meeting and worked all night writing up their plans in longhand. They did not ask for a stenographer because the operation was top secret.

The Americans had another meeting with Colonel Laurent and his Belgian aides on Friday the 13th. Then they went back to their bases. The machinery was now in motion, and it affected, in one way or another, thousands of men scattered across half of the world.

Colonel Laurent was almost certain the men would not be sent to Stanleyville. He felt that the operation was fraught with so many political consequences that it would, in all likelihood, be called off. But it was his job to get ready, in case the paratroopers were needed, so he returned to his headquarters in Namur, a town on the Meuse River, thirty-five miles southeast of Brussels.

Laurent sent for the commanding officer of the First Battalion—Major Jean Mine. The First Battalion was stationed in another city—Diest, about thirty miles north and east of Brussels. As it turned out, Mine was already in Namur. He had come to ask Laurent if he could take two days' leave so he could visit his elderly parents, who were living in a village in the Ardennes forest.

Major Mine, forty-two years old, was a husky and balding man, nearly six feet tall. He was friendly and easygoing and presided over the First Battalion like a sort of benign headmaster. Mine had been a professional soldier for twenty-five years. He participated in the futile Belgian defense against the German onslaught in 1940, was captured and spent a year and a half in a German prisoner-of-war camp. But he escaped, made his way to England and joined a Belgian infantry brigade that was being formed there. Mine landed in Normandy with the allied forces and fought in France, Belgium and Holland. It was his pleasure to participate in the liberation of Brussels. After the war, he became a paratrooper and made 150 jumps. Like most of the other officers, he had served in the Congo.

One big problem which confronted Laurent and Mine was that one company of the First Battalion was on ceremonial guard duty at the Royal Palace in Brussels and was scheduled to remain there until Monday the 16th. The entire battalion, moreover, had been scheduled to participate in a parade in Brussels on Sunday, the 15th—a parade marking the birthday of King Baudouin. Laurent was under orders to maintain top secrecy. He did not want to pull the men away from the palace or withdraw the battalion from the parade because it would arouse suspicions. But the battalion might be ordered to move out any day.

As it turned out, the departure was finally set for Tuesday, the 17th. The battalion paraded in Brussels that Sunday. The company that had been guarding the palace was relieved on Sunday, a day early. All of the men were brought back that afternoon to their base in the Citadel of Diest, a damp nineteenth-century fortress that is shrouded in fog most days of the winter. The men were confined to barracks. Phone and mail service were cut off, and the men were told they were going on a NATO exercise.

The first battalion was to be reinforced for the Stanleyville operation with one company of the second battalion. Although the officers and noncoms in each battalion were all professional soldiers, the privates were young men who were doing their national military service and who had volunteered as paratroopers. Those in the first battalion had had eleven and a half months of training; those in the second, only five and a half months.

While the men waited in Diest, they got their weapons and other equipment ready. Because of the weight problem, they could not take heavy mortars along. They would, in fact, be very lightly armed. They were expected to make up for it in speed and surprise. The paratroopers would take just four armored jeeps, each of which was equipped with three light machine guns, and eleven little tricycle-type vehicles that can carry three men cross-country. Everyone in the battalion was a fighting man; typists and cooks, for example, doubled as mortar crews. Each man was given an FN 7.62 automatic rifle—the standard NATO weapon—with one hundred rounds of ammunition as well as two grenades. Others had machine guns, 83-mm. bazookas, grenade launchers and 60-mm. light mortars.

Colonel Laurent packed his personal belongings. He took his pistol and a notebook to be used as a battle diary. Inasmuch as the paratroopers had to travel lightly, he left behind his binoculars. He did take a bathing suit, for use at Ascension Island, and an old raincoat he had used in the Congo in former years.

"I'm leaving for an operation, but a final decision has not

been taken on whether we will go through with it," Laurent told his wife. "We are simply going to a camp to get ready."

Mrs. Laurent was a paratrooper's wife. She had been reading about Stanleyville in the newspapers. She did not have to ask; she knew what was afoot.

Early in the evening of Saturday the 14th, Colonel Burgess Gradwell, the commander of two C-130 squadrons based at Evreux, a town in Normandy, returned to his home near the base. Gradwell was tired; he had been in Germany on Air Force business that day and he looked forward to a quiet weekend with his wife and two teen-age children. But the phone rang. Gradwell was told to report in the morning to the headquarters of his unit, the 322nd Air Division, in Châteauroux, France. There went his weekend.

Next morning, Gradwell was plagued first by bad weather and then by mechanical troubles. It was not until Sunday evening that he arrived at Châteauroux. He went at once to the Operations Command Post of the base, where he was met by his superior officer, Brigadier General Robert D. Forman. The general handed Gradwell a copy of the Dragon Rouge plan that had been drawn up in Brussels a few days previously.

"Pack your bags, boy; it looks like you're going," Forman said.

Gradwell, who was forty-five years old and came from Oneida, New York, was a small man—five feet six inches tall—who bubbled over with good spirits. He had been in the Air Force for twenty-four years and had flown transport planes all that time. He moved men and cargo around during the campaigns in North Africa, Sicily, Italy and France. For a time he flew supplies to Tito's partisans in Yugoslavia. He dropped arms to Polish patriots during the Battle of Warsaw. In 1960, Gradwell was one of the American pilots who airlifted UN troops to the Congo. Next year, during the Tshombe secession, he flew Irish troops of the UN command to Katanga. On one such mission, his plane, a C-124 Globemaster, was hit nearly twenty-five times by Tshombe's soldiers while coming in for a landing at Elisabethville. Gradwell unloaded the Irish soldiers and then limped back to Kamina on three engines.

After receiving the Dragon Rouge plans, one of Gradwell's

first tasks was to assemble the planes. Some were on routine missions elsewhere in Europe; one was in Libya. All were called back to Evreux and serviced.

The C-130E, nicknamed the Hercules, is not particularly large as modern transport planes go. But it is a highly versatile aircraft. Built by Lockheed and costing more than $2.2 million each, these planes can carry sixty-four fully-equipped paratroopers or ninety-two ordinary passengers or cargo, or various combinations of each. They can take off from rough airstrips less than three thousand feet in length, climb to altitudes in excess of thirty thousand feet and cruise at six miles a minute—all with heavy payloads.

As part of the preparations for the Stanleyville mission, two HC-97 air-rescue planes, a version of the C-97 transports, were readied. One would be stationed at Ascension, the other at Léopoldville. If a C-130E went down at sea, the HC-97's would drop life rafts and other supplies and would also drop rescue personnel by parachute. A fleet of nine C-124 Globemaster transports was also told to stand by to carry food and other supplies. Four other C-124's were to be sent directly to Kamina, carrying two big tank trucks that would refuel the C-130Es on the ground.

There were a thousand details to arrange. Someone, for example, suggested that portable loudspeakers, or bullhorns, be taken along so that the troops could call to hostages who might be hiding in houses in Stanleyville. After a flurry of phone calls, Air Force officers located twelve bullhorns and put them aboard. Ten tons of C-rations were collected to feed people who would be evacuated. The U.S. Army in Europe supplied 550 cots, as well as tents, for the paratroopers to use while at Ascension. Then an officer remembered that the island is covered with volcanic ash and rock; it might not be possible to drive ordinary wooden tent pegs into the ground. After another flurry of phone calls, the U.S. Army came up with steel pegs.

There was another detail. The Simbas might shoot some of the hostages. The Belgian paratroopers were bringing three doctors with them. The U.S. Air Force assigned one of its flight surgeons to the mission; he packed a complete set of operating equipment, as well as intravenous fluids, compression bandages and splints.

* * *

At six o'clock on the evening of Saturday the 14th, Radio Stanleyville announced that "Major" Paul Carlson had been sentenced to death by a "war council tribunal." Carlson, the announcer said, had been defended by Congolese lawyers "of his own choosing." The announcer added that the Stanleyville government had agreed "in principle" to an offer by Michael Hoyt, the U.S. consul, to "negotiate" Carlson's fate.

Carlson knew nothing of the "trial." Neither had Hoyt made any offer of "negotiations." The Simba authorities made that up of whole cloth, but they knew what they were doing. They were holding a loaded pistol at Carlson's head and telling the outside world and especially the American government that he would be murdered if the advance on Stanleyville were not halted.

In Alhambra, California, Dr. Carlson's elderly mother, Mrs. Ruth Carlson, suffered a heart attack. She had not been told of the death sentence, but she collapsed from the strain of worrying about him.

On the same day that Radio Stanleyville announced the death sentence, the newspaper *Le Martyr* published on its front page a statement from Gbenye which said:

> We hold in our claws more than 300 Americans and more than 800 Belgians, who are kept under surveillance and in secure places. At the slightest bombardment of our region or of our revolutionary capital, we shall be forced to massacre them.
>
> All Americans and Belgians living under our protection have written and signed their last will. We shall send these documents shortly to their respective destinations. The security of these individuals is subject to the retreat from the Congo of the Belgians and the Americans who massacre our people continuously.
>
> We shall make fetishes with the hearts of the Americans and the Belgians and we shall dress ourselves in the skins of the Belgians and the Americans.

After the announcement on Saturday, Radio Stanleyville fell silent for several days about Carlson's fate. But his plight

214

caught the attention and sympathy of millions of people. He was not the only person in Stanleyville who was threatened with death, but his case seemed especially poignant. He had gone to the Congo to help the Congolese people, and, after taking his wife and children to safety, he had gone back to Wasolo, "the lost corner," rather than abandon his patients.

On Monday the 16th, Secretary of State Dean Rusk sent a message to Jomo Kenyatta, the prime minister of Kenya, who headed the Congo committee of the Organization of African Unity, asking Kenyatta to use his influence to have Carlson spared. Rusk said: "The United States government declares unequivocally that Dr. Carlson is not in any way connected with the U.S. military and has been engaged only in his activities as a medical missionary. Dr. Carlson is a man of peace who has served the Congolese people with dedication and faith for three and a half years, taking care of the sick and wounded including members of the rebel forces. His execution on charges which are patently false would be an outrageous violation of international law and of accepted standards of humanitarian conduct."

Rusk also urged Kenyatta once more to try to induce the Stanleyville regime to admit a Red Cross delegation.

That same Monday, the U.S. and Belgian governments, worried over the fate of Carlson and the other hostages and alarmed at the increasingly desperate tone of Radio Stanleyville, flashed the word to Colonels Laurent and Gradwell. They were told to move out to Ascension Island on Tuesday the 17th.

The first C-130E took off from Evreux at 7 P.M., followed, at ten-minute intervals, by fourteen others. The planes headed northeast, crossing over the French provinces of Normandy, Ile de France and Picardy. After an eighty-minute flight, they were over Kleine-Brogel, a NATO base in northeast Belgium, close by the border with Holland. The airfield was obscured by fog and rain and the planes had to land by radar. A "follow-me" vehicle led them to a hangar where Colonel Laurent and his paratroopers were waiting.

Gradwell and Laurent introduced themselves. The paratroopers and their equipment were loaded into the planes. Although the senior officers knew that Stanleyville might be

215

their ultimate destination, the Belgian paratroopers were told only that they were going "to southern Europe or perhaps a bit further." American crews were told at each stop only what their next destination would be. Gradwell, meanwhile, was in contact with U.S. Air Force headquarters in Wiesbaden. There was some delay. Then an officer at the other end of the line said:

"We have just received the signal: Go."

The first plane, with Gradwell and Laurent aboard, took off at 10:30 P.M., climbed to nearly twenty thousand feet and headed southwest twelve hundred miles to Morón de la Frontera, in Spain. They stopped ninety minutes for refueling at Morón, during which time the inquisitive airman got a look at the red berets of the paratroopers, and then took off for Ascension. They had to make a long detour around the bulge of West Africa, flying, all the time, at more than five miles above the Atlantic. There was one minor difficulty: the third plane, or "Chalk Three" as it was known in Air Force parlance, developed trouble in one of its engines and had to return to Morón on the remaining three. The maintenance plane accompanied it back to Morón and mechanics quickly fixed the engine. Then Chalk Three and the maintenance aircraft followed the others to Ascension. The little armada flew all the rest of the night and the following morning, touching down at Ascension just after one o'clock on the afternoon of the 18th. They had come 4,298 nautical miles from Kleine-Brogel. Now they would wait for further orders.

Ascension Island is in the middle of nowhere. Volcanic in origin, it stands out as a tiny speck in the South Atlantic, eight degrees below the equator and nearly two thousand miles off the mouth of the Congo River. The island is just thirty-four square miles in size.

Ascension was uninhabited until 1815, when a detachment of British sailors arrived to help guard Napoleon, who had been exiled at St. Helena, seven hundred miles to the southeast. During World War II, the American government built an airstrip on Ascension to serve as a refueling station for bombers that were being ferried from South America to Africa. In recent years, the U.S. Air Force has operated a missile-tracking station on the island.

Desolate and lonely though it was, Ascension was a paradise to the Belgians and Americans who had just come from a chilly, fogbound European winter. The weather was warm. The men sunbathed, swam and went fishing. They caught some strange-looking fish and cooked them at a beach party.

The paratroopers, who ordinarily live a Spartan existence, were amazed and delighted at the facilities provided by the Americans. The men were fed juicy American steaks—all they wanted. There were free movies. Each paratrooper was given $10 and they swarmed into the canteen to buy American beer, cigarettes, candy and other items. The cots did not arrive the first day; they had been put aboard the C-124's, which fly only half as fast as the C-130E's. The men slept on the ground, under tents, the first night.

But there was work to do. Each morning, the paratroopers went through their fitness exercises. The American officers were amazed. In one exercise, for example, the paratroopers did deep knee bends—with another paratrooper perched on their backs. Under the guidance of American officers, the men practiced jumping from the C-130E's—on the ground. They had never jumped from C-130E's before and had to familiarize themselves with the plane.

Hardly any of the Americans spoke French, or, for that matter, Flemish, the other official language of Belgium. But most of the Belgians were fluent in English.

On one occasion, the Belgian officers were briefed on what they could expect to find in Stanleyville by an American named John Clingerman. He had been Michael Hoyt's predecessor as the American consul in that city and had left on July 15, less than three weeks before the Simbas arrived. Clingerman showed the Belgians maps of Stanleyville and marked out thirteen places where hostages might be found—the various hotels and Camp Ketele and other military installations. Each officer was given a copy of the map. Clingerman cautioned the Belgians that the Congolese civilian population was not particularly hostile. And he mentioned the names of various people in Stanleyville to whom the paratroopers could turn for advice—among them Monsignor Fataki, the Congolese prelate; José Romnée, the ex-paratrooper who was the leader of the city's business community; Peter Rombaut, the honorary British consul; and Joseph Guerlach, the acting French consular agent.

Ascension Island was incommunicado. All cable and mail service was interrupted in an effort to preserve top secrecy. Belgium is a tiny country and the departure of its elite battalion was bound to arouse suspicions. In an effort to keep things secret, the Belgian government announced that the men were on a NATO exercise. But newsmen nevertheless learned that the paratroopers had been airlifted to Ascension. And so, reluctantly, the Belgian government was forced, on Friday the 20th, to acknowledge that the men were poised at Ascension for a possible drop on Stanleyville.

Both the Belgians and the Americans at Ascension were aghast at the news leak. Now the Simbas would know of it as well. Perhaps they would fortify the airfield with heavy machine guns. Said one American general: "It was like setting up a shooting gallery. I thought they'd call off the operation after the news got out. It was like dropping men to their deaths."

15

MAJOR CARLSON MUST DIE

"Monsieur Nothomb, you are a lucky man!" the Simba guard exclaimed as he put the young baron into a solitary-confinement cell in Stanleyville's central prison. "Did you know that our beloved leader, Monsieur Lumumba, was imprisoned in this very cell—*your cell*—in 1959?"

Nothomb gave the guard a sour look. But the Simba was not being sarcastic; he spoke in hushed and reverential tones. The cell was a Simba shrine. There was a footprint in the concrete pavement in front of the door—a footprint, the Simbas vowed, that had been made by the imprisoned Lumumba while the concrete was still fresh. All day long, a steady stream of Simba prisoners and guards came to the door of Nothomb's cell. They knelt in adoration. Then they kissed the footprint.

The Belgian consul had been put into solitary as a result of one of those absurdities which seem to flourish in the Congo. Nine months before, Nothomb and his vice-consul, Paul Duqué, had shared an apartment in Léopoldville. Nothomb came home late one night and found that Duqué was still out. So, as an idle joke, he wrote a little note and left it on Duqué's bed: "Soldier Duqué, report tomorrow at the office of Commandant Nothomb and explain your absence."

Duqué chuckled mildly when he saw the note—after all, it was not very funny. He put it in his pocket and forgot about it. Nine months later, after Nothomb and Duqué had

219

been put into prison, the Simbas took Duqué to the Immoquateur to search his apartment. They sifted through mounds of papers and found the note, which, mixed in with other papers, had been brought to Stanleyville by Duqué.

The Simbas gleamed with suspicion. It was proof, they told each other, that the Belgian consul was really a soldier! A *mercenary! A spy!*

"No, no," Duqué wailed. "It's just a joke. The consul could not be a commandant—he's too young for that."

"This is a case for the Sûreté," the Simba leader declared.

Nothomb was put in solitary while the Sûreté investigated the matter. Congolese efficiency being what it was, the Sûreté apparently forgot all about it. They forgot all about Nothomb as well, and he remained in solitary, day after day.

Solitary confinement is a dire punishment for any man. But for Nothomb, who loved people and loved to talk, it was sheer agony. The cell itself was luxurious by prison standards. He had a cot and mattress and a washbasin. There was a little courtyard, surrounded by a high wall, in front of the cell door and Nothomb could venture out into the courtyard if he wished. But he was all alone, left to his thoughts.

The Simbas had a radio in the room next to Nothomb's cell. It was turned in to Radio Stanleyville at full volume. All day long, Nothomb lay on his cot and listened while Simba announcers screamed for Belgian and American blood. The "newscasts" were followed by wild blasts of Congolese cha-cha-cha, the same records, played over and over again. Soon Nothomb felt like screaming. The Simbas never turned the radio down, much less off.

Nothomb went through one of the worst moments of his life during his stay in solitary. A note was slipped to him saying that all of the Belgian women and children were to be brought to the prison and that a massacre would begin in a few hours. He suspected that the Simbas had written the note in an attempt to crack his psychological resistance, but there was always the possibility that the report was true. There was no way to find out. He sank into profound gloom. It was only after several days had passed that he learned a well-meaning but misinformed Belgian had sent the note.

One morning Nothomb looked up to see a bloodthirsty

Simba officer named Commandant Placide Kitwunga standing
in the cell door.

"May I sit down?" Kitwunga said, almost deferentially.

"Certainly," Nothomb said, trying to sound as if he were
utterly unconcerned.

Kitwunga parked himself on Nothomb's cot. "Monsieur
le Consul, could you help me?" he said. His eyes were wide
and imploring.

"Certainly—what do you want?" Nothomb replied.

"Well, I have been sent personally by General Olenga to
see you," said Kitwunga. "Do you have passports at your
consulate? We need nine passports."

"Yes, I have passports," Nothomb said. "But they're
Belgian passports."

"Don't you have any Congolese passports?"

Nothomb was beginning to enjoy the conversation. "Commandant, what do you think? The Congo has been independent since 1960. How could we Belgians have Congolese
passports any more?"

Kitwunga was crestfallen. He stared at the floor, then
said: "Do you know where I could find Congolese passports?"

"The ministry of foreign affairs in Léopoldville!" Nothomb
exclaimed in triumph.

"What shall we do?" Kitwunga wailed. He was plainly
frightened. "We need passports."

It was clear to Nothomb now that Olenga and his top
aides were getting ready to flee the Congo. It was, of course,
absurd that they would ask their prisoner for assistance. But a
lifetime of psychological dependence on white people is not
erased overnight. Nothomb, for his part, relished ridiculous
situations of this sort. Quite apart from his delight in mis-
chief, he saw this as an opportunity, albeit a faint one, to get
rid of Olenga and those others and thus possibly spare
Stanleyville's white community from the massacre which
seemed bound to come.

"Commandant, there's no problem at all," Nothomb said,
beaming at his visitor. "You are a sovereign state. You can
make your own passports."

"But we need little books," Kitwunga protested.

"Not at all," replied Nothomb. "You can print them on a
single piece of paper. When the Congo became independent

in 1960, they didn't have books for passports, so they use single pieces of paper, with the name and photograph of th bearer of the passport. You can do the same."

Kitwunga brightened. "But what would these pieces paper say?"

"That's easy," Nothomb said with a beatific smile. H took a pencil and a piece of paper and wrote: *"Passepor République Populaire du Congo."* Then he filled in som of the wording of a Belgian passport. "Have it printed an you've got passports!" Nothomb exclaimed.

"Wonderful!" said Kitwunga. "I'll tell General Oleng immediately. Thank you very, very much."

Kitwunga bowed and scraped his way out of the cell.

Later on, General Olenga visited the prison to free Simb prisoners who were needed at the front. A guard who wa friendly to Nothomb asked Olenga if Nothomb could be take out of solitary and put back into the cell with the Americans Olenga agreed. Hoyt, Carlson and the other Americans wer delighted to see Nothomb; they had worried greatly abou him during his absence.

The prison was filling up. One day thirty-five Belgia men were brought in. They had been held hostage in th Sabena Guest House, but now they were moved to the priso so they could be guarded more closely.

By this time, all Belgians in Stanleyville were either i custody or in hiding—all except for Doctor Barlovatz. Th elderly physician continued to circulate around the city, eve to the prison. The Simbas had forbidden any visits, but th prison director was an old friend of Doctor Barlovatz an friendship, intensified by a bribe, succeeded in opening th doors. During one of his visits, Barlovatz remarked wit bitter irony that he had just heard a radio broadcast from Nairobi in which Jomo Kenyatta declared that he had bee assured by the Simba leaders that Stanleyville's foreigner were in "no danger."

Barlovatz kept the men supplied with books, but one da the books failed to arrive. Nothomb discovered that the priso authorities had impounded them. "There was a book among them which insulted our republic," a guard declared.

The book was *Un Pays Sans Justice—A Country Without Justice*.

The men were lounging on their plank beds one afternoon when Ernie Houle, who had been to the latrine, came running back to the cell, driven by Simbas who were beating him with rifle butts. Then a high-ranking Simba officer, Colonel Martin Kasongo, lurched into the cell, so drunk he could hardly stand.

"Who are you?" he said to Grinwis, who had gotten to his feet near the door.

"The American vice-consul."

Kasongo slapped Grinwis in the face with his full strength. Grinwis reeled. Kasongo struggled to keep his balance.

Turning to Hoyt, the colonel said, "Who are you?"

"The consul."

He slapped Hoyt in the face, but Hoyt knew what to expect and rolled with the blow.

Kasongo went down the row, slapping each man in the face—Dr. Carlson; the three radio operators; the two conscientious objectors; Massacesi, the honorary Italian consul; Makaroff, the Belgian civilian; and Patrick Nothomb. The drunken Simba came to the last man—Paul Duqué who tried to duck. This so enraged Kasongo that he knocked Duqué down and kicked him several times.

Kasongo left. As usual, the cell door was locked at 6:30 P.M. Now it was dark. The twelve men were nervous. At about seven o'clock, they heard someone rattling the door. They were always afraid when the Simbas rattled the door at night but now they were terrified. They felt certain that the Simbas were coming to kill them.

The door opened. In walked Christophe Gbenye

"Have you been mistreated?" the president asked.

Nothomb told him what Kasongo had done.

Gbenye turned to an aide. "Call the military police," he said. Gbenye lingered a moment. "Maybe I'll have you taken out of here and put in a hotel," he said. He left. The door was locked.

Next morning Martin Kasongo was brought to the prison and put into solitary confinement.

Each day the tempo of prison rumors increased. The ANC was nearing the city; Stanleyville would fall at any time;

the Simba government was collapsing. The prisoners suspected that these rumors were exaggerated, yet they knew the end was near. Excitement mounted—and, with it, dread of a massacre.

The prisoners discussed plans of what they should do if the city started to fall to the ANC. Some decided they would rush their guards and get their guns. One or two prisoners would probably be killed in the process, but there were nearly fifty Europeans in the prison by now and so there was no doubt about the outcome of the struggle. Then, the men would barricade themselves in the prison until the ANC arrived.

But it was an agonizing problem. If they overwhelmed the guards too soon, the other Simbas in Stanleyville would attack the prison and kill them all. If they waited too long, the Simbas might arrive at the prison in such great numbers as to make it impossible to overwhelm them. Then, in all likelihood, the Simbas would kill everyone.

Some of the Belgians proposed bribing the guards. But even if the guards were neutralized, Simba troops or the *jeunesse* might come to the prison and massacre all of the men.

On November 16 Michael Hoyt celebrated his thirty-fifth birthday. The Barlovatzes and Jenkinsons each sent him a little birthday cake.

The next day was an uneventful one. But the following day, Wednesday the 18th, the day the paratroopers landed on Accension Island, was one that the Americans would never forget.

At about nine o'clock, they heard the noise of a large crowd in the distance. Soon it was an uproar, punctuated with shrieks and yells. The Americans sensed that it had something to do with them. None of them, Carlson included, knew that the missionary had been condemned to death four days previously. But they had heard rumors that he had been accused of being an American major and a spy.

At ten o'clock, the guards told the Americans to come to the prison office.

"Should we bring our things?" someone asked.

"No, nothing," a guard replied.

At the prison office, a Simba wrote down the names of

the eight men—Michael Hoyt and the four other consular personnel, Dr. Carlson and Gene Bergman and Jon Snyder, the two conscientous objectors. The men were taken outside and put into two vehicles—a covered jeep and a Volkswagen. Simbas climbed into the vehicles and they started off.

"Where are you taking us?" Hoyt asked one of the Simbas.

"To the Lumumba Monument," the Simba replied. And then he added, in a matter-of-fact tone: "To be killed."

Huddled in the back of the jeep, Grinwis turned to Hoyt and said, "This is it; this is the end."

The vehicles proceeded slowly along the street to the monument, three blocks away. The street was lined with Congolese civilians, three, four and five deep, men, women and children. They howled curses at the Americans and shook their fists. *"Mateka!"* they screamed. Thousands of other civilians were jammed into Lumumba Square. The city's post office overlooks the square and its roof and balconies were thick with people. The whole town, it seemed, had turned out for the show.

The two vehicles halted in front of the monument. The mob surged forward, but was held back by Simba military police. The men in the Volkswagen were taken out and thrust into the covered jeep. The eight men were packed in so tightly they could hardly move. Half a dozen armed Simbas ringed the jeep and tried to hold the mob back. Even so, the civilians managed to get at the Americans. They reached into the jeep and clawed at the faces of the Americans with fingernails. They burned them with lighted cigarettes and twisted their prison beards. They jabbed at them with pins and knives. A Simba officer came up to the jeep and struck Don Parkes, the radio operator, just over the eye with a metal bar. Blood gushed down Parkes's face and onto his shirt.

Several Simbas milled around the jeep. "We're going to eat you," they shouted above the tumult. The mob whooped with glee. The Simbas brandished machetes and pointed to the genitals of the men, indicating that they would be castrated. They made motions of slitting their throats. Several boys who seemed to be about ten years old joined in the sport. They made motions of cutting flesh from the arms of the Americans and eating it.

It was then that the men learned why they had been brought to the monument. The Simba authorities, desperately in need of scapegoats, had announced that they had captured American mercenaries at Kindu—mercenaries who were to be executed at the monument that day.

"Which one is the major?" the civilians kept screaming, referring to Carlson.

Gene Bergman, the twenty-one-year-old conscientious objector, kept thinking, over and over: "I don't know how they are going to kill us, but I hope they'll do it real quick, rather than cut off first the hands and then the arms and legs like the Simbas sometimes do."

After this part of the ordeal had lasted fifteen minutes, the Simbas ordered the eight Americans out of the jeep. A roar went up from the mob. The men were made to line up, single file, in front of the steps that led to the hallowed photograph of Patrice Lumumba, next to the beautiful blood-red flowers. The screams of the mob were deafening. The Simbas had their machetes and their automatic weapons ready. Hoyt looked out at the sea of wild faces. He noticed among them Martin Kasongo, the Simba colonel who had been jailed by Gbenye for slapping the Americans around and who had now evidently been restored to grace. Hoyt also caught a glimpse of Commandant Oscar Sengha, the Simba officer who had done so much in the past to help the Americans and who also had been jailed for a time. But there was nothing Sengha could do now.

Just then General Olenga shouldered his way through the crowd. He glanced at the Americans, but, as Hoyt noticed, he never looked them in the eye. Olenga carried on a heated exchange with the Simbas. One officer seemed to object to what the general ordered; Olenga suddenly knocked him to the ground. The guards told the Americans to get back into the jeep. Olenga had canceled the executions. The mob roared angrily.

The relief of the Americans was short-lived. The driver of the jeep had gone off with the keys. The eight men were jammed in the back of the jeep for another fifteen minutes while the mob howled for their blood. The guards became afraid that the mob would overpower them. With the help of some civilians, they started to push the jeep away from the monument. The mob ran alongside the jeep, screaming, *"Mateka!"* A Simba struck at the canvas side of the jeep with a rifle butt, and the blow caught Paul Carlson in the middle of the back. "Oh, that was a good one," he gasped. The guards pushed the jeep for two blocks. By now the mob had thinned out. They stopped the jeep and continued to wait for the man with the keys.

Michael Hoyt had gone through more horror that morning than most men see in a lifetime. But now a new and more exquisite terror came over him. He experienced intense claustrophobia from being packed so tightly in the jeep. There were two men sitting almost on top of him. "Please, please, shift your weight," he shouted to them. He became frantic. "Please!" The men managed to shift their weight slightly. Hoyt's panic ebbed.

After fifteen minutes, the key to the jeep was finally found. A Simba officer told the men that he was taking them to see Gbenye at the presidential palace. "You're really lucky," the officer said as the jeep rolled along the tree-shaded avenues of the city. "You're lucky that Monsieur Gbenye is our president; he's the one who saved you."

When the Americans arrived at the palace, they saw another screaming mob—this one of about four thousand persons—on the front lawn. But this mob was under better control. They were lined up in groups. The *jeunesse* were drawn up in ranks. So, too, were the Nationalist Women. Another group consisted of deputies to the provincial legislature. Each section was controlled by military policemen.

The Americans were ordered out of the jeep and lined up single file. They were photographed. Then they were marched through the mob to the palace. The Simbas and civilians cursed at the Americans and brandished knives to indicate they would be castrated. They shouted, *"Mateka"* and *"Kufa*—die!" But the military police held the mob back.

Gbenye was on a balcony of the palace, speaking in French into a public-address system. The eight Americans were halted just beneath him.

"Major Carlson has been tried and condemned to death," Gbenye was saying. "He is a mercenary! We captured him at Yakoma. He was leading American troops there. We were going to execute him last Monday, but we have postponed the execution because of an appeal from Jomo Kenyatta."

Gbenye added that Carlson would be executed the following Monday—November 23—unless "negotiations" with the Americans were successful.

Paul Carlson blanched as he listened to Gbenye. It was the first he had heard about a death sentence. He drew a small Bible from his pocket and handed it to Jon Snyder, who was standing next to him. "Give this to my wife," Carlson said.

While Gbenye was continuing his speech, the mayor of Stanleyville put an automatic weapon against Ernie Houle's head. The mob took this to mean that Houle was the "Major" Carlson about whom Gbenye was speaking. They pointed at Houle and shouted. Gbenye told the mayor to put the weapon down. Someone else reached up with a pen knife to cut Houle's ear off. Gbenye saw that, too, and motioned the man away.

Gbenye harangued the mob for forty-five minutes, in Lingala as well as French, while the Americans stood there beneath him. Then he ordered the mob to step back. The Americans were put back into the jeep and returned to prison.

Carlson was stunned by the death sentence. He took a barbiturate pill to calm his nerves. Michael Hoyt tried to cheer him up. "They won't execute you," Hoyt said. "You're their trump card. They won't play it. The fact that they want negotiations is an encouraging sign for all of us. Don't worry—we'll all get out alive."

Hoyt was not entirely convinced by his own words, but he felt he had to do something to console Carlson.

"Let's have a moment of prayer," Carlson said.

The men bowed their heads. After the prayer, Carlson treated the cut over Don Parkes's eye.

Seventy vehicles were lined up at the ferry landing. The river was half a mile wide and the ferry was a small one, capable of carrying only a few vehicles at a time. It took several hours to get all of them across. Once they were on the other side, the order was shouted down the line. The vehicles started out, groaning along in second gear at ten miles an hour. Great clouds of fine dust, the red dust of the Maniema, billowed skyward.

Thus it was that Lima One left Kindu, crossed the Lualaba River and set out on the last leg of its journey to Stanleyville, some 250 miles away. It was November 18—the day when Michael Hoyt and the other Americans were taken to the Lumumba Monument and the Belgian paratroopers landed at Ascension Island.

Lima One had paused for thirteen days in Kindu. Most of its vehicles were in sad shape when they arrived in Kindu, victims of a thousand potholes and quagmires on the road up from Kongolo. There had been only one mechanic to service them all. And Commandant Liégeois had been under orders to wait for reinforcements. As is the custom in the Congo, they were slow in coming. But eventually Michael Hoare's mercenary unit was bolstered by another commando, bringing its strength to 120 men. And a second major unit, known as Lima Two, arrived in Kindu with three hundred Africans and fifty French-speaking white mercenaries. (Lima Two got its name from the fact that its commander, Commandant Robert Lamouline, also on loan from the Belgian army, also had a last name beginning with the letter L.) Lima Two, however, was not ready to move out on the 18th, so Lima One went first.

Although Liégeois continued as commander of Lima One, both it and Lima Two now had a new overall commander—Frédéric Vandewalle, a fifty-two-year-old Belgian colonel who had spent a quarter of a century in the Congo. He had been an officer in the Force Publique. During the secession in Katanga, he served as one of Tshombe's military advisers. Then, in August, he had returned to the Congo at Tshombe's invitation, to help reorganize the ANC.

Vandewalle's biggest worry was the European hostages in Stanleyville. He knew from broadcasts by Radio Stanleyville that they might be massacred at any time. Yet there was a good chance that if he struck quickly enough he might take the city before the Simbas had a chance to carry out their threat. This was, after all, what had happened in Kindu. Vandewalle knew that the paratroopers were standing by at Ascension Island. But the plan at that time was that they would be used only if it became clear that the column of mercenaries and ANC troops could not reach the city soon enough.

Vandewalle's idea was to take Stanleyville in a Kindu-type operation. His columns would roar into the city at high speeds. A detachment would be sent to the center of town to find the hostages. Others would race across the city and secure the airport. Still others would take the Tshopo River bridge, so as to prevent the Simbas from pouring in reinforcements from the north. Lima Two would attack Camp Ketele. Then men would pincer in from the airport, the bridge and Camp Ketele to deal with remaining resistance in the center of town.

There were enormous risks. Even if the column arrived quickly enough to avert a massacre, the hostages still would not be out of danger. There were sixteen hundred foreigners in Stanleyville. The column would have to find, assemble and protect them until they could be flown to safety. And Vandewalle had fewer than two hundred reliable men—the English-and French-speaking white mercenaries. The six hundred ANC troops in the column might, or might not, be of any use.

Vandewalle was a prudent man. He knew the mercenaries well. He assigned to himself the job of guarding Stanleyville's banks once the column reached the city.

As Lima One moved north along the right bank of the Lualaba, the armored vehicles in front kept spraying stalled vehicles, clumps of trees, huts and anything else that seemed suspicious. On several occasions, the Simbas put improvised armored jeeps in the road—smack in the middle of the road—to await the column's approach. Each time Lima One saw them in the distance and each time it blew the occupants of the armored cars to eternity.

One of the biggest dangers to the mercenaries was that they would be shot by their ANC auxiliaries. Whenever a weapon was fired by the lead vehicles, most of the ANC troops in the rear would open up with a furious barrage, firing wildly in all directions. Many closed their eyes before squeezing the triggers. Miraculously, the mercenaries survived.

From time to time, the column shot and killed people along the roads. One Congolese stood up from a clump of high grass and fired a pistol at the column, hitting an ANC soldier in the arm. He was riddled to pieces with machine-gun fire. Another man was taking a bath in a stream. When he saw the column, he bolted in panic. He was brought down by another furious fusillade.

Most of the time, though, the column saw no one along the road. The villagers heard the column coming and fled into the jungle. When the column passed through a village, cooking fires were still burning. Washing fluttered on clotheslines. Dogs and chickens scurried around. Sometimes there were a few old people on hand, too old and tired to run.

But there were few villages. Most of the time there was nothing but the rain forest, gorgeous and ghastly, on either side of the road. Trees soared to nearly two hundred feet. During those infrequent moments when the column had halted and the machine guns were still, the warblings of songbirds could be heard. The heat and humidity were stifling. The dust was blinding. Minutes after leaving Kindu, the men were covered with red dust. They were terrified of ambushes, but there was more than one way to die in the Congo. There was no doctor and a slight nick from a bullet could, because of blood poisoning, be just as lethal as a shot in the heart.

Major Hoare had a passionate hatred—beards. He insisted that his men shave every morning. He also ordered them to pray to God each day. They were not exactly the religious sort and one suspects that not too many of them prayed. But they did shave; Hoare saw to it. That was about the extent of their ablutions. At night the men would tumble out of the trucks, too exhausted to wash their bodies or clothes, have a meal of cold C-rations and then spend the night sleeping fitfully in the backs of the trucks or on the ground.

As the South African mercenaries bumped along in the trucks, they sang "Sarie Marais," a folksong of the Boer War. And, to the tune (more or less) of "We're Marching to Pretoria," another Boer War song, they sang:

You go fast, we'll go fast,
Straight through the Congo.
For we're marching on to Stanleyville,
To Stanleyville, to Stanleyville,
For we're marching on to Stanleyville,
And we don't give a bugger for
Joe Kenyatta, Tom Mboya, Julius Nyerere,
Old Nkrumah, Joshua Nkomo, Michael Hoare and all.

The little ditty was a piece of racial impudence, yet in a way it had a deeper significance. In a very real sense, South African power was reaching now from its northern border, the Limpopo River, to the Congo River. There were only 120 men in Hoare's column, yet they were the backbone of Lima One. They were ill-trained, ill-disciplined and ill-equipped, yet they were striking deep into the heart of rebel territory nearly the size of France. They had inflicted heavy casualties on the Simbas with scarcely any casualties of their own. Nothing in the Congo could stop them. Nor, for that matter, was there anything anywhere in tropical Africa that could stop them.

In Washington, U.S. officials came to a difficult decision. At Jomo Kenyatta's request, Gbenye had postponed the execution of Paul Carlson for one week. But Gbenye still insisted that he would have the missionary doctor killed on November 23, unless the U.S. government entered into "negotiations" with the Simba regime. It was, of course, blackmail of the most outrageous sort. But Carlson's life, as well as the lives of other Americans in rebel-held territories, hung in the balance. The State Department instructed the American embassy in Léopoldville to radio this message to Gbenye:

"We stand ready at any time for discussions to insure the safety of United States nationals now in the Stanleyville area."

The message also asked that Gbenye provide communications facilities for Hoyt.

Lima One rolled into Punia, a tin-mining center, on November 20. There was no resistance from the Simbas. Several ANC soldiers amused themselves when they arrived in town by shooting a German shepherd dog with their automatic weapons. The animal howled, rolled in the dust and died. Those were the only shots fired in Punia.

From Punia, the column barreled on to the Lowa River, a big tributary of the Lualaba. The ferry was on the far side of the river. So, too, were the Simbas. The Simbas let loose with a mortar barrage. But that did not stop Lima One's advance. While the men laid down a heavy return fire from machine guns, one group crossed the Lowa in four small boats powered by outboard motors and established a bridge-head on the far bank. They also brought back the ferry, which had been damaged. A Greek mercenary named Basil, who had been a mechanic in Elisabethville, spent the rest of the day repairing it.

Next morning the ferry was fixed. But it was a small craft and it could take only one vehicle across the Lowa at a time. The operation went on till well after nightfall. Then a Katangese soldier shouted, "White man fell in the water." The merce-naries swarmed to the ferry landing, but there was nothing they could do. Basil had fallen off the ferry and had been swept to his doom in the fast-moving current.

That night a chorus of anguished screams rang out from the jungle. The men leaped to their feet and grabbed their weapons. But then they smiled and put their weapons down. The screams came from a family of chimpanzees who were annoyed by the intrusion and hoped to frighten the column away.

The following morning—Sunday the 22nd—the last vehi-cle had been taken across. Just then, Lima Two appeared. Lima One was ordered to go ahead, take the town of Lubutu and wait for Lima Two to catch up.

Frenchie had by then rejoined the column. The Ferret had remained behind in Kindu for repairs, and Frenchie had been ill with malaria. But now he was back in action. His associates said he was suffering from a bad case of nerves as well. His .30-calibre machine gun blazed almost continually from the turret of the Ferret. Whenever the column encoun-tered a truck that was stalled in the road, all of the vehicles would halt. Frenchie would plaster it with a few hundred rounds. Then, with the Sons of Bitches covering him, he would move up to the stalled truck to investigate.

Every few hours the column was lashed with driving rain. Vehicles slithered off the road and bogged down. But the Sons of Bitches were equipped with takeoff gears and winches and thus were able to pull the other vehicles out of the mud.

The column took Lubutu at nightfall that day with no

resistance from the Simbas. The men took up positions in a hospital and other government buildings on a hilltop. Stanleyville now was only 144 miles away. There was a good road all the way. Some of Hoare's officers urged him to continue straight through to Stanleyville. But Hoare had orders from Vandewalle to remain in Lubutu until Lima Two could catch up. Vandewalle feared that there were too few white mercenaries to take Stanleyville quickly enough to avert a massacre. He wanted to have as many men as possible arrive in the city simultaneously—even if some were undependable Katangese troops.

In the middle of the night, there was an alarm at the hospital. A truck drove into Lubutu with its headlights blazing and pulled up in front of the hospital. Someone opened fire at it. Several Simbas jumped from the vehicle shouting, "*Mai, mai,*" and disappeared in the darkness. When the mercenaries found flashlights, they discovered there was a dead Simba officer in the back. With him was a boy of ten or twelve who had a crude bandage on his arm, covering a gunshot wound. The officer had brought the boy, who was his son, to the hospital for treatment; he had not known that Lubutu had fallen to the government forces.

The youngster cowered in the back of the truck. A mercenary got into the truck, put a pistol against the boy's head and shot him dead.

Hoare was furious when he learned of the killing.

Michael Hoyt and Paul Carlson, together with the other American prisoners, had a quiet day on Thursday the 19th—the day after they were taken to the Lumumba Monument. They rested on the planks that served as cots, still racked with horror over their narrow escape from death at the hands of the mob. During the day the men received a visit in their cell from a Greek doctor. He told them that the events at the monument the day before had been anything but spontaneous. Placards had been put up in town earlier in the week proclaiming that there would be a public trial and execution of captured American mercenaries. And there had been similar announcements on the radio.

The men had been spared by General Olenga. No one, of course, knew what went on in Olenga's mind at the time,

ut the assumption was that Olenga knew that if the men
vere killed he would lose any chance of being able to bargain
or a cease-fire. Curiously enough, it was the last time any of
he Europeans saw the general in Stanleyville. He presum-
bly had gone out to organize the defense against Vandewalle's
column.

The Americans, however, had been reprieved only for
he moment. Carlson in particular was doomed—his execu-
ion was set for Monday.

At the town of Isangi, about one hundred miles down-
tream from Stanleyville, the killings had already begun. On
he 19th, the Simbas killed two nuns, one an American and
ne a Belgian, and a Dutch priest. Many other nuns were
tripped, beaten and raped. The American nun was Sister
Marie Antoinette, fifty-one, of Bellmore, Long Island.

At noon on Friday the 20th, a Simba officer took Hoyt
rom the prison and put him in an auto. When Hoyt saw the
nan, fear welled up once more—for perhaps the thousandth
ime. The officer was one of those who had taken him and the
ther Americans to the monument two days earlier. Now
omething else was afoot.

The officer drove rapidly through the streets of Stanleyville.
Ie was very nervous, and his eyes kept darting back and
orth as he drove. Hoyt was relieved to a degree when he saw
hat they were not heading to the monument. Rather, he was
aken to Gbenye's presidential palace.

A mob of about two dozen Simba military police swarmed
round the car with rifles and sticks, howling furiously. They
anked Hoyt from the car and chased him at a run into the
palace. Hoyt stopped in front of a door to an office where a
nan was standing. When Hoyt had recovered his wits, he
aw that the man was Gbenye.

"Come in," Gbenye said. A smile blossomed across the
resident's face. "Come in, Monsieur Hoyt."

Hoyt followed Gbenye into the office and sat down at a
lesk. Gbenye took a chair on the opposite side. He folded his
ands and beamed pleasantly at his visitor.

Hoyt had been in prison six weeks. He had a ragged
eard. His hair grew down over his neck. His clothing was

frayed. But Gbenye had not summoned the American cons
to gloat over his plight.

"I've received a message from your ambassador
Léopoldville," Gbenye said. "He has offered to begin negot
ations with my government over the American citizens
Stanleyville."

This, then, was the reason for Gbenye's good cheer. H
blackmail threat to murder the hostages unless talks wer
opened seemed to be working.

"Your ambassador said that I should tell you what cond
tions I wish to establish concerning the negotiations," Gbeny
added. "But I'm not going to deal with you and I'm not goir
to reply to your ambassador directly. What I've decided to d
is to send a message to our representative in Nairobi instruc
ing him to arrange the negotiations."

Hoyt stared at the president with cold and hard eyes. H
was not taken in by Gbenye's efforts to be charming. To
many things had happened for that.

"Oh, yes," Gbenye said as if it were an afterthought. '
think it would be a good idea if you would send this messag
to your ambassodor in Léopoldville."

Gbenye handed over a piece of paper on which a me
sage was written in French. He told Hoyt to translate it int
English. It was made clear that Hoyt had little choice whethe
he would send it. The military policemen, standing just ou
side the doors, shouted threats at Hoyt and waved the
rifles. The message said in part:

> PAUL CARLSON CAPTURED AND CONDEMNED TO DEATH
> STOP ALL AMERICAN CITIZENS GATHERED IN SEVERAL RE-
> GIONS OTHER THAN STAN STOP ASK YOU PARTICULARLY
> INTERVENE EFFECTIVELY WITH TSHOMBE TO OBTAIN
> CEASE FIRE DURING THESE NEGOTIATIONS OR RISK COM-
> PROMISE DESIRED RESULTS STOP IN NAME ALL AMERICAN
> CITIZENS IN POPULAR CONGOLESE REPUBLIC REQUEST
> INITIATION NEGOTIATIONS WHICH CONSTITUTE OUR LAST
> CHANCE STOP IN CASE OF DELAY I SAY FOR MYSELF AND
> MY COMPATRIOTS GOODBYE STOP

Hoyt signed the message. He knew the embassy woul
realize that it had been written under duress. That wa

important. The point was that the message would serve to ert the embassy to the gravity of the situation.

Gbenye beamed with satisfaction. He had gotten what e wanted from his captive. He informed Hoyt that he would ve the Americans taken out of prison that day and moved the Victoria Residence, an apartment hotel. This was not act of compassion on Gbenye's part. There had been talk at Jomo Kenyatta or other representatives of the OAU ould visit Stanleyville to check on the condition of the white stages. Gbenye wanted to exhibit them in the best possible ght.

At seven o'clock that evening, the Simbas came to the ison. Patrick Nothomb and several other Belgians had already been taken to the Victoria Residence. Now the eight mericans and about twenty-five Belgians—all of the white en who remained in the prison—were lined up single file. nd then, carrying their belongings, they were marched ree blocks, through the sweet-scented nighttime streets, to e Victoria Residence.

16

BURN THE PRISONERS ALIVE

When Michael Hoyt, Paul Carlson and the other Ame
cans arrived at the Victoria Residence, they found the lob
jammed with men. Most were Belgians; a few were Ame
cans. The stairway leading to the upper floors was filled w
women and children. A Simba colonel was screaming at t
crowd in Lingala. Hoyt did not understand Lingala and so
turned to Carlson.

"What's he bellowing about?" Hoyt asked.

Carlson turned to Hoyt. There was terror in his ey
"He says he is going to kill us all," the doctor replied.

The Simbas had assembled all of the Belgian and Ame
can hostages in the Victoria. The men had been brought fr
Camp Ketele and the other outlying places where they h
been held the last three weeks. The women and children h
been moved to the Victoria from the Hôtel des Chutes a
the Congo Palace. In all there were 280 Belgians and
Americans. And there was one other person—Raoul Massace
the honorary Italian consul whose misfortune it was that t
Simbas had captured an improvised armored car which th
figured was of Italian origin.

The purpose of assembling the hostages in the Victo
was to impress Jomo Kenyatta or other representatives of t
Organization of African Unity with how well Gbenye w
treating his "prisoners of war." But now Kenyatta let it

known that neither he nor any other OAU representative was coming to Stanleyville. It was, he felt, too dangerous.

The Simbas still hoped to use the hostages in bargaining a cease-fire, which, in turn, would save their regime from destruction. But events were moving at a frenzied pace now. The column of mercenaries and ANC troops reached Punia that day. The Belgian government announced that the paratroopers were poised on Ascension Island. The Simba regime was dying. But even a dying lion can be very, very dangerous.

Just before Hoyt and Carlson arrived at the hotel, the Simbas got word of the fall of Punia. Gbenye flew into a rage and ordered all of the hostages taken to outlying jungle villages pending the outcome of the "negotiations" in Nairobi. The men were put in the lobby and the women and children on the stairs. Some of the Simbas wanted to kill the hostages then and there. That was the moment when Hoyt, Carlson and the others arrived.

One Simba officer screamed in Swahili: "The Americans have bombed us. President Gbenye is very angry. We are waiting for trucks. Then we shall take you out into the jungle and kill you. We shall kill all of the men, but we shall kill the children, too, because if we don't, they will come back in twenty years to avenge you. And we shall kill the mothers, too, because otherwise they would be unhappy."

That was only logical—to the Simbas.

For a long time, many of the hostages had simply refused to believe that they would be killed. But now they saw through to the awful truth. Some of them would, in all certainty, die. Those who believed in God spent their time in prayer. Those who did not believe in God pondered the mathematical odds of being able to survive somehow.

A Belgian man huddled with his wife in a corner of the lobby. He was on the verge of cracking up. A stranger sat down next to the couple and cracked a few jokes in heavily accented French. "I'm a doctor," the stranger said. "Let me have a look at you."

The stranger examined the Belgian. "You're just suffering from nothing more than a bad case of the jitters," he said. He gave the man some pills to calm his nerves.

The Belgian couple stared at their benefactor. "Aren't you Dr. Carlson, the American missionary?" they said.

"Yes," he replied. "I am supposed to be a mercenary. I am due to be shot on Monday."

It was characteristic of Paul Carlson that he spent his time looking after the other hostages. Among them were two Belgians who suffered heart attacks because of the strain. One man had been beaten so severely by the Simbas that he could hardly walk. His back was raw and he had a nasty head injury. At least two other Belgians had bullet wounds inflicted by the Simbas.

That evening Radio Stanleyville screamed that Carlson was "an adventurer, a Yankee major, a murderer and a war criminal."

The hours ticked away. Now it was after midnight. Several trucks and buses had been brought to the Victoria, but the Simbas did not order the hostages into them. Then a Simba lieutenant summoned Hoyt and Nothomb.

"I want you to send a message to your governments," the lieutenant said. "It's your last chance."

Nothomb's spirits rose. He had been convinced that the Simbas would kill the hostages that night. But messages to Washington and Brussels were, of course, powerful magic. It meant that the Simbas would, in all likelihood, postpone the slaughter.

Hoyt and Nothomb, together with their vice-consuls, David Grinwis and Paul Duqué, retired to a small room just off the lobby and spent an hour composing another message urging the Belgian and American governments to obtain a cease-fire "without delay." The message also said: "All American and Belgian citizens residing in territory controlled by the People's Government of Stanleyville are alive as of November 21 and they will so remain if an immediate end is put to Belgian and American military aid to the Léopoldville government."

The diplomats handed the message to the Simba officer.

"Fine," he said.

The four men, together with the other male hostages, spent the rest of the night huddled on the lobby floor. They got no sleep.

In the morning, the Simbas told everyone to go to rooms upstairs. Michael Hoyt started to shave off his prison beard. He had hardly started hacking away at it when the Simbas ordered him and Nothomb down into the lobby. They were taken on foot to the radio station nearby, where they were forced to read the message in English and French. Then they were taken in a jeep to the airport control tower, where Nothomb read his message again, beamed, this time, to the control tower at Bujumbura.

From the control tower, the two men could see that the airport was guarded by a large detachment of Simbas. They had obstructed the runway with barrels and vehicles from which the wheels had been removed.

After returning to the Victoria, Baron Nothomb spent many an anxious hour peering from his windows. There were virtually no Congolese civilians on the streets, but hundreds of Simbas swarmed past. Nothomb noticed that many were boys of only ten or twelve. The Simbas had been sustaining heavy casualties, and many of the older ones were dead.

Michael Hoyt, who was in another room, finished shaving. An itinerant Portuguese barber pitched up at the Victoria that morning, hoping to make a few francs, and he gave Hoyt a haircut of sorts.

Along with Paul Carlson, there were five other American missionaries in the hotel. Among them was Clifford Schaub, the thirty-six-year-old evangelist who came from Pittsburgh and who had been held at Camp Ketele. When Schaub was brought to the Victoria Residence, there had been a joyous reunion with his wife Helen and their two sons. Mrs. Schaub and the boys had been held in the Hôtel des Chutes. When the boys saw Schaub they said, "Daddy, we've been praying for three weeks that you'd be brought back."

Phyllis Rine, the plain-looking young girl from Ohio who had come to the Congo to teach African children the Bible, shared a room with the Schaubs. On one occasion, the Schaubs talked about what they would do if they survived. Schaub remarked that conditions might be too unsettled to remain in the area. Perhaps, he said, the family ought to go back to the United States for a while.

"What do you think you'll do, Phyllis?" Schaub asked.

"I don't want to leave the Congo," she replied. "If I can't work in Stanleyville, I'll work with our mission in Bukavu."

The other American missionaries in the Victoria were Al

Larson, the regional chief of the Unevangelized Fields Mission; Del Carper, who had lived in a world of near-silence ever since the Simbas took his hearing aid, and Charles Davis, the one-time juvenile delinquent from Boston.

The center of attention was Paul Carlson. As the world waited to see if Carlson would live or die, President Johnson sent a message of sympathy to his relatives in California. The Belgians and the Americans were impressed with Carlson's composure in the face of death. Each day Carlson met with the other American missionaries in Schaub's room for prayer. Often he recited a favorite verse of the Bible—II Timothy 4:17: "Notwithstanding the Lord stood with me, and strengthened me; that by me the preaching might be fully known, and that all the Gentiles might hear; and I was delivered out of the mouth of the lion."

During the few days that they were together, Charlie Davis, who was something of an evangelistic ball of fire, became very friendly with Carlson, who was, in many ways, quite the opposite type of man. Once, when they discussed the death sentence, Carlson told Davis: "I live from day to day. I take each day as it comes. After I have lived that day, I thank the Lord for that day and that it was given to me for work."

Carlson was more and more convinced that he would die. Once, in an effort to cheer him up, Al Larson said: "Now, look, Paul, when you meet President Johnson, don't forget I'll be with you—let me shake his hand, too."

Carlson looked down at the floor and said, "Don't worry, Al. I won't be seeing him."

Paul Carlson was not the only man who felt that death was near. So, too, did Colonel Opepe. From what the hostages could gather, Opepe had fallen out of favor with General Olenga and had lost his post as the number two man in the Simba army, though he continued as a high-ranking officer. Olenga, it was felt, suspected that Opepe was too friendly with the Europeans.

Opepe had become a nervous wreck. He lost weight and his face was haggard. Some of the Belgians proposed a deal with Opepe: if he would protect them, they in turn would see that he was not killed by the ANC. Although Opepe was interested, he never committed himself. It was, of course, highly risky. The Simbas would kill him if they got wind of it. Even if he did succeed in saving the Europeans, the ANC might kill him anyhow, despite protests from the Europeans. Opepe knew well the murderous instincts of the ANC; he was, after all, a veteran of twenty-four years in the Force Publique and ANC.

Soon after the hostages were taken to the Victoria, Colonel Opepe had a haircut and then visited Monsignor Fataki.

"Here I am, Monsignor, looking my very best for the last time," Opepe said.

The seventeenth American in the Victoria Residence was a stranger to most of the others. His name was Guy Humphreys, and he did not come from Stanleyville. He owned a plantation one hundred miles away. Humphreys seldom visited Stanleyville. He had few friends, and was so close-lipped about his personal affairs that the others puzzled over him.

But some of the missionaries knew him. Whenever his name was mentioned an uncomfortable silence came over them. Humphreys was an ex-missionary. He had come to the Congo seventeen years previously, preached for eight years, then resigned. It was never very clear to the others why Humphreys had given up mission work. Humphreys himself said only that he wanted to make some money so that he could set up a mission program free of control from mission boards back home. Although the missionaries did not care to talk openly about Humphreys, it was clucked confidentially that he had been known to smoke cigarettes and that he even partook of spirituous beverages from time to time.

Guy Humphreys was a strange man. He was small—five feet seven inches tall and weighing just 123 pounds. He was forty-seven years old, but he was hard as nails and had the stamina of a man half his age. Humphreys had a wife and children, but they had returned to the United States long ago. He himself had not been back home in eleven years. He lived with the Congolese, miles from any other white man. And he spoke Swahili like a Congolese.

Only a few white men who come to Africa ever really get to know Africa. They come as missionaries, diplomats, businessmen or teachers, and settle in the cities or at mission stations where they usually are surrounded by most if not all of the comforts of modern living. Life for them goes on pretty much as it would back home.

Humphreys was an exception. He was fascinated with Africa—the real Africa, the beautiful and savage Africa of the rain forest. During his years in the Congo he made countless hunting trips into the jungle, often for weeks at a time. He went on foot, accompanied only by native guides, covering as much as twenty-five miles a day along trails known only to ivory poachers and the infrequent white hunter.

Humphreys shot many an elephant in the Congo jungles. For a time his rifle kept a mission school of 150 children supplied with elephant meat. He explored areas into which few if any white men had ever ventured. On the occasion, at the behest of Belgian colonial officials, he and three other white men journeyed for days up a remote river and discovered a spectacular waterfall. Its existence had been reported by natives, but, until then, no white man had confirmed that it did, indeed, exist.

On a thousand and one enchanted nights, Humphreys lay in a hammock and listened to the sounds of the jungle. There were soft, caressing calls from nocturnal birds, the sounds of monkeys scurrying through trees, the rustle of the wings of big bats. A hundred thousand insects chirped, sang, whined, trilled and made noises like the sawing of wood.

And there were other, more startling, sounds. Elephants made the jungle shudder with their trumpet cries; crocodiles groaned from river banks and often a hippopotamus joined in with a deep bellow. Sometimes a magistrate monkey would let loose a bloodcurdling cry that resembled the roar of a lion.

Many men have come to grief in the jungles of the Congo, but Humphreys was never harmed. On one occasion, he had a close call. He was hunting in the moonlight, wading barefoot in a small stream, when suddenly he saw a slight movement near his foot. Switching on his flashlight, he saw that he had almost stepped on a horned viper—a ghastly snake, two feet long and as thick as the calf of a man's leg, whose bite is highly venomous.

After leaving missionary work, Humphreys became a trader. For a time he tried his hand at gold mining, but he went broke. Later he operated a fleet of trucks. Then in 1962 he acquired a plantation. It was potentially a most valuable holding—there were some 425 acres of young coffee trees which ordinarily would have been ready for harvesting in two years. But the Belgian who owned it was getting out of the Congo; he felt it was too dangerous to remain at that lonely outpost. Humphreys took it over with an agreement that he would pay the Belgian one hundred tons of coffee—worth well over $40,000—when the trees matured.

It was a rough existence. Humphreys often was threatened by the *jeunesse* and even by his own workmen. But he stuck it out.

In August, a week after Stanleyville fell to the Simbas, fifteen ragged ANC soldiers arrived at Humphreys' plantation, having retreated the hundred miles from Stanleyville on foot. They were terrified of being captured by the Simbas. At gunpoint, they forced Humphreys to drive them in his truck to Boende. The trip took two days, during which time neither Humphreys nor the soldiers had anything to eat.

"Merci, beaucoup," the soldiers said as they alighted at Boende. Humphreys stared at them glumly, then turned the truck around and headed back. As he found out later, he was lucky that the ANC had kidnapped him; a band of Simbas arrived at the plantation four hours after they left. They had come, they informed Humphreys' workmen, to kill the American *bwana*.

Humphreys got only as far as Ikela, a town on the Tshuapa River, when the front axle broke. He finally got the axle fixed. But then the same ANC soldiers who had kidnapped him returned to Ikela from Boende, with orders to defend Ikela, and, to acquire spare parts for their own vehicles, they stripped Humphreys' truck.

Humphreys was stranded in Ikela. He still could have gotten out to Léopoldville by other transportation, but, like so many other foreigners, he felt that, although there would be difficulties, he would be able to manage under the Simbas somehow.

The Simbas took Ikela two weeks later, scattering the ANC. When they learned that Humphreys was the American who had transported the ANC, they announced that they were going to kill him. While a mob screamed, a Simba officer beat Humphreys with a rifle. The little man threw up his arm to protect himself. The rifle glanced from his elbow and the stock broke off.

Instantly the mob was silent. The officer picked up the broken stock and stared at the two pieces. "What *dawa!*" he exclaimed in amazement.

That saved Humphreys for a moment. Obviously the American was a magician. But then he went through one ordeal after another for weeks. On one occasion, he was stood up before a firing squad, but the execution was called off at the last moment. Another time he was imprisoned in a tiny room for two days without food or water. Crazed with thirst, he managed to break a pipe and get water. On yet another occasion, the Simbas tied his hands behind his back and then tied him to a Congolese whose hands were similarly bound. The Simbas beat the two men with rifles and stomped on them with their boots. One Simba drove a fist into Humphreys' liver. The pain was so intense that Humphreys was convinced the man had stabbed him with a dagger. He groaned. "White man, why do you cry?" a Simba said, mockingly. When Humphreys got his breath back, he spat contemptuously. "Who's crying?" The Simbas always admired a man who withstood their tortures; they untied him.

Humphreys was taken to the home of a Simba major. He waited all day on the steps of the front porch to hear his fate. The major's personal sorcerer befriended him and the two chatted pleasantly in Swahili. Then Humphreys was taken inside to see the major.

"If I visited America and lived there as a stranger in your land, would I have a right to have radio equipment and call my countrymen to attack your people?" the major asked.

"Major, I have no radio equipment," Humphreys said, wearily. "I not only don't own a transmitter, but I don't even know how to operate one."

The major thought for a while, then said, "You can go back to your plantation."

"But my plantation is two hundred kilometers away," Humphreys protested. "I have no vehicle. I have no papers. I won't even get one kilometer before someone will either arrest me or kill me."

"Get out," the major said.

Humphreys wandered out into the yard. The sorcerer

came up and smiled. "I'm glad that you are released," he said.

"I don't know what I'll do," Humphreys said. "I won't get one kilometer."

"That's right," the sorcerer said. He took Humphreys back to the porch. "Wait here—I'll talk to the major," he said. In a few moments, the sorcerer came back, grinning happily. "I've fixed it up," he said. Humphreys was moved to a nearby Belgian-owned plantation.

But things were hardly any better. One day a band of Simbas came to the plantation to kill "the American." A Simba captain, who was a mulatto, intervened at the last moment. "Look at him," the captain said, pointing to Humphreys. "You can see by his skin that he is not a real American." Humphreys was dark complexioned to begin with and his skin was darkened still further by years in the equatorial sun.

"Look at me!" the mulatto continued. "My father was also a European. What if this man's father was an American! He has been here for many years and he is like one of us, just like I am one of us."

The Simbas were convinced. They put their guns down.

There were other friendly Simbas as well. One was the local administrator, a former schoolteacher named Yoka, who had been sent from Stanleyville to become a civilian ruler of the Ikela area. When Yoka got wind of another plot by the Simba soldiers to kill Humphreys, he had Humphreys brought to his home. He wanted Humphreys to live there so he could guard him from the troops.

For two weeks, Humphreys was Yoka's guest. He ate his meals with Yoka and the Simba officers. Usually the Simbas conversed in Lingala, a language Humphreys did not understand. But when they talked in Swahili, he joined in their conversations. All the time, Yoka and the others were most friendly and polite to their guest.

Humphreys, for his part, was impressed with Yoka. Most Congolese whom he had known in the past were lazy and indolent, but Yoka burned with revolutionary zeal. He was up each morning at dawn and often worked till after midnight administering his little domain.

In October, Humphreys' new friends secured a pass for

him to go to Stanleyville. He had become fond of them during his stay in Ikela; they had, after all, saved his life. Yoka put Humphreys on their regular Simba courier truck and he arrived in Stanleyville on October 10.

Humphreys figured that his luck had changed. What made things all the better was that a Belgian friend in Stanleyville lent him an apartment. He laid in a supply of canned food and books, then hid in the apartment to avoid the attention of the Simbas. He figured that in time he might be allowed to leave Stanleyville, or that the Simba regime would collapse. In any case, he was safe for the moment. He remained there six weeks.

It was Humphreys' misfortune that the apartment was in the Victoria Residence. The Simbas found him when they brought the Belgian and American hostages to the building. Now he, too, was a hostage.

In the afternoon of Saturday the 21st—Hoyt and Nothomb had, that morning, broadcast the messages from the radio station and from the airport—all of the men in the Victoria Residence were ordered into the lobby. There were, in all, about 200 of them. They were ordered to get into two vehicles—a bus and a truck—that were parked in front of the building. The truck bore the clasped-hands emblem of American foreign-aid gifts; it had been given to the central government and had been captured by the Simbas. But only 110 men could squeeze into the two vehicles; the Simbas started up with them, leaving the other 90 at the Victoria.

"Where are you taking us?" Nothomb asked a Simba officer.

"To the Tshopo," he said with a grin.

But the officer was only taunting the hostages. The two vehicles crossed the Tshopo bridge and headed out into the jungle. Then the Simbas told the men they were being taken to Banalia, a town ninety miles north of Stanleyville, where they would continue to be held even if Stanleyville fell.

"You'll be guarded in Banalia by the *jeunesse*," a Simba officer said. It was a terrifying prospect; the *jeunesse* were the cruelest of all the rebels.

Paul Carlson was in the front of the bus, next to two Congolese women, one of whom was carrying a small baby.

Carlson chatted with the women in Lingala. It turned out that the woman with the baby was Colonel Opepe's wife. He had evidently taken the opportunity to move them to a safer place.

The bus, which was rather decrepit to begin with, kept breaking down because of the overload. The hostages had to get out and push it several times. Finally, in a little village seven miles from Stanleyville, the engine let out a last gasp and was still. A Simba tinkered with the engine, to no avail. Turning to the hostages, he said, "Is there a mechanic among you?"

There were five Belgian mechanics in the bus, but none moved. Then Patrick Nothomb had another wily idea. He drew close to one of the mechanics and whispered: "Introduce yourself and put that engine out of action forever."

"O.K., Monsieur Nothomb—trust me," the man said.

The mechanic worked on the engine for some time. He managed to cross wires and otherwise guarantee that it would never work again.

All the while, a Simba stood by, admiring the man's work. "Isn't it marvelous!" the Simba said. "Without the Belgians we could do nothing!"

The Simbas decided that they and the hostages would spend the night in the village. They commandeered a hut and put all 110 of the men in it. It was so crowded that no one could even sit down. After a barrage of protests from the indestructible Nothomb, the Simbas finally allowed 40 men who were either elderly or ill to sit in the bus.

It was something of a comfort to the men to know that they were not going to be executed, at least not then. But now a new and, in its way, equally terrifying prospect opened up. They envisaged that they would be moved through the jungles by the Simbas for days, weeks or even months, always one step ahead of the ANC and the mercenaries. And, in all likelihood, they would eventually wind up dead.

At nine-thirty that evening, a Simba colonel arrived at the village with three trucks. The Simbas had changed their minds about moving the hostages to Banalia. They took them back to Stanleyville instead. As they entered the city, Hoyt noticed that there was a member of the *jeunesse*, armed with a spear, stationed behind each tree. The Simbas were bracing for an attack.

When the men reached the Victoria, there were tearful reunions with their wives and children. Patrick Nothomb found a bottle of whisky and belted back a few. Michael Hoyt and some of the other Americans turned their attentions to a case of beer.

In Léopoldville and elsewhere, radio monitoring facilities were tuned constantly to Radio Stanleyville. That was the only way the outside world could get even a hint of what was going on in the beleaguered city. Now the tone of Radio Stanleyville was becoming more threatening. In one broadcast, the station declared that each Belgian and American in Stanleyville would be placed under the surveillance of three trusted members of the Lumumba party, "disappearing altogether in the event of the slightest American attack on Stanleyville."

The men who monitored Radio Stanleyville were used to wild outbursts, but even they were shocked that Saturday when an announcement was made that "the whole population is decided to devour all the prisoners in case of bombardments of our region." The announcer added that drums of gasoline had been placed around the houses where the hostages were being held. The Simbas, he said, would "burn the prisoners alive" if the United States failed to "negotiate" by the following Tuesday.

At 6:20 P.M. local time on Saturday, a message came for Colonel Gradwell at the communications center at Ascension Island. Gradwell read it, picked up a phone to his operations officers and said one word: "Go!"

The paratroopers and the air crews had been on a three-hour standby basis, but Gradwell's orders were to depart ASAP—"As soon as possible." Their destination was "Charlie" stop—Kamina—which would put them a little more than three hours' striking distance from Stanleyville.

The first plane, with Colonels Gradwell and Laurent aboard, took off from Ascension at 7:30 P.M., followed closely by the others. They flew non-stop for 2,490 nautical miles, arriving in Kamina nine hours later.

When they landed, dawn was breaking over Katanga.

17

TOO HORRIBLE TO TALK ABOUT

In half a dozen capitals around the world, there was excitement and suspense that weekend. State Department and Pentagon officials held one meeting after another. President Johnson kept in close touch with developments. There was a flurry of meetings in Brussels. Several other governments whose nationals were also being held as hostages were similarly alarmed—among them Britain, Canada, India and France. In Léopoldville, the American and Belgian embassies maintained a twenty-four-hour vigil. Newspapers emblazoned the Stanleyville story in headlines. And millions of ordinary people waited, with dread, to hear news of the fate of Paul Carlson and the other hostages.

Attention was focused that weekend not only on Stanleyville but on Nairobi, the strikingly beautiful mile-high capital of Kenya. The United States and Belgium were making one last effort, in Nairobi, to secure the release of the hostages by peaceful means. The American ambassador to Kenya, William Attwood, was ordered to meet with a representative of Gbenye to discuss the fate of the hostages. Gbenye had designated as his representative an itinerant Congolese politician named Thomas Kanza. And Gbenye had also asked Jomo Kenyatta and Diallo Telli, the secretary-general of the Organization of African Unity, to "assist" Kanza in the talks.

When Attwood received his instructions, he contacted Kenya officials immediately. They assured him that Kanza would be brought to Nairobi for talks on Saturday the 21st. The whole thing, of course, amounted to blackmail. But the lives of Stanleyville's sixteen hundred foreigners hung in the balance and particularly the life of Paul Carlson, who, Gbenye vowed, would die on Monday if the talks were not held. The American and Belgian governments were fully prepared to use the paratroopers if need be. But there was still a hope that Attwood might succeed in persuading Kanza and, through him, Gbenye, to release the hostages.

Attwood seemed a good choice for the task. Forty-five years old, he was one of the youngest and ablest ambassadors in the U.S. foreign service. He had been one of President Kennedy's New Frontiersmen and had helped write speeches for the former president during his 1960 campaign. After the election, Attwood returned to his job as foreign editor of *Look* magazine. In 1961, Kennedy chose him as ambassador to Guinea, which then seemed on the verge of becoming a Soviet satellite. Attwood's patient but blunt-spoken diplomacy was credited with helping to swing Guinea away from the Communist bloc. In early 1964, President Johnson named him ambassador to Kenya.

In dealing with Kanza, Attwood was up against some big problems. No one was certain how much influence, if any, Kanza had, in the Stanleyville regime. Kanza, like Gbenye and Soumialot, was a political down-and-outer until the Simbas conquered Stanleyville. He was one of the few Congolese whom the Belgians had ever permitted to acquire a university education—he had studied in Belgium and later spent two months in a summer seminar at Harvard. Kanza was a member of the Bakongo tribe, from the Léopoldville area. In other circumstances, he would probably have gone far in Congolese politics. But his father and Joseph Kasavubu, the president of the central government, had long been enemies and Kasavubu saw to it that young Tom was pretty well excluded from the political pickings. Kanza did serve for a while as Lumumba's representative to the United Nations and as the Congo's chargé d'affaires in London. Otherwise he was usually out of work.

Like Gbenye, Kanza had tried to wangle a job from Tshombe. He hung around Léopoldville for three weeks after

Tshombe's return from exile, awaiting the call. But the call never came.

On September 25, Gbenye appointed Kanza as foreign minister of the regime. But Kanza was not in Stanleyville; he arrived there on October 7 and spent only a few days in his new capital. Then he left on a political safari to other African countries and never returned to Stanleyville. Gbenye continued to refer to Kanza as his "foreign minister." Kanza himself had other ideas. In October, he met with Attwood in Nairobi and said he had not accepted that job because he wanted to maintain his "political flexibility."

At noon on Saturday the 21st, Ambassador Attwood showed up at the country home of Jomo Kenyatta, near Nairobi, to meet with Kanza. Kenyatta was there and so was Diallo Telli. But Kanza, Attwood learned, was in northwestern Uganda, where he presumably was busy arranging for shipments of Communist-made arms to the Simbas. Attwood spent an hour with Kenyatta and Telli. He told them that the paratroopers were poised to go into Stanleyville, but that he hoped that Kanza could secure the release of the hostages so that the paratroopers would not have to be used. Attwood was an old acquaintance of Telli's—Telli was a Guinean and the two men had known each other in Guinea. After the meeting, Telli remarked that neither he nor Kenyatta ought to get mixed up in the Stanleyville problem. "This is ridiculous," Telli said. He withdrew from the talks and, the next day, left Kenya.

In Washington and Brussels, meanwhile, concern for the hostages mounted when monitoring facilities picked up a broadcast by Gbenye over Radio Stanleyville saying that the Belgians and Americans would be moved outside the city, to an "unknown destination" in the jungle.

Kanza finally arrived in Nairobi on Sunday. He spent the afternoon conferring with Kenyatta. At seven o'clock that evening Attwood was told that Kanza would see him the following day, at Kenyatta's country home. Attwood immediately cabled the news to Washington.

Events were moving rapidly that Sunday. In another broadcast over Radio Stanleyville, Gbenye announced that the death sentence on Carlson had been stayed until Tuesday. Gbenye told the populace of Stanleyville: "If American bombardment comes to us, take your machetes and cut up foreigners in pieces."

Wild cries of "*Lumumba mai, mai*" punctuated Gbenye's speech.

The same day, Lima One arrived in Lubutu. While the men waited for Lima Two to catch up, Colonel Vandewalle flew back to Kamina in a small plane for an urgent military conference. The paratroopers had arrived in Kamina from Ascension that morning. Kamina was thick with colonels. Colonel Laurent, the paratrooper commander, and Colonel Gradwell, the U.S. air force commander, were there. So, too, was Colonel Clayton Isaacson, an officer from the U.S. Strike Command. Isaacson was in charge of the four C-130Es that had been at the disposal of the Congolese government ever since August, and he now took overall command of the operation from Gradwell.

Also in Kamina were Colonel Frank A. Williams, chief of the American military mission to the Congo, and Colonel E. Monmaert, the Belgian military attaché in Léopoldville.

The men met in a hangar to review plans for Dragon Rouge. It had been set for the following day, Monday the 23rd, but Colonel Vandewalle pleaded that it be delayed until Tuesday. He argued that if this was done, the ANC and mercenaries could arrive in Stanleyville at the same time and thus lessen the chances of a massacre. The ANC-mercenary column, he pointed out, was motorized and, with this mobility, could strike quickly into outlying areas in search of hostages. After listening to Vandewalle's arguments, Colonel Laurent swung over to the opinion that a Tuesday drop would be better.

The American officers wanted to go in on Monday, without waiting. The upshot was that no conclusion was reached at Kamina. Colonels Williams and Monmaert returned to Léopoldville to report to their governmnets.

Officials of the American embassy in Léopoldville also wrestling with the problem. They knew that it would be "politically cleaner" if the paratroopers went in Monday, rescued the hostages, then got out before the ANC and mercenaries arrived. If the paratroopers went in Monday, the operation would be disassociated from the central government's conquest of the city. There would, in all likelihood, be less criticism from other African governments. Most African governments were, of course, strongly against Tshombe and it seemed almost certain that they would ignore the humanitarian side of the rescue operation and choose to make an issue, instead, of the fact that the conquest of Stanleyville by Vandewalle's columns would destroy the "People's Republic."

But although embassy officials knew full well the political difficulties that lay ahead, they decided that it was too risky to go in on Monday. The officials wanted to have as many men as possible on the ground. They wanted the ANC and mercenaries particularly to seal off the eastern escape routes from the city. There was a very strong fear that the Simbas might flee in that direction with the hostages.

As it turned out, however, Washington and Brussels called off the Monday drop because of Ambassador Attwood's cable informing them that Kanza would meet with him on Monday morning. They wanted to wait and see what would come of the meeting.

On Monday, Paul Carlson's wife, Lois, sent a plea by radio to the Stanleyville regime, saying: "My husband came to the Congo to serve the Congolese people medically and spiritually and has no political connections or interests. His only concern is for the welfare of the Congolese people, whom he loves and with whom he works. I appeal to you as Congolese to let him return to the service of your people. I beg you as husbands and fathers to let him rejoin his family who need him and love him so much."

Attwood and Kanza met at Kenyatta's home at 11 A.M. Monday. They sat around a table covered with a zebra skin. Kanza quickly laid down his terms: the hostages would be released only if the United States and Belgium forced Tshombe to halt the advance of the ANC-mercenary column. There would have to be a general cease-fire, Kanza said.

"I am here to talk only about the safety of the hostages," Attwood said.

"My instructions are to discuss the whole Congo problem," Kanza replied.

"Since we're not authorized to talk about the same thing, I will have to seek further instructions from Washington,"

Attwood said, adding: "Will you guarantee that the hostages are safe and that they will remain safe?"

Kanza replied: "That all depends."

Attwood spent an hour pleading with Kanza. He suggested among other things that a Red Cross plane be allowed to fly to Stanleyville that day to begin the evacuation of the hostages. The Red Cross plane had been standing by in Bujumbura ever since the Red Cross's two-day visit to Stanleyville in September. Kanza replied that the Red Cross were "spies." Attwood argued that it was illegal and barbarous to hold diplomats and innocent civilians as hostages, but his words fell on deaf ears.

Jomo Kenyatta went along with Kanza to a considerable degree. Kenyatta urged the Simbas on several occasions not to kill the hostages, but, despite pleas from Attwood and U Thant, he refused to use his influence to get them evacuated. First, Kenyatta insisted, there had to be a cease-fire. The fact that the lives of the hostages would be used as blackmail to obtain the cease-fire meant nothing to Kenyatta. Some Kenya government officials said that Kenyatta agreed with Kanza that the Red Cross was a Western spy organization.

Attwood left the meeting grim-faced and returned to Nairobi to cable Washington for instructions.

The issue was simple: should the United States submit to blackmail? It might—or might not—have been possible for the United States and Belgium to pressure Tshombe into ordering a cease-fire. It was, however, always possible that the mercenaries would ignore the order. They were almost at the gates of Stanleyville, and they would not take the matter lightly if the prize were snatched from them when it was within their reach.

But even if the United States could pressure Tshombe into a cease-fire and even if the mercenaries would obey it, there was no assurance whatsoever that the Simbas would turn the hostages loose. It is in the nature of a blackmailer to demand more once he had gotten the first payment. There was a very good chance that the Gbenye regime then would up their demands. Having gotten away with it once, they might well have turned around and insisted that the whole Congo be given to them—or they would murder the hostages. There was always the possibility that they would kill the hostages anyway—or that the *jeunesse* or the civilians might do it. The rebels had already killed thirty-five Europeans —in Boende, Kibombo, Kindu, Albertville and other places.

The State Department's orders to Attwood were sent that evening. Kanza's proposals, the department said, amounted to "outrageous blackmail." Attwood was told to break off the talks. To do otherwise would have been impossible.

As Averell Harriman put it: "We couldn't let Americans be used as political hostages. If we did, no American would be safe any more in any exposed area."

At ten o'clock on Monday evening, Colonel Burgess Gradwell, the C-130E commander, was in the "Talking Bird" at Kamina. The "Talking Bird" is the air force nickname for a C-130E fitted out as a powerful radio station. The plane had been flown into Kamina with the rest of the air armada the day before. Once on the ground, it had sprouted a maze of antenna towers and offloaded auxiliary generators. From then on, the Talking Bird was in continuous contact with "Fireman"—Washington.

Suddenly the receiving equipment in the Talking Bird clattered into action. "Stand by," Fireman said. Gradwell summoned Colonel Isaacson, the Strike Command officer who had taken overall command of the Dragon Rouge operation once the planes reached the Congo. "Stand by, stand by," Fireman kept saying. Then the code word was flashed: "BIG." Colonel Laurent, the Belgian paratroop commander, also received a code word, from Brussels: "PUNCH."

The plan had been that no one could move until both signals—BIG PUNCH—were received. But now both governments had given the order. After having tried for three and a half months to get their nationals out of Stanleyville by peaceful negotiations, the two governments were going to use other means. Dragon Rouge was on.

The American air crews swarmed into the C-130E's. The paratroopers, who had been resting on the floor of a hangar, were alerted. The first plane would launch at 2:45 A.M., followed at close intervals by the others. It would take three hours and fifteen minutes to reach Stanleyville. And the drop was planned for 6 A.M.—dawn. At that hour they would catch the Simbas groggy—and yet have enough light.

The column of mercenaries and ANC troops was also getting ready to move. Colonel Vandewalle, the Belgian officer who had taken overall command of Lima One and Two, returned to Lubutu by helicopter at 4:30 P.M. on Monday. Lima One had been waiting at Lubutu for Lima Two to catch up. Then, just as Vandewalle arrived in the town, Lima Two pulled in. Vandewalle was ready; his column was bunched up now. He called the officers together—Major Hoare, the mercenary chief; Commandant Liégeois, the head of Lima One; and Commandant Lamouline, who commanded Lima Two.

"We're leaving at once," Vandewalle told them. "The paratroopers will probably jump at Stanleyville at six o'clock tomorrow morning. We want to arrive there at the same time."

Just then a furious tropical storm broke over Lubutu. The rain came down in blinding sheets, cutting visibility to a matter of yards. While the column waited for the deluge to abate, some of the mercenaries stripped off their clothes and took showers in the rain.

At 5:30 P.M., Lima One and Two rolled out of Lubutu. The Ferret, manned by Frenchie and his Congolese driver, was in front, followed by the Sons of Bitches. Stanleyville was just 144 miles away, and there was a new, almost complete road all the way. Work had stopped when the Simba rebellion erupted, and the road had not been paved. But it was level and wide and nearly an *Autobahn* by Congo standards.

It rained all that night, a fine, persistent drizzle. The men were soaked to the skin. Even at their best, the mercenaries were not exactly the happiest people on earth, but now they were overwhelmed by added discomfort and gloom.

At 10 P.M., the column halted. It was pitch dark and still raining, but someone had spotted a vehicle which he took to be a Simba armored car in the road just ahead. A bazooka was brought up. The bazooka operator was unable to take proper aim because of the darkness. A mercenary held a lighted match aloft so that the man could line up the after and fore sights. He fired three shells. Two of them hit the target. There was a terrific explosion, followed by a violent display of pyrotechnics. As it turned out, the vehicle, a Mercedes sedan, had been filled with ammunition. A Simba officer who

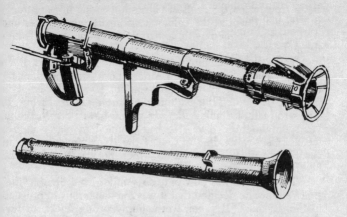

Bazooka A.Y. M9

had been in the car was cut in two by one of the bazooka shots.

The column had to wait five minutes, until all of the ammunition in the Mercedes had exploded. Then the vehicles skirted the hulk of the car—it was glowing, red hot, from the explosions—and continued the journey to Stanleyville.

Soon after midnight, the Simbas struck again from ambush. Hidden in the jungle, just a few yards back from the edge of the road, they waited until the armored vehicles had passed, then opened up on the trucks. They shot one South African sergeant through the head, killing him instantly. Another mercenary was wounded. The rest of the column raked the jungle with tremendous bursts of fire. The Simbas never fired again. They had either fled, or were dead.

The column started up again, groaning along at ten miles an hour in the rain. Occasionally they passed through a darkened and deserted village, but most of the time there was nothing but dripping jungle on either side of the road.

At 3 A.M., the convoy neared another village called Gene-Gene. Frenchie spotted a crude roadblock. He sprayed it with his .30-calibre machine gun, then knocked it down with the Ferret and drove on. The column followed. Just then, the

Simbas opened with a tremendous barrage. Some seemed to be in trees or on the roofs of village huts; long lines of tracer fire flashed down at the column. Again the mercenaries and ANC troops replied with a barrage of their own. Things calmed down.

The column counted heads. Another man had been killed—George Clay, a South African-born correspondent for the National Broadcasting Corporation. Clay, who lived in Nairobi, had joined the column just fourteen hours earlier, to cover the fall of Stanleyville. He would have been forty-one years old in three days. He had planned to marry in two weeks. Clay was riding in one of the trucks in the column, recording sounds of the battle, when he was struck in the head by two bullets.

The column was now only sixty miles from Stanleyville. But Vandewalle decided that it was too dangerous to proceed in the darkness. His men were simply sitting ducks for further Simba ambushes. He called a halt until daybreak.

The mercenaries crawled under the trucks and tried to sleep. But they were wet and cold; the equatorial jungle can be very cold during a rainy night.

The mercenaries knew now that the paratroopers would reach Stanleyville first. If there was any glory to be had from capturing the city, it would not go to them. But it made little difference to most of them. There would nevertheless be plenty of loot, more loot, as it turned out, than the mercenaries had ever dreamed existed.

For the ANC soldiers in the column, there was a prospect not only of loot, but also of the pleasure of the *ratissage*, the exacting of vengeance in the old tribal fashion.

All day Monday, Stanleyville's white hostages waited with rising suspense and dread to learn whether they would live or die. They were, of course, used to tension and fear, but now it was all too plain that their ordeal would soon be resolved. They knew from radio reports that the column of mercenaries and ANC troops was at Lubutu and that the paratroopers had been at Ascension; they did not know that the paratroopers were now at Kamina. They knew also that talks were to be held in Nairobi. But many if not most of them had little hope that the talks in Nairobi would lead to their release. Quite apart from anything that Gbenye might do, the civilians and the ordinary Simba troops had been whipped to such a fury by Radio Stanleyville that it seemed highly likely they would slaughter the hostages themselves. Like Dr. Frankenstein, Gbenye had created a monster.

Although Paul Carlson was not particularly happy that Monday, he was in far better spirits than he had been for days. He had expected to die Monday, but now that day had arrived and nothing had happened. Carlson had no time, however, to rejoice. He spent the day looking after sick people in the Victoria Residence.

Late Monday afternoon, the Simbas took Michael Hoyt, Patrick Nothomb and Raoul Massacesi, the honorary Italian consul, to Gbenye's palace. They also picked up Peter Rombaut, the honorary British consul. The rebel president met the four men in a reception room. He radiated good cheer. "Have a beer," he said. A servant trotted out with several bottles and placed them on a table.

There was also a well-dressed man in the room. He was dark-skinned, but did not appear to be Congolese. Gbenye brought him over to the four consuls. "This is Monsieur Hugh Scotland," Gbenye said in French. "He wants to interview you."

"Good afternoon, gentlemen," Scotland said in perfect British-accented English.

Scotland was, it turned out, a thirty-eight-year-old Negro from Trinidad with a British passport. He had a home and an English wife in London, where he had worked for a time as a theatrical agent. Scotland told Hoyt and the others that he was now a free-lance journalist and photographer, that he had come to Stanleyville overland from Nairobi and that he had spent two weeks touring the Simba-ruled areas. He said that he wanted to write a story on how the whites were being treated in Stanleyville. Scotland added he would tape-record the interview and that he would take the tapes to Nairobi "to assist in the negotiations." Scotland did not mention it, but he was also a fringe character in the shadowy world of Congolese politics. He was a friend of Kanza's. According to Tshombe, Scotland visited Tshombe while the latter was living in exile in Madrid in a futile attempt to arrange a political deal between Tshombe and Kanza.

After Gbenye had introduced Scotland to the four men, he got up to leave. "Oh, no, you stay with us," Scotland said. Gbenye sat down. Patrick Nothomb noticed that the president was not wearing his pistol that day. "Ah, hah," Nothomb whispered to the other men. "You see, our president is trying to allure Mr. Scotland that he is a good man, a true head of state."

Scotland switched on a tape recorder. Turning to Nothomb, he said, "What do you think of Monsieur Gbenye?"

What Nothomb thought was certainly not something that he was going to mention in Gbenye's presence. But the baron was a wily diplomat and so, smiling innocently, he said: "It is most difficult to judge Monsieur Gbenye now because a civil war is going on. But I am sure that after the war he will be well known."

And then Nothomb added, under his breath: "In exile or in jail."

Scotland turned to Hoyt. "What do you think about American interference in the Congo?" he asked.

Hoyt ignored him.

Scotland turned to Massacesi. "What do you think about Italian policies in the Congo?" he said.

"What?" said Massacesi.

"Well, is your advice followed by your government?" Scotland said.

Massacesi looked at Scotland with bewilderment. "I never made a policy," he said. "I came here to make roads."

"But Italian armored cars were found in the Congo," Scotland cried. "What about that?"

"I don't know—I'm a workman, not a politician," Massacesi said.

After the interview, the four consuls went with Scotland to the ballroom of the palace. It was an enormous room, more than one hundred feet long, built for Stanleyville's colonial governors. A row of glass windows looked out on the Congo River, half a mile wide. The Simbas were having a big party. Two "revolutionary orchestras" were taking turns at loud blasts of Congolese music, including some new revolutionary ditties that had just been composed. Among them were "Long

Life to Soumialot and Olenga" and "Oh, Beautiful People's Army."

There were several dozen high-ranking Simba officers and civilian officials in the ballroom. They milled around, chatted with each other and listened admiringly to the revolutionary songs. The four consuls took a table in the corner. More beer was brought to them. Then one of the revolutionary orchestras played a new number. The consuls guffawed quietly as they listened. The song was entitled "I Was in Prison but Now I Am Free."

The Simbas were having a great time. Servants kept trotting into the room with more beer. Scotland busied himself recording the new revolutionary songs. The four consuls sat quietly in the corner. On one occasion, Michael Hoyt looked up and saw, to his horror, that Alphonse Kinghis was standing nearby, staring at him. Kinghis was the first president of the Olenga regime, the man who had staged the macabre executions at the Lumumba Monument. Now Kinghis was wearing a long robe—his vestment as bishop of the Kitawalist sect. He stared at Hoyt for a few moments. Hoyt remembered that Kinghis had threatened him, long ago, at Camp Ketele. But then Kinghis moved away.

Some of the Simbas shook their fists at the four white men, but most came over to their table, shook hands—there was no longer any alarm about losing one's *dawa*—and chatted pleasantly. Scotland also sat with the four white men for a while. "Nice party—nice people," he observed. Hoyt drew close to him and whispered: "Be careful what you do or say. Our lives—and yours—are in great danger." Scotland seemed unnerved by this.

At nine o'clock, Gbenye sent word that the four consuls could leave if they wished. Scotland shook hands. He said he would see them in the morning. He would come to the Victoria Residence, he said, and take photographs of their quarters. Peter Rombaut went home. Inasmuch as he was British, he was not among the hostages at the Victoria Residence. But Hoyt and Nothomb, together with the unfortunate Massacesi, were taken back to the Victoria.

That evening, Lucy Barlovatz telephoned Hoyt and Grinwis at the Victoria—the telephones remained in working order all through the Simba occupation. "I understand that

Thursday is a big American holiday—what do you call it, Thanksgiving?" she said. "So I'm going to cook you two pygmy turkeys."

"Pygmy turkeys?" Grinwis said.

"Oh, you foolish boy—*chickens*," she said.

Paul Carlson visited Charlie Davis that evening. They prayed together, then they talked. Carlson said he held no bitterness against the Congolese for what had happened. "If I get out of this, I want to come back and work with these people again," Carlson said.

Patrick Nothomb retired to the room which he shared with eight other Belgian hostages. One man was reading Robert Ruark's *Something of Value*, a novel about the Mau Mau in Kenya.

"It's no time to read that book," Nothomb said, jokingly.

In the middle of the night, the man awoke, screaming in terror. The other men switched on the light.

"What's the matter?" they said.

"It's horrible, horrible—the Mau Mau," the man said.

"What about them? What did you dream about them?" the others asked.

"It's too horrible to talk about," the man said. He was still shaking with fear.

"It's just a dream—go back to sleep," the others said.

It was about 3:30 A.M. when the man had the nightmare. Four hours later he lay dead in the street near the Victoria Residence, his body riddled with Simba bullets.

18

THE RED DRAGON

With their powerful turboprop engines screaming in unison, the first five planes of the Dragon Rouge armada took off from Kamina precisely on schedule at 2:45 A.M. They climbed rapidly to fifteen thousand feet of altitude, then headed north and slightly west to a rendezvous point. The whole operation was carried out with split-second timing. Seven other C-130E's were standing by at Kamina. They waited until 3:15 A.M. Then, one after another, they shrieked down the runway, lifted off and headed out into the African night.

The first five planes, or Chalk One to Five in Air Force parlance, each carried 64 Belgian paratroopers, a total of 320 men. Among them were Colonel Laurent, Major Mine and other senior Belgian officers. These 320 men would jump when the planes came in over the Stanleyville airfield. It was their job to secure the field and clear it of obstructions. Then, if all went well, the other seven planes would land.

The other seven were lined up in accordance with how their loads would be used. Chalk Six and Seven were bringing the four armored jeeps—to be used in spearheading the dash into the city to reach the hostages—and four radio jeeps, for mobile communications. Chalk Eight and Nine each carried 64 paratroopers. They were rigged for jumping, if necessary, but the plan was that they would land in the planes if possible. Chalk Ten was loaded with the little three-man tricycles. Chalk Eleven had miscellaneous equipment. Chalk

Twelve, the last plane to land, was the hospital plane. It had an Air Force flight surgeon and six hundred pounds of medical equipment aboard.

One other C-130E was aloft over the Congo that night. That plane—Dragon Chief—had left Kamina an hour earlier. Aboard it was Colonel Isaacson, the overall commander of Dragon Rouge; he had gone on ahead to check weather conditions.

The armada was heading for a rendezvous over Basoko, a town situated at the confluence of the Aruwimi and Congo rivers, one hundred miles downstream from Stanleyville. The planes would link up there with the two B-26 fighter-bombers, piloted by Cubans. Then, with the B-26's in the lead, they would fly up the river to Stanleyville. If the Simbas had ringed the airfield with anti-aircraft guns or other heavy weapons, the B-26's would go in first to soften up the defense. Otherwise, the B-26's would hold their fire.

As the planes droned on, a gibbous moon appeared in the east-northeast, drenching the night sky with a golden glow. But then lightning flashed across the sky. Glowering masses of dark clouds loomed ahead. On command from Colonel Gradwell, who was aboard Chalk One, the armada altered its course and circumnavigated the storm.

The Belgian officers were impressed by the skill of the American navigators. None of them had ever been to Stanleyville, much less Basoko, before. They were from Massachusetts, Georgia, the Dakotas, California. They had taken off in the middle of the night from Kamina, which was in itself a strange place to them, and had set out to find a tiny town in the midst of the African wilderness—a town that none of them had ever heard of before.

But the navigators nevertheless plugged the planes into Basoko with precision. Miles out, the confluence of the two rivers showed up on radar screens. At 5:30 P.M., Gradwell's plane was over Basoko. The armada made a big circle to the left, to allow the planes to bunch up. The B-26's were there already, circling in wait. Gradwell was in radio touch with Colonel Isaacson, who was also circling, thirty miles from Stanleyville, watching the weather pattern.

"It looks good—press on," Isaacson said.

With the B-26's in front, Chalks One to Five headed up

the river to Stanleyville, now just thirty minutes away. Chalks Six through Twelve were not far behind.

In Washington, some sixty officials of the State Department and other government agencies were gathered in the Operations Center of the State Department for what would be an all-night vigil. There is a seven-hour time difference between Washington and the eastern Congo; it was 7:45 P.M. Monday evening in Washington when the planes took off from Kamina.

The vigil was maintained in a large conference room in the Operations Center. A huge map of Stanleyville hung on the wall. Officials had marked on it the likely places where the hostages might be held—the Central Prison, Camp Ketele and the various hotels. There were several charts on the walls as well. One showed the number of planes in the rescue armada. Another gave a breakdown of the paratroop battalion. Another had been prepared for later use. It would show casualties—how many dead, how many wounded.

Midway in the evening, Secretary of State Dean Rusk arrived at the Operations Center. With him were Under Secretary George Ball and Averell Harriman, then Under Secretary for Political Affairs. The three men had just come from a dinner at the German embassy that was given for Foreign Minister Gerhard Schroeder, who was visiting Washington at that time. Rusk, Ball and Harriman were wearing dinner jackets and black ties. They peeled off their jackets and sat at the conference table in their shirt sleeves, waiting for the news.

As the hours ticked away, tension mounted. Aides kept bringing in coded messages. The planes had left Kamina and were nearing Basoko. But the big question remained unanswered. Could the paratroopers get into the city in time to save the hostages?

At the LBJ ranch in Texas, President Johnson and his staff stayed up until 4 A.M. getting reports on the progress of the rescue mission.

At about the same time that the planes reached Basoko, the mercenaries and ANC troops were getting ready for the final dash into Stanleyville. The column had halted for several hours at Gene-Gene, the village where George Clay was killed in the Simba ambush. Now, just before dawn, they were set to move out. First there was a detail that needed attention. As a reprisal for the ambush, the men set fire to the village. A couple of dozen grass huts went up in flames, lighting the predawn sky like an enormous bonfire.

As the village burned, the mercenaries captured two Congolese, a man and a woman. The mercenaries asked Michael Hoare what to do with the captives. Hoare gave the order. The man and woman were marched through the burning village to the edge of the jungle. Then they were—set free!

A group of South African mercenaries was sitting in the mud alongside their trucks when Frenchie came along, singing loudly. "It's my birthday!" he said. He had two bottles of brandy. The men looked around to see if Hoare was present —he became furious if he caught any of his men drinking on duty. But Hoare was somewhere else, so Frenchie and the South Africans drained the bottles.

As the column started up, the South Africans decided they wanted more to drink. They had a bottle of Scotch, but they were afraid that Hoare would see them drinking from it. Then they hit upon a solution: they picked up some coconuts, filled them with whisky and passed the coconuts from man to man.

Hoare never did figure out why his men had taken such a sudden passion for coconut milk that morning.

It was just sixty miles to Stanleyville from Gene-Gene, and the last twenty-four miles were paved. The column proceeded "Belgian style" all the way. They sprayed every hut, every clump of vegetation, every abandoned vehicle, every crossroads.

"Twenty minutes!" the American loadmaster shouted. He was standing in the back of Chalk One and had just gotten word from the pilot, through his earphones, that the plane was twenty minutes from the drop zone.

"Vingt minutes!" the Belgian jumpmaster shouted. Because of the roar of the engines, his voice could be heard only by those paratroopers nearest him. He repeated the message with hand signals. Sixty-four men were watching him in-

tently. When they saw the hand signal, those paratroopers assigned to carry general-purpose bags hitched them in place just below their reserve chutes. The bags weighed up to one hundred pounds. They contained ammunition, special weapons and other things that are part of a paratrooper's gear.

The five planes were lined up Indian file, twenty seconds apart. Stanleyville's airfield is to the west of the city and so, to preserve as much of the element of surprise as possible, the planes were coming in from the west. Ever since Basoko, they had been dropping altitude; now they were down to a mere seven hundred feet. Paratroopers jump from higher altitudes during training operations. But this time Colonel Laurent wanted them to jump as close to the ground as possible. There were two reasons for this: it would minimize the time the men would be dangling from their chutes, perfect targets for waiting Simbas. And the lower the men jumped, the less they would be dispersed on the ground.

"Ten minutes!" the American loadmaster shouted.

"*Dix minutes!*" the Belgian jumpmaster repeated.

Up front in the cockpit, the American navigator was finishing a series of calculations. His job was to figure out the CARP—the Computed Air Release Point. He had to take into consideration the direction and velocity of the wind and the speed and altitude of the plane. From this he would determine the exact moment when the men would be told to jump.

"Six minutes!"

"*Six minutes!*"

A red warning light flashed on next to the jump doors on either side of the plane. The American loadmaster opened the two doors; they slid back into the ceiling of the aircraft. The loadmaster put a small platform in each doorway. The platforms extended partly out of the plane and would make it easier for the men to jump clear of the fuselage. The loadmaster also extended sets of wind deflectors from each doorway.

The Belgian jumpmaster was similarly busy. "Prepare for action," he shouted, in English. Belgian paratroopers still retain certain English commands from their World War II days in Britain. "Outboard sticks stand up!"

The men were sitting in four long files. Those on the outside stood up and folded their seats back.

"Inboard sticks stand up!" The other two files rose and folded back their seats.

The men were facing the jumpmaster in the rear of the plane.

"Hook up!"

All sixty-four men hooked the snap fasteners on their static lines to anchor line cables that ran overhead the length of the plane.

"Check static lines. . . . Check equipment."

The men went over their equipment and also checked the equipment on the back of the man in front.

"Stand in the door!"

The lead men mounted the platforms and stood in the two open doors, holding on to the frames.

The plane shuddered. The pilot had lowered the landing flaps to slow the plane down; it had been flying at 230 knots and now it slowed down to a mere 125 knots.

"One minute!"

"Une minute!"

Chalk One reached the CARP seconds before 6 A.M. The navigator gave the signal. The red lights went out. Green lights flashed on. Instantly the paratroopers started tumbling out of the two doors, thirty-two men from each. In just twenty-five seconds, all were gone.

Chalk One roared down the length of the field and across an adjacent golf course, then turned to circle back. Chalk Two and Three were over the field now, disgorging their paratroopers. The air was thick with great billowing canopies. Chalks Four and Five were coming in from the western end of the field.

As Gradwell watched, the Simbas opened up from the ground with .50-calibre machine guns. Chalks Two through Five all were hit several times as they came in over the field. But the damage in each case was slight.

Gradwell also saw that the field was littered with barrels and with about ten wheelless vehicles. This would pose a big problem. The obstructions would have to be removed before Chalks Six through Twelve could land.

With Chalk One in the lead, the little armada circled then came back over the field, again at seven hundred feet. This time they dropped bundles of weapons and other equip ment by parachute. Again the Simbas hit some of the planes with their heavy machine guns. But the damage was minimal.

Chalks Two through Five now were finished with their work. They headed to Léopoldville, where they would stand by for the evacuation. Chalk One, with Gradwell aboard, continued to circle the field and radio reports to Kamina, for relay to Washington.

The two B-26's that had accompanied the planes in from Basoko had not been needed. They left without firing a shot. Dragon Chief, with Colonel Isaacson aboard, roared in over the runway at one hundred feet to see what was going on, then turned and headed for Isaacson's headquarters in Léopoldville.

It took just forty seconds for the paratroopers to reach the ground. The first to touch down were Sergeants Julien Derwaerder and Marcel Dominique. They were both machine gunners, both twenty-seven years old, both attached to headquarters company. As soon as they had gotten rid of their chutes, they found their machine guns, which had come down in separate chutes, and set them up.

It had taken just eighty seconds for all of the 320 men to jump from the five planes. But they were scattered all along the airfield and golf course—a distance of more than a mile and a half.

The men regrouped. Colonel Laurent, who had jumped from Chalk One, ordered headquarters company to clear the field of obstructions. There were between three and four hundred steel drums on the runway, each filled with water. Working quickly, the paratroopers rolled the drums away. The wheelless vehicles posed a bigger problem, but there was no time to try to find a truck to tow them away. Gangs of paratroopers heaved and pushed and finally managed to roll the vehicles from side to side until they got them off the runway.

Eleventh Company was sent to seize the airport control tower and the nearby Sabena Guest House. There were perhaps thirty Simbas in the tower. They traded fire with the paratroopers for a few moments, then fled. Resistance at the Sabena Guest House also faded away.

A squad was sent to silence the Simba machine guns that had fired on the plane. The Simbas saw the paratroopers from

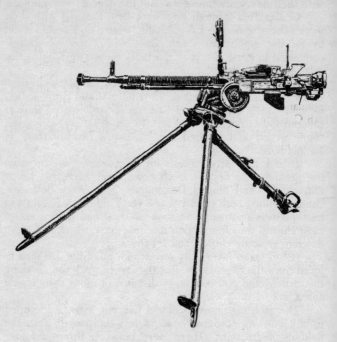

Chi-Com .50 Cal. Type 54

a distance and ran. They took with them one machine gun, but left another that was too heavy to carry. It turned out to be a .50-calibre weapon—made in Communist China.

The seven other C-130E's were near Stanleyville, waiting for orders to come in. After Colonel Laurent saw that the field was clear and that the Simbas had been driven off, he radioed to Colonel Gradwell, who was still circling overhead, and said it was all right for them to land.

Chalk Six had had mechanical troubles and was behind schedule. Chalk Seven was the first plane to land. It touched down at 6:45 A.M., just forty-five minutes after the first paratroopers had landed, bringing two jeeps and some paratroop-

272

ers. It was followed by Chalks Eight and Nine, each fully loaded with paratroopers.

A telephone was ringing in the control tower. It rang perhaps a dozen times, then stopped. Now it started ringing again. A paratrooper finally picked it up.

"The Simbas have assembled the white people at the Victoria Residence. Come quickly," a voice said in French.

It was now a few minutes before seven o'clock. Not all of the planes were down yet. But Major Mine, the battalion commander, was alarmed by the telephone call. He ordered 11th Company to move out to the city at once—on foot. The two jeeps that had just been unloaded from Chalk Seven went with them.

The airport was two miles from town. The two jeeps went first. The men followed, running all the way. They were shot at continually by Simbas who were hidden in houses and in the elephant grass that lined the road in places. The paratroopers laid down a murderous return fire with their automatic rifles.

The company entered the city on the Avenue Monseigneur Grison. They advanced along the street in leapfrog fashion. While the rest of the company laid down a blast of fire, a few men would run to the next corner. Then they would cover the rest as they came up.

The men reached the corner of the Avenue de l'Eglise. A white man darted out of a building and rushed up to them.

"Hurry, hurry—murder is being committed," he shouted.

19

DAY OF WRATH

"Oh, oh, there's hell to pay now," Donald Parkes said. Parkes, one of the radio operators, had been awakened at 6 A.M. by the roar of the C-130E's. He looked out the window of his apartment in the Victoria Residence—he was on the fifth or top floor and had a clear view of the city. In the distance, he saw the C-130E's come in low over the airport, dropping the paratroopers.

Parkes woke up James Stauffer and Ernie Houle, the other two radio operators. "There's hell to pay now," Parkes said. "The Simbas said they'd kill us if Stanleyville is invaded. They'll come to our rooms now and shoot us down in cold blood."

Stauffer got up, went over to the refrigerator and opened a bottle of beer. As the men watched, they saw the C-130E's circle and come back for a second pass, dropping bundles on the airfield. The two B-26's also were circling in the distance.

It was 6 A.M., Tuesday, November 24, the 111th day since Stanleyville had fallen to the Simbas. For 111 days the city's foreigners had prayed for deliverance; now it had come, bringing with it the prospect that some or all of them would die.

The paratroopers were only about three miles from the Victoria Residence. But there were thousands of Simbas as well as civilians between the paratroopers and the hostages, and Christophe Gbenye had vowed that if the paratroopers came the hostages would be massacred.

274

Someone switched on Radio Stanleyville. "We have been stabbed in the back by the Belgians and the Americans," the announcer was screaming. "Take your machetes and kill the white people. *Kill the white people!*"

Parkes went up on the roof of the Victoria Residence for a better view. He remained there for nearly half an hour. He saw the first plane land—Chalk Seven. Then he went back to the room and rejoined Stauffer and Houle.

Michael Hoyt and David Grinwis were in an apartment three floors below. Like everyone else in the Victoria, they had been awakened at 6 A.M. by the roar of the planes. The two men dressed and shaved. The Belgians with whom they shared the room started to drink beer. The men could not see the parachutes from their floor, but Grinwis concluded from the number of planes that it was a paratroop drop.

Grinwis proposed that the men organize to resist the Simbas. There were several armed Simbas in the corridors at the time. But they were not on their guard. They walked along unconcernedly, trailing their weapons. It would be easy, Grinwis pointed out, to overpower one or more of the Simbas. With even one automatic weapon, the hostages could defend the Victoria, or at least the upper floors, until the paratroopers reached it.

Hoyt felt that this would only provoke Simba reprisals against other Europeans. He figured there would be so much confusion and panic among the Simbas that they might well ignore the hostages in their haste to flee the city. And Hoyt, like the others, had been threatened with death so often that he had begun to believe that it could never really happen.

There were 298 white hostages in the Victoria that morning—280 Belgians, 17 Americans and Massacesi. About 100 of the hostages were women and children. A few of the men talked of resisting the Simbas, but no one did anything about it.

The will of the hostages had been paralyzed. They had lived for 111 days at the whims and caprices of primitive people who were utterly unpredictable. The hostages had given up trying to outguess their captors; they had settled back into passive fatalism.

Paul Carlson shared an apartment on the top floor with Gene Bergman and Jon Snyder, the young Mennonites. After they heard the planes, the three men sat on the edges of their beds with bowed heads and prayed.

"If this is my day to die, then I am prepared," Carlson prayed. "I ask only that You comfort my wife and children."

Several Belgian men were also living in the flat. They prepared a breakfast of bread, butter, jam, bacon and coffee. The three Americans joined them.

Charlie Davis shared a room with Al Larson, the head of the Unevangelized Fields Mission, and Del Carper, the man whose hearing aid had been confiscated. After the planes came over, the men prayed and read their Bibles. Davis pondered the 24th chapter of Proverbs: "Rejoice not when thine enemy falleth, and let not thine heart be glad when he stumbleth."

It was 7 A.M. The paratroopers were starting their dash into the city. The Simbas went through the corridors of the Victoria Residence, ordering the hostages out into the streets.

Clifford Schaub, the missionary from Pittsburgh, was in an apartment with his wife, Helen, and their two children, Tammy, eight years old, and Mark, six. Also with Schaub was Phyllis Rine. The two boys were not dressed and Schaub started to help his wife dress them. But a rebel interposed.

"Kwenda," he said in Swahili—"go." Schaub went downstairs. The women and children would follow.

Guy Humphreys, the wiry little ex-missionary, was in another apartment with a Belgian couple by the name of Bodson. Bodson was an employee of a Belgian business firm. He had been in the Congo many years. He was to have retired on a pension in mid-August, but then, a few days prior to his scheduled departure, Stanleyville was overrun by the Simbas. Bodson was very ill; he had had a heart attack almost every day that he was confined to the Victoria Residence.

When the Simbas came to Humphreys' apartment, Bodson was in bed. He protested that he was too ill to go down into the street. The Simbas waved Humphreys on ahead.

As Charlie Davis went downstairs, he met Paul Carlson. Both men had taken their Bibles with them. Davis, in addition, had thought of bringing along his toothbrush. "I don't know what today is going to be," Carlson said to Davis. "I just have a feeling, however, that today, one way or another, this whole thing is going to be over."

The hostages formed up in a group in front of the hotel. There were about 250 of them, many of them babies in arms. About 50 others stayed behind in the Victoria. They had hidden on the roof and in closets and cupboards. The Simbas had been in too much of a hurry to search the building carefully. Many of those who had hidden had been on the upper floors and had seen the parachutes. Those on the lower floors did not know that rescue was near.

There were about a dozen Simbas in front of the hotel, armed with automatic rifles. In command was Colonel Joseph Opepe. The spirits of the hostages rose when they saw Opepe—because of his reputation of being friendly to the Europeans. And, more important, he had been interested in making a deal under which he would surrender the hostages in exchange for his own life.

Opepe had a rifle slung over his shoulder. He was wearing slacks and a sport shirt. Those who had known him in the past could hardly recognize him that morning. He had lost a great deal of weight. His face was haggard. He was plainly worried.

Patrick Nothomb came out of the Victoria, followed by Paul Duqué, his vice-consul. As everyone waited to see what Opepe had in store for them, some of the Simbas taunted them: "Your brothers have come from the sky. You will be killed now."

Some of the hostages had brought blankets with them, thinking that the Simbas were going to take them to outlying villages.

"You don't need blankets—you're going to die," the Simbas said.

Opepe made a speech to the hostages. "You are going to pay because of the bombers. We are going to march you to the airport and let you die under your own bombs," he said.

The Simba soldiers said: "Let's kill them now."

"No, we will use them as a shield," Opepe said. "We will put them in front of us so that the paratroopers will be unable to enter the city."

Nothomb hung on every word and gesture from Opepe. He was heartened, to a degree. He suspected that Opepe was

277

stalling for time, that he really intended to surrender the hostages to the paratroopers. If Opepe had wanted to kill them, Nothomb concluded, he would have done so then and there.

Hoyt and some of the others thought otherwise. If Opepe really meant to protect their lives, he would have kept them in the hotel, rather than expose them to danger on the streets, Hoyt felt.

On Opepe's orders, the white people were lined up three abreast in about eighty ranks. "March!" Opepe said.

The column started out at a funeral pace down Avenue Sergeant Ketele. No one spoke. A few children cried. A baby howled. Exotic tropical birds warbled.

The street was lined with gorgeous mango trees, huge canopies of deep green leaves. It was a residential street, and on each side were rather run-down bungalows that had served as the homes of lower-echelon Belgian officials in colonial times.

The column reached Avenue Gouverneur Meulemeestre, crossed the intersection and continued on down Avenue Sergeant Ketele. Hoyt, Grinwis, Nothomb and Duqué were near the head of the column. Paul Carlson and the other American missionaries were in the middle. So, too, were the radio operators—Parkes, Stauffer and Houle. Phyllis Rine and Mrs. Schaub, together with the two Schaub children, were further back. They were the only American women and children in the column.

Colonel Opepe walked alongside the hostages. About a dozen Simbas with automatic weapons were spread out along the column.

As Patrick Nothomb marched along, he spotted a young Simba who had been at the beer party for Hugh Scotland at Gbenye's palace the night before. And the Simba noticed Nothomb.

"Colonel, you have to kill him immediately," the Simba shouted to Opepe. "He is the Belgian consul and he has sent a telegram to his government to send the paratroopers this morning." Then, pointing to Hoyt, the Simba said, "And there's the American consul who has been negotiating—see where it's brought us."

Other Simbas shouted: "Yes, kill them now."

Opepe continued to stall. "No, not yet," he said.

The Simbas looked at Opepe with what appeared to be growing suspicion.

The column marched along in silence another block. This one was lined with the same run-down bungalows but it was shaded with palm trees instead of mangoes. They reached Avenue Lothaire. Avenue Sergeant Ketele comes to a T-junction end at Avenue Lothaire and the column started to turn right into Avenue Lothaire.

The hostages and Simbas heard a tremendous burst of gunfire. It came from paratroopers who were working their way into the city along Avenue Monseigneur Grison. The Simbas ordered the column to halt and sit down. They sat down, some of them in Avenue Lothaire and some, not having turned the corner, still in Avenue Sergeant Ketele.

The firing grew louder. The paratroopers were only a matter of blocks away.

The Simbas were nervous. "You have to kill them now," they told Opepe. "The paràs are coming."

Some people sitting near Opepe recalled that he replied: "The first one of you who kills a white man I will kill immediately."

Two Simba officers raced up. They were apparently fleeing the oncoming paratroopers.

"We're going to shoot them now," they said.

"Shoot them?" said Opepe. "That's too easy. We're not going to shoot them. We'll get spears and knives and cut them up."

The white people watched Opepe intently. If there was any salvation, it would come from him. To all appearances, he was still stalling.

A pickup truck arrived. In it were several Simbas including Bubu, the mute ex-boxer who was one of Soumialot's entourage. Bubu made excited grunts and gestures signifying that paratroopers were coming, and that the hostages should be killed immediately. Opepe ordered him to return to the fight. He left.

Opepe turned to the hostages. "Haven't I protected you all this time?" he said. "Why have you allowed your brothers to come? I've watched over you, but now I can no longer take responsibility for you."

279

The firing grew louder. The paratroopers were only a few blocks away. Looking ahead to the next intersection, the hostages could see that Simbas were fleeing down the Avenue de l'Eglise to get away from the paratroopers.

It is not too clear exactly what happened then. Some of the survivors say that Bubu returned, in a rage, and opened fire point blank at the hostages. Others said that a teen-age Simba standing near the head of the column opened fire first. At any rate, all of the dozen Simbas soon were firing wildly into the 250 people who were sitting in the street.

Several people toppled over, dead or wounded. The Simbas paused for a moment. None of the whites screamed, none spoke. The only sound was the moaning of the wounded. Many of the hostages still could not believe that it had finally happened. Then the instinct of survival asserted itself. Scores of hostages jumped to their feet and ran. The Simbas fired one fusillade after another.

Michael Hoyt and David Grinwis ran down a driveway. Hoyt fell down; his legs could not go fast enough for the momentum of his body. He got up, ran, fell down again. A man running next to him was hit in the back by a bullet and fell over on his face dead. Grinwis also fell down twice, but then got up and continued running.

Hoyt ran past a shed filled with lumber. He reached a low wall. He started to go over it, then pulled back. It was too dangerous to expose himself. He crouched behind the wall. Bullets were whizzing around him. He heard the Simbas shouting in Lingala and Swahili.

When Grinwis got to his feet the second time, Hoyt was gone. Grinwis ran into a courtyard behind an apartment building. He saw an open door and darted in. It was, he discovered, a servants' toilet. Grinwis's hands and legs were bleeding from falling in the gravel driveway. But he paid no attention to that. Suddenly there was a burst of firing nearby. Something banged on the door. "Oh, God, I've had it," Grinwis said. The door swung open. In came a large black dog. The dog was terrified. It had broken loose in panic over the firing and was dragging a long rope. In a moment, a second dog, a tiny, white animal, scurried into the toilet. He was followed by a Belgian carrying a large pillow. Grinwis heard more shots, more cries, more groans outside.

Patrick Nothomb ran behind an abandoned building when the massacre started. Five other people had taken refuge there. One, a three-year-old boy, was screaming. His mother tried to hush him up, fearful that he would attract the Simbas. But the boy would not stop screaming. One of the men had been hit in the lips with a bullet. Another had been shot in the arm. Nothomb took his handkerchief and put a tourniquet on the man's arm. In the process, Nothomb was covered with the man's blood.

When the first shots were fired, Paul Carlson, Al Larson and the other missionaries lay flat on their faces in the streets. Then, when the Simbas paused for a moment, Larson shouted, "Let's go."

The men ran across the street, to a small, yellow-colored bungalow. There was a concrete wall, five feet high, around the porch. Larson and Jon Synder, the conscientious objector, leaped over the wall. Larson broke down the door and they dashed into the house.

Paul Carlson started to run to the rear of the house, but he saw a Simba and returned to the front. Charlie Davis went over the wall onto the porch. Then Carlson started to follow. He got one foot and one knee on the top of the wall. Davis reached out to assist him. His hand was perhaps five inches from Carlson's hand. But Carlson dropped back. Davis figured that Carlson had decided not to risk exposing himself, that he was huddling at the foot of the wall.

Davis raced into the house. He darted from room to room, looking for a place to hide. He saw a closet and dived into it. There were seven other people in it already—among them Larson, Snyder and a small Belgian girl.

The eight people had picked the worst possible place in which to hide. The closet had a glass door; they were plainly visible to anyone on the outside. A Simba burst into the house. He walked past the glass door and out into the back yard, where he shot a Belgian woman twice. Then he returned to the house, passed by the glass door and left, without noticing the people in the closet.

Guy Humphreys, the ex-missionary, ran with the rest of them when the massacre began. Two Belgians ran with him, one on either side. As they raced along, the man on Humphreys' right turned a somersault and fell dead with a bullet in the back. The man on the left fell with a bullet in his mouth, spitting torrents of blood. Humphreys flung himself behind a palm tree. As he watched, a Simba came up to two other men who were lying on the ground and shot them to death.

Humphreys got to his feet and ran again. He dashed into the servants' quarters behind one of the homes. There were several Belgians in the room, including a child who was crying. They, like Nothomb's group, were afraid that the child's cries would bring the Simbas. But they could not silence him.

Humphreys was a tough little man. He resolved that he would not die passively. He picked up a brick and crouched by the door of the room, waiting to smash the brains of the first Simba who entered.

When the massacre started, Mrs. Helen Schaub grabbed her two sons by the hand and ran with them through a yard. Phyllis Rine had been with her, but Mrs. Schaub did not have time to see what Miss Rine did. Dragging her two children along, Mrs. Schaub eventually got to a run-down garage. She hid with them behind a mound of old auto parts. A Belgian couple darted into the garage, carrying a small baby. They all huddled together. Timmy Schaub, the eight-year-old, kept crying for his father. The Belgian man, who spoke English, kept telling the boy: "Don't worry; your daddy is all right."

Théo Papazoglakis was one of those who remained lying in the street while the Simbas fired. Several days before, Papazoglakis had prepared a final letter in Greek for his wife in which he said: "If I die, I will not be a victim of the African people but rather a victim of ignorance." Papazoglakis' brother, Antoine, lay in the street nearby. Simba bullets tore into Antoine's arm, shattering three inches of bone. Théo was not harmed.

Both Phyllis Rine and Ernie Houle remained lying in the street. At one point, Houle looked up. He saw that Miss Rine's leg was almost shot off by a burst of fire. Miss Rine sat up and looked at the ruined leg. Then she lay back, closed her eyes and bled to death.

Several people died trying to shield their children with their bodies.

One woman who fled with her baby into a nearby yard was driven back into the street by spear-wielding Simbas. A Simba threw his spear at her head, but it struck only a glancing blow. The woman lay down in the street, covering the baby with her body. A Simba came up with a rifle, held it against her and fired repeatedly. The woman was killed. The baby survived.

A Belgian man named Ferdinand Mascaux threw himself atop his eighteen-month-old son. Mascaux was killed. The child was drenched in his father's blood, but unharmed.

Adrien Desmyttere, a twenty-three-year-old headwaiter, was near the head of the column when the Simbas started shooting. Looking back, he saw his young wife, Liliane, who was holding their eight-month-old daughter, Nellie. Suddenly Mrs. Desmyttere fell to the pavement, blood gushing from her chest. Desmyttere ran to her. She was dead. He snatched up the baby and, with bullets whipping around them, dashed away unscathed.

As fourteen-year-old Chantal Brinkmann watched, the Simbas killed her mother. Then Chantal's ten-year-old sister, Sonia, threw herself on her mother's body. The Simbas opened fire again, killing the child. Chantal's father moved toward her with his arms open, intending to shield her with his body. A Simba speared him in the neck, wounding him mortally.

Max Dubuisson, a twenty-seven-year-old engineer, and his wife, Katie, twenty-five, hurled themselves on their daughter, Monica, when the firing started. It was Monica's fourth birthday. As people around them screamed and fell, Dubuisson tried to dig his fingers into the pavement. The firing stopped. The Dubuissons were not harmed. But then Dubuisson heard a rebel say, "Now let's turn them over and finish off the ones who are left alive." To his horror, Dubuisson saw that several Simbas were coming over to where he and his wife and daughter lay.

Just then a white man in a red beret came around the corner from the Avenue de l'Eglise. More white men followed. *"Les paras!"* someone cried. The paratroopers saw what was happening. They shouted and ran toward the hostages, firing from the hip at the Simbas, who turned and fled.

Charlie Davis, Al Larson and Jon Snyder, who were

huddled in the glass-doored closet with the Belgians, heard the firing stop, but they were afraid to venture out. Minutes passed. Then they heard a voice say, in English: "But I know they're in there." There were footsteps in the house. The glass door swung open. It was Gene Bergman, the other conscientious objector, who had lain unharmed in the street during the slaughter. There were two paratroopers with him.

Davis grabbed both paratroopers in an embrace. The paratroopers kept saying, in French, "You are safe now. Everything is all right. Don't worry."

Davis went out to search for Carlson, who, he figured, must have taken refuge at the foot of the wall. Davis jumped over the porch wall. He landed inches from Carlson's riddled body. He had been shot while trying to scale the wall. There were five bullets in his chest, one in his head, one in his leg.

Davis took Carlson's body in his arms. He broke into tears. "They killed him, they killed him," Davis kept saying. Gene Bergman came up and took Carlson's Bible from his pocket, to give to his wife.

The bitter tragedy of Carlson's death was that the Simbas had not singled him out for execution. He was slain at random by a Simba who was trying to kill as many white people as possible. The real murderer was Christophe Gbenye. It was he who had arrested Carlson at Buta on trumped-up charges of being an American major and spy. Gbenye had condemned Carlson to death after a fictitious trial. If it had not been for Gbenye, Carlson would have been back in Wasolo that day, looking after his Congolese villagers.

After the paratroopers had driven the Simbas away, those whites who were still alive came out of hiding. They ran back to the corner of Avenues Sergeant Ketele and Lothaire, took a look and gasped. Twenty-two people lay dead at or near the intersection, under the great canopy of palm trees. Twenty of the dead were Belgians—two young girls, four women and fourteen men. The other two were Americans—Phyllis Rine and Paul Carlson.

Forty other persons, all of them Belgians, were wounded. Five of them died later.

As far as anyone could tell, none of the Simbas who carried out the massacre was killed by the paratroopers. They all ran at the last minute.

There were pools of blood on the asphalt paving at the intersection. The intersection was littered with shoes; people had run so fast that they had leaped out of them.

The paratrooper chaplain, Father Pierre Van der Goten, who had jumped from Chalk One, arrived at the intersection and gave the last sacraments to the dead and dying.

Some of the survivors hugged the paratroopers; others wept. Little children, many in pajamas, ran around hysterically with their hands over their heads, thinking that this would protect them from any more bullets. Husbands and wives raced around looking for each other and for their children. From time to time, there was a wail of grief when someone finally found—among the dead—the person for whom he had been searching. Many of the paratroopers were also in tears.

When Major Mine arrived at the scene, he took one look, gritted his teeth and said: "*C'est le Congo.*" Then Mine ordered the survivors into a nearby building, to safeguard them from sniper fire.

There were many joyous reunions when people found that their loved ones were safe. Clifford Schaub found that his wife and two sons had not been harmed, but his joy was short-lived; it was then that he learned that Phyllis Rine was dead.

When Guy Humphreys came out of hiding, he saw a Belgian woman, Mrs. Verwilghen, carrying her nine-year-old daughter. The child was bleeding profusely. Humphrey knew the Verwilghens well from his years in Stanleyville.

"Give her to me," Humphreys said.

He took the child in his arms and ran down the street. "Where's the first-aid station?" he shouted to the paratroopers. They motioned him to a store nearby. But, before Humphreys reached the store, the child shuddered twice and died in his arms.

Humphreys took the tiny body into the store, laid it on the cement, then cried like a child. Mrs. Verwilghen was beyond tears. She had lost her husband as well that morning. She said not a word to anyone.

Later, Humphreys volunteered to lead the paratroopers to another part of the city. On the way he passed the Victoria Residence and saw the body of his friend Bodson, the man who had heart trouble and who had had only a few days before retirement when the Simbas took Stanleyville. The Simbas had forced Bodson from his sickbed and had gunned him down in the street. Mrs. Bodson was shot on the stairs of the Victoria and had fallen down into the lobby seriously wounded.

When Baron Patrick Nothomb returned to the street from his hiding place, he, too, broke into tears. But then he got control of himself; he had work to do. Nothomb moved from one corpse to another, putting identity tags around their necks. Many of them were almost unrecognizable; their faces were frozen in the final moment of terror.

The wounded were loaded into vehicles—among them the pickup truck which Bubu had abandoned minutes earlier. With paratroopers guarding the vehicles, they were taken to the airport.

When Michael Hoyt came out to the street, he met Colonel Laurent. And he found that Grinwis and the other members of the consulate were safe. As the men were talking, a three-wheeled vehicle rolled up. Out jumped John Clingerman, Hoyt's predecessor in Stanleyville. Clingerman embraced the men, shook hands and said, over and over, "God, am I glad to see you." Then he said: "Where's Mike Hoyt?"

"You're shaking hands with him," someone replied.

Clingerman looked again. Hoyt had lost twenty-five pounds, and his customary crew cut had grown into a shaggy mop. And he was not wearing his glasses.

Clingerman told Hoyt and Grinwis to leave for the airport at once. They protested that there were people to be helped. "Your orders from Washington are to leave," Clingerman said. "The United States has spent a million dollars in rescuing you guys and we don't want you killed now. I'll take care of the evacuation of the other Americans."

Hoyt and most of the other Americans set out on foot in a long column of people walking slowly to the airport. The column was guarded by a dozen paratroopers. Charlie Davis read aloud from his Bible as he trudged along. Mrs. Verwilghen walked near Hoyt, supported by two Belgians. She stared vacantly ahead all the time.

All day long, columns of Europeans and Asians streamed

out to the airfield. They came in groups of fifty, a hundred, two hundred, each guarded by paratroopers. Most had lived in Stanleyville many years; some had been born there. Now they were leaving the city forever, taking with them only the clothes on their backs.

The paratroopers combed the city, searching for all of the foreigners. One patrol continued on from the scene of the massacre to the Victoria Residence, where they rescued the fifty people who had hidden on the roof and in their rooms when the Simbas ordered the others into the street.

Another patrol went to the Sacred Heart Mission, where they found fifty nuns and priests. The Simbas had come to the mission earlier that morning, looking for the priests. But they had barricaded themselves in a shower room. No one was harmed.

The patrol continued on to the Hôtel des Chutes. There they found three Europeans, including the hotel manager, who had hidden in the cellar with his Congolese employees. The hotel otherwise was empty except for stacks of arms and ammunition the Simbas had left behind.

The patrol went to the Central Prison. The guards had fled, leaving the prison gates open, but the prisoners were too terrified to come out. The paratroopers saw that there were no foreigners in the prison and left.

Patrick Nothomb and José Romnée, the ex-paratrooper who had been the leader of Stanleyville's business community, went with the paratroopers on many such rescue missions. Some Europeans had barricaded themselves in their homes and were so terrified that they refused to come out even when Nothomb and Romnée called to them. Often the paratroopers had to break down doors in order to rescue everyone.

Some people were hidden in attics, others had crawled into sewers.

Camp Ketele, the lair of Nicolas Olenga, the lord of the Simbas, was abandoned without a fight. It was littered with weapons, helmets and uniforms that the Simbas had dropped in their haste. General Olenga had vanished. So, too, had Gbenye and Soumialot.

The paratroopers set up a roadblock next to Camp Ketele and awaited the arrival of the mercenaries and ANC. At 10:30

A.M., a green flare arched skyward. The mercenaries had reached the end of their fantastic, twenty-three-day journey from Kongolo. They shot off the green flare as a prearranged signal so the paratroopers would hold their fire.

With Al Larson, the missionary, serving as a guide, the mercenaries made a wild dash to the headquarters of the Unevangelized Fields Mission, at Kilometer Eight, to rescue twenty-five people, most of them women and children, who had taken refuge there. But the Simbas had gotten there first. The Simbas shot and killed Hector McMillan, the missionary from Avonmore, Ontario, and they wounded McMillan's two teen-age sons. The others were not harmed. They included Larson's wife and child and Charlie Davis's wife and two children. The mercenaries took them all to the airport.

Colonel Burgess Gradwell, the C-130E commander, circled the field for two hours that morning. Under his direction, five C-130E's landed one after another and offloaded men and equipment. Parking facilities were limited—the field could hold only two of the big planes, or, with a little squeezing, three—and Gradwell ordered each plane to take off for Léopoldville as soon as it was empty.

Then a Simba machine gunner hit Gradwell's plane seven times. The bullets holed a fuel tank and knocked out a hydraulic line. Gradwell had to head for Léopoldville.

Chalk Six and Chalk Twelve, the hospital plane, were still on the ground, waiting, with engines running, for refugees and wounded people. Then the first group of refugees arrived at the field. The paratroopers hustled them on board Chalk Six. As they did, the Simbas opened fire with heavy machine guns from the nearby jungle. Several bullets struck the plane, puncturing a port fuel tank. The pilot did not know that the plane had been hit. He opened the throttle and roared down the runway, then took off, fuel streaming from his wings.

Three vehicles, meanwhile, had rolled up to Chalk Twelve, accompanied by paratroopers. When the crew members looked into them, they gasped. The vehicles were filled with twenty people who had been wounded in the massacre. Some had arms and legs almost torn off. Others had great gaping wounds in their bodies. Many of the crewmen wept as they helped the paratroopers transfer the wounded to the plane.

Chalk Twelve waited to see if any more wounded were coming. All the while, bullets were whizzing past as the Simbas and paratroopers traded fire. Minutes ticked away. Inside the plane, Lieutenant Colonel George Banning, a thirty-nine-year-old flight surgeon from Washington, D.C., was working on the twenty wounded people. Banning finally leaned out of the plane and shouted: "We've got to go. We can't wait any longer. These people are dying."

Chalk Twelve started to taxi out, but a barrel blocked the runway. A paratrooper saw it, ran out under fire and knocked it aside. The pilot opened the throttle and the big plane took off to Léopoldville. There were several doctors on the ground who could look after other wounded people.

The twenty patients on Chalk Twelve had been sent on ahead, for they were the most critically wounded. There was blood all over the floor. The men tending the wounded were drenched. Dr. Banning moved rapidly from one to another, administering morphine to calm them down. He put compression bandages on some to stop the bleeding. Others were given intravenous fluids to make up for blood loss.

A wounded man said, "I'm really in pain." Attendants turned the man over. Blood spurted several feet across the aircraft; the man had been shot in the back. Another man who had been shot in the mouth sat on the edge of a stretcher, holding a cup to catch the blood. People in shock do strange things; he was afraid he would mess up the floor.

A Belgian paratrooper who had been wounded in the fighting had also been put aboard the plane. He put his arm around a wounded woman and comforted her. Another man, who had been shot in the side, refused to lie down. He insisted on sitting next to his wife, who lay on a stretcher with her leg shattered. The man paid no attention to his own wound, but rather kept asking Banning about his wife's condition. One man had been shot in the chest. The bullet came out of his mouth. He died in the arms of an American officer.

Among those on the plane was Théo Papazoglakis, who had brought his wounded brother, Antoine, to the airfield. After Antoine's arm wound was dressed, Théo assisted in caring for the others.

Most of the time, not a word was spoken by anyone. The

wounded were too much in shock to talk. The crew members could not think of much to say.

A massive airlift continued all day. Planes came in from Léopoldville in a steady stream to take the refugees away to safety. The C-130E's returned on many such missions. Sabena and Air Congo sent commercial airliners. French, Italian and British planes also arrived.

It was while the whites were waiting at the airfield for evacuation that they heard a report that Colonel Joseph Opepe had been killed by his own men soon after the massacre because they regarded him as a traitor to the Simba cause.

Many of the whites were saddened by the report. They had come to respect Opepe and were convinced that he really did try to spare their lives.

The mercenaries and the ANC were running wild in Stanleyville. They shot every Congolese they saw. They looted homes and stores. When Patrick Nothomb finished gathering up Belgian nationals, he returned to his apartment in the Immoquateur to pack his belongings. But the mercenaries had gotten there first; the apartment was bare.

The mercenaries burst into offices and stores. Using dynamite and acetylene torches, they broke into safes and helped themselves to whatever cash remained. One group invaded the wine cellar of a hotel and drank it dry. A mercenary patrol paid a visit to the city zoo. They found that the lions were ravenously hungry. Gleefully, they released the lions, who ran off into the city.

The ANC and mercenaries blew up the Lumumba Monument. The ANC went on a rampage in the native quarters, dragging people from their houses and shooting them. The ANC entered the local headquarters of the Lumumba party— the Mouvement National Congolais. They saw a hand reach out of a wardrobe, trying to close the wardrobe door. The soldiers fired. The door swung open and a man tumbled out dead. The soldiers went from room to room. They gunned about twenty-five men who were trying to hide in closets or beneath desks. A few survivors were taken outside and killed in the driveway.

Colonel Laurent, the mild-mannered commanding officer of the paratrooper regiment, was horrified. "I never saw such a bloodbath in my life," he said. "No prisoners were taken. They were shot up, cut up or beaten to death. It was brutal."

Laurent did not want the young paratroopers to see what was going on. He ordered his men to return to the airfield as soon as they had rescued everyone. All were withdrawn from the city by five o'clock that afternoon.

One paratrooper was fatally wounded in Stanleyville. Two men were wounded by gunfire and three were injured in the drop. None of the American airmen was hurt.

When darkness made it impossible to continue the evacuation, there still were several hundred people at the airfield, waiting to leave. They spent the night in the hangar.

Now there was only one American refugee left in Stanleyville—Guy Humphreys. And this was, in a way, appropriate. The ex-missionary was the one who had been in the Congo the longest. He was the only one who really knew the great rain forest that encircled the city. Humphreys did not want to leave. He would rather have gone back to his plantation. But he knew that it was impossible for the moment.

Patrick Nothomb was still in Stanleyville. He felt that he could not leave until all of the Belgian civilians had been evacuated. The jaunty little baron had displayed great courage during the last 111 days; he had come close to death so many times that he had almost lost track of them. He had worked night and day to do what he could to protect the Belgians and other foreigners. Now Nothomb was exhausted emotionally and physically. He was terrified as he huddled in the hangar, listening to sporadic exchanges of gunfire between Simba snipers and the paratroopers. Whenever a shot was fired, Nothomb shook violently. He dreaded that he would be killed by a stray bullet. He was almost convinced it would happen. "After all I've been through, to die now would be stupid, stupid, stupid," he kept telling himself.

Nothomb wanted to scream. But he could not allow himself that luxury; he was still the Belgian consul, and he could not upset the others, who looked to him for leadership.

Even the worst nightmare eventually comes to an end. Finally it was morning, a glorious, sparkling morning. The jungle emerged from darkness in all its splendor. Humphreys and the other refugees were flown out of Stanleyville. By then, sixteen hundred foreigners of seventeen nationalities had been evacuated from the city—twelve hundred whites and four hundred Asians.

One of the C-130E's that took off that morning carried twenty-two wooden coffins, containing the bodies of Paul Carlson and the other people who were massacred under the palm trees at the corner of Avenue Sergeant Ketele and Avenue Lothaire.

Baron Nothomb took one last look at Stanleyville. He had come to the city for what he had thought would be an uneventful two weeks. And now, at last, it was time to go. At eleven o'clock, he boarded a plane. The pilot revved up the engines and took off. The plane headed out over the great brown flood that is called the Congo River, the river that Stanley had explored nearly a hundred years earlier, the river on whose banks the Belgians had built the lovely little city of Stanleyville.

The pilot set a course southwest over the wilderness for Léopoldville, where Baron Patrick Nothomb's wife and two little children were waiting for him.

20

EPILOGUE

Two days later—Thanksgiving Day in the United States—the C-130E's went into action again. The code name for this operation was Dragon Noir, the Black Dragon. Seven planes were used—four of them carrying paratroopers and three with armored jeeps and other equipment. The big planes took off in a stream from Stanleyville's airfield at 4:15 A.M. and set a course for Paulis, 225 air miles to the northeast. Intelligence officers had reported that several hundred whites were being held hostage in Paulis and that they were threatened with death.

Unlike Basako, where the Aruwimi spills into the Congo River, there were no natural landmarks around Paulis. But the American navigators nevertheless plugged their planes into the town at 6 A.M., precisely on schedule. The ground was blanketed by heavy fog, but the pilots were able to catch a glimpse of the airfield—a dirt strip only 4,100 feet long—through swirls in the fog.

The armada made one big circle. Then the first four planes came in over the airfield at 600 feet, just twenty seconds apart. As they did, 256 men tumbled out. A sergeant was wounded in the chest by ground fire as he stood in the door, waiting to jump. Rather than block the door, he jumped anyway. The troopers were dead tired. They had been on standby alerts or in action for many days. Some were almost asleep when they poured from the planes.

The fog was so dense that when Colonel Laurent's parachute opened he looked around as he dangled from the harness, squinting and said, "God damn it, I can't see the ground."

Despite the fog hazard, the troopers landed safely. The Simbas made a half-hearted attempt to defend the airstrip, then fled. The runway was cluttered with steel barrels, but the paratroopers quickly rolled them aside. At 6:30 A.M., Colonel Laurent radioed that it was safe for the equipment planes to land.

A Dutchman who worked in the local brewery met the paratroopers at the airstrip. He said that all of the white men in town were being held in a Roman Catholic mission and that the Simbas intended to kill them. Without waiting for all of the planes to land, the paratroopers raced to the mission. There they found fifty white men, unharmed.

But no one was in a mood to rejoice. Prior to the rescue, the Simbas had killed twenty-two white hostages—twenty-one Belgians and an American missionary. Witnesses said the slaughter was carried out as a result of Gbenye's final radio broadcasts ordering the Simbas to execute all whites in rebel territory.

The killings began Tuesday night—Tuesday was the day when Stanleyville's hostages were rescued. The American, Joseph W. Tucker, an Assemblies of God missionary from Lamar, Arkansas, was the first to die. Survivors said he was bound, then slowly beaten to death. Eleven Belgians were similarly slain that night and ten more the next day. All of the bodies were dumped into a river.

Just before they withdrew from Paulis, the Simbas shot and killed a Belgian housewife.

The Simbas were even more savage in dealing with their fellow Congolese. Estimates were that between two thousand and four thousand persons were murdered by the Simbas during the occupation of Paulis. One method was to force the victims to drink gasoline. Then their stomachs were cut open and they were set afire.

Throughout the morning, patrols combed the town, collecting white people and bringing them to the brewery for protection. Among those rescued were Mr. Tucker's wife and three children. One paratrooper was killed during these operations. Other patrols, riding in trucks escorted by armored jeeps, raced to outlying plantations and mission stations, some of them twenty miles away, picking up all of the Europeans they could find. By nightfall, there were nearly three hundred people in the brewery.

The patrols into the surrounding countryside continued next morning. But the paratroopers were up against a deadline. The C-130E's were due to return at noon to pick up them and the people they had rescued. One major pleaded with Colonel Laurent for more time so that he could lead a patrol to a plantation forty miles away where several Europeans were known to be hiding. But Colonel Laurent had his orders and he had to refuse permission. The major broke into tears. The rest of the Europeans would be abandoned to the Simbas.

The evacuees, by now increased to 355, were taken under guard to the airstrip. The first C-130E touched down at noon. The airstrip could accommodate only one plane at a time and so each was hastily loaded, then ordered aloft.

At 2:56 P.M., the last plane was ready to go. This was the most difficult moment of the operation. The Belgian officers had to make sure that everyone was aboard. If any of the men were left on the field, the Simbas would kill them after agonizing torture. The officers and noncoms counted heads several times, then gave the signal. Everyone was aboard. A chain of "battle simulators"—a string of powerful firecrackers that duplicate the noises of machine guns and mortars—was set off at one end of the field to confuse the Simbas. Then the plane roared down the runway and took off.

Within minutes, the Simbas moved back into Paulis. It was not until twelve days later that the ANC and mercenaries captured the city.

All along, American and Belgian officials had anticipated some criticism from other African countries over the rescue operations. As it turned out, African reaction exceeded anything that had been expected. A number of African countries, themselves only a hop, skip and a jump more civilized than the Simbas, exploded into a frenzy of anti-Western racism, which the Communists quickly exploited.

In Nairobi, a mob that had been whipped up by the

government radio demonstrated near the United States and Belgian embassies carrying placards that said, "Hang President Johnson." While police dragged their feet in Cairo, a mob of black African students, aided by Egyptians, stormed the United States Embassy and burned down a 27,000-volume library of the U.S. Information Service. Again with government connivance, a mob of African, Asian and Russian students attacked the American, Congolese, Belgian and British embassies in Moscow, causing considerable damage. There were similar riotous demonstrations in Czechoslovakia, Bulgaria, China and Indonesia.

Jomo Kenyatta, the prime minister of Kenya, was more restrained than many other African leaders in denouncing the rescue mission. He said he was "appalled" by it. Julius Nyerere, the president of Tanzania, saw in it another "Pearl Harbor." Kwame Nkrumah, the Marxist-minded dictator of Ghana, who has been repeatedly accused by his neighbors of meddling in their affairs, said that the Congo rescue mission was a "flagrant act of aggression against Africa."

At the request of eighteen African countries, the UN Security Council was called to hear their complaints about the rescue mission. Among the more astonishing statements made at the meetings was the remark of the foreign minister of Mali, who declared that the rescue operations were the work of the same "forces" who were responsible for the assassination of President Kennedy, the murder of Patrice Lumumba and the death of Dag Hammarskjold, who was killed in an airplane crash in Africa in 1961. The foreign minister of the former French Congo told the Council: "The famous humanitarian operation of Stanleyville has now proved to us that a white, especially if his name is Carlson, or if he is an American, a Belgian or an Englishman, is worth thousands upon thousands of blacks. Thus . . . the most ruthless and most scandalous aggression of our era has just been committed."

Interestingly enough, one African rose in the Council to defend the operation—Jaja Wachuku, the foreign minister of Nigeria, the most populous and progressive state in tropical Africa. Wachuku deplored the barbarity of the Simbas. "The Africans," he said, "are hospitable people and do not commit this type of act as a matter of routine. The African is not perfect, as no human being is perfect. But I want to state this here—the majority of African states . . . do not support this type of conduct."

Wuchuku pointed out that the very countries which were complaining the loudest about the rescue missions were themselves responsible for much of the turmoil in the Congo, for they had been giving support to the rebels. Nigeria, Wachuku added, found the use of South African and Rhodesian mercenaries distasteful. He suggested, however, that it was not Tshombe's government that was to blame for the fact that they were in the Congo, but "rather it is the fault of those who made it possible or drove them to such measures."

Replying to the criticism of the rescue mission, Adlai Stevenson, the United States representative, declared: "I have served in the United Nations from the day of inception off and on for seven years. But never before have I heard such irrational, irresponsible, insulting and repugnant language in these chambers; and language used, if you please, to contemptuously impugn and slander a gallant and successful effort to save human lives of many nationalities and colors.

"But even such a torrent of abuse of my country is of no consequence compared to the spectre of racial antagonism and conflict raised in this chamber. . . . Racial hatred, racial strife, has cursed the world for too long. I make no defense of the sins of the white race in this respect. But the antidote for white racism is not black racism. . . .

"We have no apologies to make to any state appearing before this council. We are proud of our part in saving human lives imperiled by the civil war in the Congo."

One reason for the violent outbursts from so many African governments was that they were strongly anti-Tshombe. And the paradrop did make it easy for Tshombe's forces to move into Stanleyville. But there was a deeper reason as well for the African reaction. The drop on Stanleyville served as a painful reminder to them that their independence is a fragile thing, dependent upon the good will of outside powers. Black African countries have virtually no military or economic strength. This they realized most forcefully on the morning of November 24, when 545 paratroopers of a small European country, riding in just twelve airplanes, managed, at the cost of the life of just one soldier, to seize the capital of a rebel state and scatter the defenders.

*　　*　　*

The Belgian and American officers who carried out the Dragon Rouge and Dragon Noir operations had considered a plan for a third rescue mission as well. Although precise details had never been worked out, the general idea was to drop paratroopers on Bunia, where there was an excellent airstrip. After the field was secured, other planes would land with more men and equipment. Then the paratroopers would set out overland in comandeered vehicles to Watsa, nearly two hundred miles to the north, where they would search for other whites.

But such an operation was never carried out. The paratroopers were flown directly back to Kamina after the Paulis operation. They remained there two days, then returned to Belgium, via Ascension Island.

There still were about a thousand Europeans remaining in the hands of the Simbas. Many people in the Congo and elsewhere in the world were stunned—and furious—over the withdrawal of the paratroopers. They felt that the American and Belgian governments had knuckled under to ignorant criticism and contrived riots in African and Communist countries, and that the two governments had sacrificed the remaining Europeans so as to appease "world opinion."

American officials, defending the withdrawal, said that they and Belgian officials felt that a third operation was militarily unfeasible. They were not certain there were any concentrations of foreigners in the two cities. Both the paratroopers and the American airmen were fatigued by then, the officials added. They pointed out that there was no assurance that there would be any vehicles available in Bunia. Moreover, the officials said, the road from Bunia to Watsa winds through steep hills that could have been defended easily by the Simbas. This, the officials argued, would mean getting into a land war, which they had never intended.

Many military men, both American and Belgian, disagreed with the diplomats over the feasibility of the Bunia-Watsa operation. They said it could have been carried out without any great difficulty.

Some officials said privately that the African reaction did play an important role in the decision to abandon any further rescue missions. Others denied that it did.

And so, amid bitter controversy, the two governments pulled out of the Congo.

On Friday, the mercenaries stormed across the Congo River to that portion of Stanleyville that lay on the left bank. They made a grisly discovery: the Simbas had murdered twenty-eight white hostages there soon after the right bank had been seized by the government forces. Most of the victims were priests and nuns. Only six people survived.

Striking out from Stanleyville, Michael Hoare's mercenaries, the men no one liked or loved, made many quick stabs into Simba-held territory to rescue the whites who remained in rebel hands. In just one week, the mercenaries saved about six hundred of them.

But the Simbas continued to exact their vengeance on helpless hostages. On November 30, the mercenaries reached Bunia. A nun and three priests had been murdered. Forty-seven ANC soldiers who had been captured by the Simbas, as well as 122 Europeans, were freed. Almost every soldier had been mutilated by the Simbas—ears were cut off, toenails torn away and noses sliced. Isangi fell to the mercenaries on December 10; six whites had been killed there. The mercenaries got to Banalia on December 18. The town was deserted. The bloodstained clothing and identity papers of some of the resident Europeans were found at the ferry landing. The mercenaries concluded that sixteen resident Europeans had been killed at the landing and that their bodies were thrown into the river.

The town of Bafwasende fell to the mercenaries on December 19; they found that fourteen Europeans had been slain. Wamba fell on December 29; the Simbas had killed about thirty whites there. When the mercenaries reached Mungbere on December 30, they found ten victims.

It was many weeks before the outside world learned of what had happened in Watsa, the other town involved in a possible third operation. Then, late in February, eight Belgians reached Bunia after trekking 150 miles through the wilderness. They brought news that the Simbas had massacred about thirty Europeans in Watsa, including twelve nuns. A paradrop would not have saved them; they were killed while the paratroopers were still in Paulis.

In all, more than three hundred whites, eight of them Americans, were killed by the Simbas. Their deaths were tragic, but they were only a small part of a greater tragedy that had gripped the northeast Congo. The Simbas had killed tens of thousands of Congolese, and the ANC and mercenaries had also killed a great many. The northeast Congo had become one vast graveyard.

After the fall of Stanleyville, Christophe Gbenye fled to the Sudan, then made his way to Kenya. Reporters found him drinking beer in a bar in the African quarter of Nairobi. Wild-eyed, he declared that he was afraid of being caught by "American spies and stooges."

Jomo Kenyatta and other officials of the Kenya government received Gbenye warmly and acclaimed him as a "heroic nationalist." While in Nairobi, Gbenye fired off several communiqués. In one he denied that he had ever held anyone hostage. He declared his Simbas had killed "five hundred mercenaries and paratroopers" in Stanleyville, and that they had shot down "ten American planes." It was great stuff; the Kenyans lapped it up. But Kenyatta was a man with a great deal of common sense. Soon he became disenchanted with his guest. He saw from Gbenye's erratic and irresponsible behavior that he was not quite the enlightened "nationalist" he had imagined him to be.

In the months that followed, Gbenye apparently returned to the Congo on a few occasions. He spent the rest of his time in Cairo, Algiers and other African capitals.

Gaston Soumialot also skipped out of the Congo after Stanleyville fell. He appeared in Khartoum, the capital of the Sudan, and later in Cairo and Algiers. Together with Gbenye, he set up a "Supreme Council of the Congolese Revolution," with headquarters in Cairo. But soon Gbenye and Soumialot were quarreling and the council fell into impotent disorder.

Hugh Scotland, the Trinidadian who was a friend of Kanza and had been the guest of honor at Gbenye's party the night before the paradrop, went through a fantastic adventure. When a paratrooper patrol neared Gbenye's palace, a car suddenly roared down the road. The paratroopers signaled for it to stop, and when the driver accelerated they opened fire, killing the driver and a man in the front seat. In the back seat, they found a man and woman, neither of whom was hurt. The man was Scotland.

The paratroopers took Scotland under guard to the airport. He asked to see Michael Hoyt. "Save me," Scotland said, throwing his arms around Hoyt. Scotland feared that he would be turned over to the ANC, to be dealt with in their fashion. At Hoyt's request, the paratroopers put Scotland on an evacuation plane.

But his troubles were not over. When the plane arrived at the airport in Léopoldville, Scotland got into a car with a British diplomat to be driven to town. Just then a limousine arrived, with Tshombe in it. Tshombe happened to glance into the other car and he remembered Scotland as an intermediary for Kanza in Madrid. On Tshombe's orders, Scotland was thrown into a central government prison. Much later he was released and, after being expelled from the Congo, returned to England.

Soon after the rescue missions to Stanleyville and Paulis, Algeria and Egypt airlifted large quantities of arms to the Simbas. The arms were of Soviet, Chinese and Czechoslovakian manufacture, and had apparently been given to Egypt and Algeria as part of the Communist military aid program. Diplomats were convinced that the Soviets and Chinese had agreed to replace what the two countries gave to the Simbas.

The arms were flown to the southern Sudan, then were taken overland into the northeast Congo. But the arms made little difference to the outcome of the struggle. In early 1965 the mercenaries, led by Michael Hoare, struck out in a new campaign and, by the end of March, seized all of the northeastern corner of the Congo, sealing off further shipments of arms via the Sudan or Uganda.

General Nicolas Olenga remained in Aba, the northeastern-most town in the Congo, until a few hours before it fell to the mercenaries. Then, together with the tattered survivors of his army, he fled into the Sudan.

By then, the Simba uprising had been pretty well crushed. Scattered pockets of resistance remained. Thousands of automatic weapons and rifles were still in the hands of surviving Simba bands. The basic problem of the Congo—that it is virtually ungovernable—had not changed. But the Simba movement as such was no longer a major threat.

The scattered rebel leadership enlisted little sympathy from other African countries. In Cairo, President Nasser at first tried to patch up the feud between Gbenye and Soumialot but like Tweedledee and Tweedledum, they seemed to enjoy butting their heads together. Then in September 1965, following a street brawl in which two Simbas were killed, Egyptian police collared the remaining rebels and hustled them out of the country. Reportedly they found refuge in Tanzania. Meanwhile, General Olenga, trying to revive his waning influence, had denounced both the Gbenye and Soumialot factions—only to wind up in a Khartoum jail for allegedly plotting with the Sudan's own rebel movement.

The Simbas had started out like a column of *siafu*, the Swahili name for driver ants, destroying everything in their path. Now, like the *siafu*, they were gone, leaving behind only ruins to show where they had been.

The Belgian paratroopers and American airmen received heroes' welcomes in Belgium. King Baudouin decorated Colonel Gradwell, the American C-130E commander, and Colonel Charles Laurent, the paratroop officer, with the Order of Léopold II. Expressing warmest thanks to the American airmen, the king said: "The hundreds of civilians who were saved, and their families, will never forget you."

Commandant Albert Liégeois, the Belgian officer who led Lima One all the way from Kongolo to Stanleyville, was seriously injured in a plane crash at the Stanleyville airfield several days after the city was taken. As he lay in pain on a stretcher, some Congolese filched his fountain pen from his pocket. Liégeois was flown to Brussels, where he spent many weeks recuperating in a military hospital.

Baron Patrick Nothomb returned to Brussels soon after being evacuated from Stanleyville. Then he and his wife took a Christmas vacation in Cannes, on the French Riviera. A relative lent the couple a palatial apartment overlooking the harbor. The baron quickly bounced back to his jaunty self and spent many long sessions in Cannes's most elegant restaurants, making up for lost eating time. The vacation over, Nothomb returned to Léopoldville to finish out his tour of duty. There, his clothing in gorgeous disarray and his hair flying about wildly, he continued to shower charm on Europeans and Congolese alike.

Michael Hoyt and the other American consular personnel returned to the United States on Thanksgiving Day. After a rest in Tucson, he was assigned for a two-year tour of duty in the Operations Center of the State Department in Washington —the center that served as a command post during the rescue mission to Stanleyville. David Grinwis, the vice-consul, went back to Africa on a new assignment—as a member of the American Embassy in Lagos, the capital of Nigeria.

Hoyt and Grinwis, as well as Ernie Houle, James Stauffer and Don Parkes, were awarded the Secretary's Award, the highest award in the State Department, for their heroism in Stanleyville.

Among the American missionaries who returned to the United States was Charlie Davis. In the months that followed, Davis pounded the circuit from church to church all over the United States, preaching the gospel and telling about the life and death of Paul Carlson. Davis's wife, Muriel, who had been pregnant all through the Simba occupation of Stanleyville, gave birth in February to a healthy girl named Susan McMillan Davis, in memory of Hector McMillan, the Canadian missionary who was slain at Kilometer Eight.

Guy Humphreys remained in the Congo. He took a job in Léopoldville, waiting for the day when he could go back to his plantation deep in the jungle. Africa had become too much a part of Humphreys' life for him ever to leave.

Stanleyville had become a ghost city. When I visited it seven weeks after the massacre, every shop window in town was smashed. Every store, except one, had been looted bare. The exception was, of course, a bookstore. The mercenaries carried out the first wave of looting, blasting open just about every safe in town. Then the ANC followed. Finally, the civilians descended on the stores and made off with what little remained.

The streets were littered with wrecked cars, garbage and broken glass. Once in a while a military vehicle could be seen on the streets, but otherwise they were empty.

There were many women and children on the streets, each wearing a strip of white cloth on the forehead to indicate undying allegiance to the new regime. But there were few men. Stanleyville was full of widows. Many of the men who survived had fled into the jungle. Others, victims of the ANC vengeance, were buried in shallow graves just outside town.

The damage in Stanleyville was of a curious sort. Physically it amounted to little more than broken windows and blasted safes. The real damage went far deeper. Virtually all of the city's European population had fled, most of them never to return. It was they who had built the city and kept its modern economy operating. Now they were gone and the economy had collapsed; now there was no real reason for Stanleyville's existence.

Each day crowds of young Congolese men ventured out timorously and gathered in front of the office, store or factory which had employed them, hoping that the European owners would come back so they could resume work. But the Europeans were not coming back. There was no work; there was only hunger.

The American consulate seemed as picturesque as ever. In the distance, canoes of Congolese fishermen were shooting the rapids of the Stanley Falls with incredible speeds. But, up close, I could see that the consulate was still a shambles. Nothing had changed since the day when Michael Hoyt and the others had been dragged off to Camp Ketele, to begin their long period of imprisonment. The glass doors in front were smashed. Walls were marked with bullet holes. The vault in which Hoyt and the others had taken refuge when the Simbas took Stanleyville stood upon, its doors scarred by bullets. The flagpole lanyard, severed by a bullet long ago, still flapped in the breeze. The mercenaries had taken over the consulate as their headquarters. A .37-mm. cannon, captured from the Simbas, was planted on the lawn, and a box of .50-calibre ammunition lay in the driveway.

I went to the Victoria Residence, then walked down Avenue Sergeant Ketele toward the intersection with Avenue Lothaire. The day was hot and muggy. The equatorial sun burned fiercely overhead, but the great mango and palm trees provided a restful shade. Congolese children were playing in the street at the intersection, unaware that events that had happened there had made world headlines.

Several Congolese cycled by, chattering and laughing. A man walked past, followed by his wife, who carried an enormous load on her head and a baby slung across her back—it is not a man's business to carry things in Africa. Music came, faintly and dreamily, from a far-off radio. Birds warbled and the scent of tropical flowers was in the air.

On the corner was a small, yellow-colored bungalow, with a low wall around the porch. That was the porch wall over which Paul Carlson tried to climb. It still was marked with bullet holes, and bloodstains. Despite torrential rains, there still were bloodstains in the street as well.

There were a few white civilians in Stanleyville who had been evacuated in the American planes and who since had drifted back to see what they could salvage of their belongings. But the looting had been so thorough and the mood of the city was so depressing that they were preparing to leave again.

There was one other white civilian who had never left Stanleyville—Dr. Alexander Barlovatz. The elderly, white-haired physician had sent his wife, Lucy, to Léopoldville on an evacuation plane, but he himself had declined the offer to leave. Why had he remained? "I couldn't leave my Congolese patients," Barlovatz explained. "It was my duty to stay; the Congolese are human beings."

Doctor Barlovatz was one of the few white men in the city who was not carrying a gun. He continued to make his rounds of the European and Congolese quarters of the city, driving a battered automobile that was marked with Red Cross emblems. The Congolese never bothered him, but the mercenaries did. On one occasion, several drunken mercenaries knocked him about in the dining room of the Hôtel des Chutes after accusing him of being friendly with the Simbas.

One Sunday I had dinner at the Barlovatz home. Dinner consisted of only a scrawny chicken, covered with catsup. But Mrs. Barlovatz, who had returned from Léopoldville some time before, nevertheless presided in the manner of the grand hostess. Explaining her return, she said: "The reason I came back was that I heard my husband not only was cooking his own food but that he was eating it. I was in danger of becoming a widow. I came back; I had no choice."

Relaxing over a liqueur after the meal, Dr. Barlovatz was visibly wearied. He had been in the Congo a long time, more than forty years, and he had seen many a dream and hope crushed to nothing. "I used to like the Congolese a lot," he said. "Now I like them less. But there still are many of them whom I like very much. Yes, I would like to leave Stanleyville. But it is impossible; I just cannot abandon my patients."

One other man remained in the Congo—Dr. Paul Carlson. He was buried in the village of Karawa, next to the headquarters of the church he served—the Congolese Church of Christ. Mrs. Carlson and their two children flew in from the Central African Republic for the funeral. But they were not alone. Down the rivers and along jungle paths came more than one thousand Congolese, simple villagers, many so poor that they owned little more than the clothes on their backs. They wanted to show that they had not forgotten *Monganga Paul*.

ABOUT THE AUTHOR

DAVID REED has spent more than five years in Africa as a journalist during the last 35 years. He spent two years in Kenya during the Mau Mau uprising of the 1950's on a journalistic fellowship and speaks fluent Swahili. He was in the Congo, as Zaire then was known, as a staff writer for U. S. News & World Report, during the anarchy that followed its independence from Belgium in 1960. He returned to the Congo in 1964 as a Roving Editor for the Reader's Digest, to cover the events in this book. Reed has reported from more than 100 countries around the world and has covered a dozen wars, most recently in Angola, Nicaragua and Cambodia. He lives in Tidewater Virginia and when not traveling and writing, spends his time sailing on the Chesapeake Bay.

Join the Allies on the Road to Victory
BANTAM WAR BOOKS

William L. Shirer

A Memoir of a Life and the Times Vol. 1 & 2

☐ 34204 TWENTIETH CENTURY $12.95
       JOURNEY, The Start 1904-1930
☐ 34179 THE NIGHTMARE YEARS, $12.95
       1930-1940

In Volume 1, Shirer recounts American/European history as seen through his eyes. In Volume 2, he provides an intensely personal vision of the crucible out of which the Nazi monster appeared.

Anthony Cave Brown

☐ 34016 BODYGUARD OF LIES $12.95

The extraordinary, true story of the clandestine war of deception that hid the secrets of D-Day from Hitler and sealed the Allied victory.

Charles B. MacDonald

☐ 34226 A TIME FOR TRUMPETS $11.95

The untold story of the Battle of the Bulge.

John Toland

☐ 34518 THE LAST 100 DAYS $12.95

The searing true drama of men and women caught in the final struggles of the epic conflict, World War II.